HEROES

AND

PHILOSOPHY

BUY THE BOOK,
SAVE THE WORLD

Edited by
David Kyle Johnson

WILEY

John Wiley & Sons, Inc.

Copyright © 2009 by John Wiley & Sons, Inc. All rights reserved

Published by John Wiley & Sons, Inc., Hoboken, New Jersey
Published simultaneously in Canada

For general information about our other products and services, please contact our Customer Care Department within the United States at (800) 762–2974, outside the United States at (317) 572–3993 or fax (317) 572–4002.

Wiley also publishes its books in a variety of electronic formats. Some content that appears in print may not be available in electronic books. For more information about Wiley products, visit our web site at www.wiley.com.

Library of Congress Cataloging-in-Publication Data:

Heroes and philosophy : buy the book, save the world / edited by David Kyle Johnson.
     p. cm.—(The Blackwell philosophy and pop culture series)
    Includes index.
    ISBN 978-0-470-37338-5 (paper)
      1. Heroes (Television program) 2. Superheroes. 3. Conduct of life.
  I. Johnson, David
    PN1992.77.H
    791.45'72—d

2009007426

Printed in the United States of America

10 9 8 7 6 5 4

CONTENTS

ACKNOWLEDGMENTS

Godsends

We wish to thank the employees of the Company (Wiley), especially Connie Santisteban and Lisa Burstiner, for all their hard work and dedication. Additionally, thanks to the artists who redrew our illustrations; it's a good thing there is someone out there with "Mr. Isaac's" power for artistry—because it's not us! Thanks also goes out to William Irwin, the Takezo Kensei of the Pop Culture and Philosophy world; every power and "Phil-'n'-Pop" book can be traced back to his genius.

Kyle wishes to specifically thank William Irwin for his revisions and for giving Kyle the opportunity to edit this book. (I enjoyed it!) Special thanks go to the heroes (contributors) for their dedication, clear writing, and openness during the revision process—and for putting up with the now infamous "deadline debacle." Kyle wishes to especially thank his mother for her useful feedback on each and every chapter, the use of her super-proofreading powers (too bad those aren't genetic), and for always pushing him to be special but not having a collection of snow globes—because we all know that it was the snow globes that really pushed Sylar over the edge.

INTRODUCTION

The Wonder of Heroes

Heroes is more reflective than your average television show. Consider the following philosophical quote, which opens the pilot episode as well as the first season finale:

> Where does it come from, this quest? This need to solve life's mysteries, when the simplest of questions can never be answered. Why are we here? What is the soul? Why do we dream? Perhaps we'd be better off not looking at all. Not delving, not yearning. But that's not human nature, not the human heart. That is not why we are here.
>
> —*Mohinder Suresh, "Genesis"*

In a way, this quote defines the entire series. Questions of man's purpose, of how to live one's life, are always just beneath the surface of our day-to-day existence. In fact, we are all philosophers in the sense that we all seek answers to these same fundamental questions. More important, opportunities to examine such questions can be found everywhere—even on television—if we know how to look for them.

By looking philosophically at *Heroes*, we have a unique opportunity to examine questions crucial to our existence as thinking, rational beings. Is the Company evil or good? Does Hiro Nakamura really have a destiny? Do we? Could mind reading be a power that we already have? Is time travel actually possible? If it is, could we, like Hiro, use it to save the lives of those we love? What obligations does Peter Petrelli have to his brother, Nathan? Does family really come first? Is it okay to lie in order to hide your powers or save the world? Shouldn't the heroes of *Heroes* get paid for their services?

Heroes is especially useful for dealing with philosophical questions, because we usually prefer these questions to be addressed in narrative. From the fables of Aesop to the stories of the Bible, the narrative form provides a powerful way of learning and remembering moral lessons. *Heroes* in particular provides us with a rich world of weird situations, powers, and characters whom we know and love and can use to ask and answer our questions. What role does memory play in personal identity? Could the Haitian erase a person by erasing his or her past? What is the right way to understand Peter's power, and could we already have it? Could the rise of superpowers break down society? How seriously should we take fringe scientific works, like Chandra Suresh's *Activating Evolution*? We'll even ask about the show itself. It shares many elements with stories that came before it; could Tim Kring be guilty of plagiarism—or something worse?

So prepare to dive into the world of *Heroes* and the world of philosophy—and to learn something along the way. And if you like *Heroes*, you can also prepare to enjoy yourself. This book is written by *Heroes* fans for *Heroes* fans—real *Heroes* fans who believe *Heroes* can stand up to its competition, unlike certain Arizona senators when running for president:

> For the next two hours you will be seeing SNL's *Presidential Bash 2008*. . . . Next week *Heroes* will return at its own normal time. . . . Right now, over at the other

networks you can find such shows like *Dancing with the Stars*, *Boston Legal*, *Two and Half Men*, and *CSI Miami*. And they will probably tell you that they are better shows than *Heroes*. And that may be so. But guess what, my friends—*Heroes* isn't on tonight. If those other networks wanted to go up against *Heroes*, they should have waited a week.

—*John McCain*, Saturday Night Live
Presidential Bash '08, *November 3, 2008*

As you open this book, open your mind. A world of adventure and knowledge awaits.[1]

NOTES

1. A special thanks goes out to Tyler Shores for his contributions to this introduction.

PART ONE

HEROIC OBLIGATIONS

ONE

ABOVE THE SOCIAL CONTRACT? HOW SUPERHEROES BREAK SOCIETY

Robert Sharp

What would happen if you committed a murder? First, law enforcement agencies would attempt to discover your transgression. If you left a weapon behind, it would be found. If you did not, forensics would still know what kind of weapon you used. If it was a gun, the remaining bullet would become evidence. If it was a knife, the hole in the victim's body would indicate the knife's size and your relative strength. In both cases, angles, positioning, and similar features are fairly easily discovered. Even the blood splatter tells a story. (I watch too much *CSI*.) Assuming you are caught, you would be tried in front of a jury of your peers—people who are considered your equals before the law—and the prosecution would use this evidence against you. Once convicted (you left so many clues!), you would go to prison, either to serve your sentence or to await your execution. From crime to punishment, your case would proceed like any other. You would be treated no better or worse than any other citizen, and you would receive no special treatment or advantage. Equality and due process are part of our legal system—at least in theory. They ensure that justice remains fair and impartial for all members of society.

But now suppose that you are not like other members of society. You have a special gift, and no one around you knows it. Perhaps you can kill a man without actually touching him—as Maya Herrera could with her devastating plague-inducing power—and no current forensics test could trace it to you. Or maybe, like Matt Parkman, you can read and influence thoughts and can sway any judge or jury into finding you innocent. Perhaps you can pass through prison walls, as D.L. Hawkins could. If you were like any of these people, you might wonder whether rule of law should apply to you at all. You are not equal to your fellow citizens; you are superior. They must abide by the rules because they have no choice. The system can destroy them. You, however, are untouchable. You have a power that will allow you to get away with whatever crimes you wish. Could society survive such people? How would the characters of *Heroes*, people with genetic gifts, affect society?

Hero or Not, Who Needs a Social Contract, Anyway?

What philosophers call a "social contract" is a binding but largely unwritten agreement between the state and its citizens that forms the basis of all political institutions. One of the first written accounts of the concept came from the philosopher Plato, whose character Glaucon says that "men decide that, [since] they can't evade [being harmed by others] and achieve [harming others without consequences], it will pay to make a compact with each other by which they forgo both."[1] Glaucon is suggesting that laws and the very concept of justice originated from the realization that it's in our best interests not to harm other people and to create a system where they will not harm us.

Plato continued the discussion of politics with an actual supervillain story: the myth of the Ring of Gyges—a ring that makes its wearer invisible.[2] Glaucon asserts that any man, just or unjust, would likely use the ring to break laws—if he could get away with it.[3] In *Heroes*, Glaucon's suspicion is supported. When Peter Petrelli first meets Claude Rains, the invisible man, Claude is engaged in petty theft—stealing things while he's invisible because he can't be caught. It seems Glaucon was right; much of our legal system depends on the fear of getting caught and being punished. Since Claude and Gyges cannot be seen, they are free to do what they want with no repercussions. In a sense, they disregard the social contract because they don't need it. But if they don't need it, they wouldn't agree to it. So is the social contract merely something that we—those of us who can't turn invisible—must agree to in order to get along with one another in society? Are those who have superpowers—who don't need the social contract for protection—not bound by it?

Maybe. Thomas Hobbes (1588–1679), in his major work *The Leviathan*, presents the civil state as an unspoken agreement between citizens and government that provides rights and security to those who live under it.[4] As Hobbes explained it, prior to such agreements there was "continual fear, and danger of violent death; And the life of man [was] solitary, poor, nasty, brutish, and short."[5] This "State of Nature" was a place of constant war, in which "every man is Enemy to every man," because each person has similar desires for the scarce resources that nature provides.[6] In other words, it's a big fight with no rules. (Sylar would love it.) According to Hobbes, we'd all want to escape this State of Nature because no one person or group could ever win the war. According to

Hobbes, people are all basically the same, both in their power and in their desires. Sure, some are a bit stronger or faster or more intelligent or cunning, but not by much:

> [W]hen all is reckoned together, the difference between man, and man, is not so considerable, as that one man can thereupon claim to himself any benefit, to which another may not pretend, as well as he. For as to the strength of the body, the weakest has strength enough to kill the strongest, either by secret machination, or by confederacy with others, that are in the same danger with himself.[7]

This means that no one person is so strong that he or she is invulnerable to other people; we are all equal, in that we could all potentially kill one another. This equality forms the starting point for Hobbes's society; it is why we enter into the social contract. Our fear of death forces each of us to concede that we cannot take on the entire world and so we'd better find a compromise. Almost no one formally signs or agrees to a social contract. Rather, we give our tacit consent to the contract by accepting its benefits.

But if "being equal with everyone else" is why we enter into the social contract, it would seem that one who is not equal—one who is superpowered—would have no reason to enter into the social contract. Claire Bennet, for example, is invulnerable. Why should she compromise with the rest of us? If we can't kill her, fear of death seems an unlikely motive for her to abide by the social contract. Likewise, D.L. could use his ability to hide in places we could not reach. Matt might be able to plant permanent suggestions in our minds. Sylar has virtually limitless power. Why should any of them bother to enter into a social contract in the first place? If they don't need the social contract, they can't be presumed to have entered into it. Thus, it would seem that they are not bound by the social contract—they are above the law.

This does not simply mean that they can break the law and get away with it; that is obvious. Rather, if the superpowered are not within the social contract, it means they are not morally bound to obey the law; they would be doing nothing wrong in breaking it. In fact, since for Hobbes the social contract was what created moral and ethical obligations, the heroes literally could never do anything morally wrong—not because they would be super-nice, but because moral laws could not apply to them. Sylar, for instance, could not be morally condemned even for murdering his own adoptive mother. Because he is not bound by the social contract, and only it creates moral obligations, he is not morally bound to not kill her.

Hobbes Debates Superheroes: Story at 11

Hobbes, however, isn't finished with our heroes yet. Remember, the key to his claims is not that people are literally equal in power, but that they are effectively equal insofar as anyone could potentially be killed by other people. Although at first glance it might seem that most of our heroes have nothing to fear from most other people, this is not the case. The most indestructible of the heroes are vulnerable to even the non-superpowered. Claire actually dies at the end of an early episode when the high school quarterback pushes her down and a piece of wood becomes lodged in her brain ("One Giant Leap"). Adam Monroe himself acknowledges that he can be killed by decapitation by someone without superpowers—something that Victoria Pratt was well able to accomplish: "I knew blowing your head off was the only way to be sure," she tells him ("Truth and Consequences").[8] D.L. Hawkins, despite his ability to pass through solid objects, was constantly injured; for example, he got shot—three times! The third time was just some random guy in L.A.—and it killed him! ("Four Months Ago"). And, of course, all of the heroes must fear the dreaded power-stealing eclipse. Everyone has something to fear and a reason to enter into the social contract.

But even if death could be avoided, superpowered people have other fears that might lead them to seek a social contract. For example, Claire worries about her family and friends; she worries about the loss of her *normal* life—her ability to control her own destiny. These kinds of concerns seem to be what John Locke (1632–1704) had in mind when he offered his own social contract theory in his *Second Treatise of Government.*[9] Locke's social contract is based on property, especially the rights one has to one's own body and the labor produced by that body—"the *work* of his hands."[10] From Locke's perspective, Claire should still be interested in a social contract, because—although her life may be safe in a technical sense—if she does not have some sort of agreement with her fellow citizens, she is still in danger of losing things that are important to her.

But there is yet another fear that all of the heroes should share: a fear of mass public action. Sylar clearly understands this in the episode "Five Years Gone." Despite being the president of the United States and amassing a large range of abilities, Sylar still does not act openly. Instead, he maintains the illusion of being someone else: Nathan Petrelli. Despite his powers, if Sylar were to openly declare his intentions, he would almost certainly be stopped. As powerful as he may be, he clearly does not like the odds of taking on six billion people at once. Peter understands this; he fears the loss of liberty that would accompany public awareness of his gifts. And based on the vision of a possible future that he sees ("Five Years Gone"), these fears are well founded. In that future, people with powers are labeled terrorists and must be registered and placed into camps. In fact, these fears are realized in Volume 4, when people with powers are tracked down by the government. If society decides they are a threat, it can take those with superpowers down.

This reveals that, as Hobbes defined it, our heroes are "equal" to everyone else—they are vulnerable to harm just like the rest of us. So it seems that our heroes do have good reason to enter into, and be bound by, the social contract.

But they might also have a reason to avoid it—for their own protection. The public disposal of the superpowered might be justified. The goal of social contract theorists like Hobbes and Locke was to create a society of equals.[11] This is relatively easy where wealth or status is concerned. Laws can be used to redistribute both or at least make sure that imbalances aren't abused to the detriment of society. But superpowers can't be redistributed by the state. The only way to maintain equality would be to lock up anyone who is exceptional and kill those you can't lock up.[12] If the disposal of the superpowered was demanded by the social contract, entering into it would not offer the superpowered any protection. Thus, it would seem that superpowered people are not bound by the social contract.

But it's hard to say what social contract theorists like Hobbes and Locke would really say about the superpowered. On the one hand, it would seem to justify action against the superpowered, as in the future of "Five Years Gone" when president Sylar isolates the superpowered for "public protection." Yet we don't have to go to alternate future timelines for such examples; in Volume 4, the government (with encouragement from Nathan) attempts to track down the superpowered for the exact same reason. But who wouldn't be afraid of people who can walk through walls, read minds, or never die? Without some control over those with powers, society might devolve back into the State of Nature that Hobbes envisioned. So it would seem that the social contract would justify protecting the public from the superpowered.

On the other hand, concentration camps for superheroes (much like the Company's) would seem to be the only method for protecting against the superpowered, because powers can't be confiscated. But concentration camps are not the kind of thing traditionally defended by social contract theory. And even if the state could confiscate powers (for example, by taking them away with the Shanti virus or a well-controlled Arthur Petrelli), this might be seen as a violation of the rights of the individual—and individual rights are something traditionally defended by social contract theory. But again, those rights are themselves dependent on a proper social contract, which seems impossible without protecting equality. It's easy to see how arguments about how to resolve these issues could go round and round.

Even an appeal to the most basic human rights, which we might say are independent of (or prior to) any social contract, does not help us avoid these difficulties. Suppose that (following Hobbes and Locke) we assume that we have a natural right to protect ourselves from undue harm. Surely, being killed or locked up simply because you were born with a gift could be seen as undue harm. But living in a constant state of fear that your neighbor can walk through your walls or read your mind could also be seen as undue harm. Where do we draw the line? Frankly, I don't know, and I'm not sure Hobbes or Locke would either—at least, where superpowers are concerned. Their reliance on basic, innate equality among human beings means that their theories can't easily deal with such issues. So for an alternative let's turn to John Rawls's (1921–2002) more modern version of social contract theory.

Rawls and the Natural Lottery: How Do I Join the Gene Pool That Makes Me Beautiful *and* Invulnerable?

Rawls still focused on equality, but he acknowledged that many people start with advantages that other members of society don't have. For example, some are born wealthier or more intelligent or stronger. The role of society, according to Rawls, is to correct these imbalances in order to ensure that everyone has a fair shot at achieving his or her goals. This doesn't mean forcing equality itself, but rather creating a system that provides equality of opportunity. Put differently, Rawls sought to correct unfairness in society by appealing to the idea that we are all part of the same social contract, which should not benefit some people more than others.

Rawls's position rests on two main principles: the liberty principle and the difference principle. The liberty principle says that society should have as much individual liberty within it as possible. To do this, we should give all people the freedom to live their lives any way they want as long as it doesn't interfere with the freedom of others to do the same.[13] The difference principle says that any political institutions that favor some people more than others should be made to favor the least fortunate, and the opportunity to be favored by society should be open to all.[14] This means that society should aim to balance out natural inequalities, to create a more fair system for everyone involved. In fact, Rawls's view is often known as justice as fairness precisely because his goal is to create a system of justice that would not favor any one class of persons more than any other.

Already we can see similar problems for our heroes. Rawls's view may acknowledge natural inequalities, but the goal is still to create equality within society itself. How can we be fair to those without powers? How can we make sure that others have the same opportunities that a person with powers has? If Peter hadn't knocked over the giant batch of formula and Hiro Nakamura hadn't torn up the formula blueprint in "Dual," we could have given everyone powers. But even then, because the formula did not give everyone the same powers (and some powers are lamer than others), this does not achieve equality of opportunity. So how, for example, could we make sure that everyone has the same opportunities that Nathan, the flying man, has? Should we distribute jetpacks to every home?

That last question seems a bit silly, but this becomes a real issue in Claire's case, once we find out that her blood can be used to heal people. This means that she *can* share her gift with society. Still, unless some way can be found to mass-produce her blood, this redistribution will be limited. According to the difference principle, we could not decide who should benefit from her blood by releasing it on the market. That would benefit only the wealthiest members of society. Somehow, everyone must be given an equal opportunity.

Again, I am unsure how Rawls would have resolved this problem, but he did provide us with a thought experiment for deciding such things. It's known as the original position, and it involves a "veil of ignorance."[15] The thought experiment asks us to imagine that we do not know our own place in society. We must then decide which arrangement for distributing the blood would most appeal to our selfish desires, given that we don't know our place in society. By starting at this original position, Rawls supposed that we could reach a fair decision that wouldn't be biased in our own favor (or in the favor of those making the decision, such as Congress members).

A lottery might seem most fair, because it doesn't favor anyone, but that's also a bit impractical. We aren't all hurt or sick. If a healthy person won the lottery, that would be a waste of good blood (an odd thing to say, I realize). So we might create a system similar to the organ transplant system, where people in need are favored by time spent on the waiting list, the probability of success (in this case, the probability seems high in all situations), whether they deserve the second chance (alcoholics are not given new livers ahead of those who did not abuse their original organs, for example), and similar factors.

This might work for Claire's blood, but none of this would make us Claire's equal. She has countless second chances. We could not redistribute that. Nor could we redistribute Matt's mental powers or D.L.'s ability to walk through solid objects.

Those unfair advantages are natural and cannot be transferred directly. Of course, as I mentioned earlier, if we had some secret power-giving formula, we could distribute it throughout society. But, again, since the formula produces different powers in different people, it would not achieve equality. (Besides, doing so might blow up the world.) So, what to do?

According to Rawls, part of the aim of justice as fairness is to correct nature's lottery, the unfair (and undeserved) advantages that some people have simply because they were born to certain families or with certain genetic traits.[16] The superpowers of the heroes fall into both groups. In theory, this means that the gifts these people have should somehow be redirected to benefit society as a whole. So, according to Rawls, since the powers can't be redistributed among the members of society, people having these powers should be required to use them for the benefit of society.

This is not a problem for most of our heroes. Many of them already do this. Hiro recognizes that his powers make him responsible for looking out for society, and D.L. rescues strangers out of car wrecks ("Nothing to Hide"). There are exceptions, however, Sylar being the most obvious. He uses his gift to amass personal power, and he's willing to kill anyone who gets in his way. He has lots of individual liberty, sure, but he uses it to interfere with the liberty of others. People like Sylar are exactly why we need a social contract, but they also represent the biggest threat to maintaining it.

Both the difference principle and the liberty principle cannot abide people like Sylar. There seem to be only three options for dealing with Sylar: neutralization, imprisonment, or death.[17] But even when his abilities are temporarily removed (Volume 2), he continues to kill to get what he wants, as when he kills Candice Wilmer ("Kindred") and Alejandro Herrera ("Truth and Consequences"). And even though he took a slight turn for the better in Volume 3, it didn't take much to turn him bad again by Volume 4. So it seems that neutralizing his powers would not be enough. He needs to be executed or imprisoned (for life) in order to protect the social contract.

Sylar, however, is not the only threat to a Rawlsian social contract. In fact, all of the people with superpowers would either need to use their abilities to help society or be eliminated in some way. The Rawlsian state is like a joint-stock company. Everyone should be receiving roughly the same benefits and have similar opportunities. Because superpowers cannot be distributed equally, some form of service would be demanded of those who had them. Yet demanding such services would infringe on personal freedom, a direct violation of Rawls's liberty principle. So Rawls's system would seem to conflict with itself in the case of superpowered people.

Do Superheroes Break Society?

Micah: Dad, how'd you get out of jail?

D.L.: Between you and me, I walked out.

Micah: Out of prison? How'd you do it?

D.L.: Ain't no jail can hold your old man.

Micah: Why not?

D.L.: 'Cause I got a secret.

Micah: Like Superman?

D.L.: Yeah. Just like Superman.

—"Better Halves"

We've seen some examples of how genetically superior humans break the paradigm for various social contract theories, but what about the bigger question? Do superheroes break society completely? I think the answer is yes.

D.L. Hawkins can easily escape from any jail. The Haitian, who can erase memories, could commit many crimes without *ever* being convicted. Claire could survive the electric chair indefinitely and overcome the toxins of lethal injection.

The fact that Adam, who has the same gift, lives for centuries indicates that imprisoning someone like Claire for life would amount to "cruel and unusual punishment." How could the legal system deal with such people?

It probably couldn't. Congress could not keep up with the various abilities that could arise, and any laws that were created would be difficult, if not impossible, to enforce. According to Hobbes, a state must be all-powerful to create and enforce internal peace.[18] This is why it must be like a Leviathan, a giant unstoppable sea creature that can overwhelm anything in its path. But it's unlikely that a state would ever be powerful enough to counter the rise of superpowers in its midst. The "explosion future" that we see in "Five Years Gone" shows the inhumanity caused by attempts to legislate superpowers. In the "exposed future" that we see in "I Am Become Death," where nearly everyone has access to powers, it is virtually impossible to police the public. As the Peter from that future says, "[A]ll the crime, murder—all ability. People can't be trusted. We're weak, jealous, violent. Abilities are the new weapon of choice."

Other factors also preclude our ability to incorporate people with special gifts into a sustainable social contract. Even basic laws would become difficult to apply. Take the concept of a duty to rescue, which some nations (and even some U.S. states) make into a legal obligation in certain cases. The idea is that citizens should help one another in cases where there is no significant risk to the rescuer. These laws, which are often confused with so-called Good Samaritan laws, apply only if the rescuer does not endanger his or her own life.[19] But a person capable of instant regeneration is seldom in any real danger, even in extreme rescues. How would courts deal with such cases? Should Claire be held accountable under rescue laws for not acting, when she clearly was not at risk?[20]

Of course, these legal questions are relatively simple when compared to the chaos that would occur within society as the result of superpowered persons. If your neighbor could read your thoughts, you would want to move to a new location. If your coworker could wipe out your memories, you would change jobs (if you could remember that the Haitian in the cubical next to you had that power). Worse, if you knew there were people around you who hid such powers, you would be in a constant state of fear. Whether or not society began as the kind of State of Nature that Hobbes described, society would almost certainly be transformed by widespread paranoia, and we would essentially be in a state of war with one another. Contracts would cease to be formed, because no one could trust the other to abide by the rules. People with such powers would have to fight to defend themselves, and life would indeed become "nasty, brutish, and short." Luckily, no one in reality has such powers.

But what if the superpowered took control? Maybe they could govern and legislate both the powered and the nonpowered successfully. Maybe, but probably not. Adam took it upon himself to improve humanity and decided that the best thing to do was to wipe it out. That hardly seems like success. The first generation of heroes (Angela Petrelli, Charles Deveaux, Bobby Bishop, and Daniel Linderman), after witnessing the massacre at Coyote Sands ("1961"), also tried to take control. First, they formed the Company—in a way, its own legal system, designed to keep those with powers under control:

> We find people, and we make sure they don't become dangerous. Now, sometimes that can mean making sure they understand entirely what they're capable of and teaching them to use their abilities for the good of mankind . . . and sometimes it can mean eliminating them.
> —Linderman, "Four Months Later"

Later, the Company planned to strengthen its control over the general public. As Linderman explains,

I was a lot younger than you when I discovered my power. And there were others too, like me, who discovered theirs. We were all confused. And we found each other. Together, we tried to make a difference to the world. And for a while, we did. It was beautiful. And then, some of my . . . friends . . . they lost their way. They used their powers for personal gain. And all the good that we'd done was—well, it amounted to nothing. And I learned that healing one person at a time was just not enough. We needed something— something to pull it down on course. Something big.

—*".07%"*

Linderman's plan, of course, was to unite the world by giving it a common threat. As he explains to Nathan, "People need hope, but they trust fear." By creating a huge explosion in New York, Linderman hoped to bind society together with a common cause. In a sense, he sought to create a new social contract, one not unlike Hobbes's vision. Fear would form the basis of cooperation and control.

But in the Company's attempt to control society from behind the scenes, it denies the very basic equality and respect that Rawls demanded for a social contract. Together, Linderman and Bob Bishop remind us of Lord Acton's (1834–1902) warning that "Power tends to corrupt; absolute power corrupts absolutely." (Both Nathan and Arthur Petrelli seem to show this as being true as well.) In order to sustain a reasonable social contract, in which every member is seen as roughly equal, such powered people could not be allowed to control society.

So it seems that despite the hype, the arising of superpowers within society would not be a good thing. We'd wish people with powers were all like Claire and Hiro—saving people from burning buildings, stopping villains, and so forth. But, in reality, they would likely break down the very fabric of society. I guess we should be glad that such things are limited to fiction—for now.

NOTES

1. See Plato, *The Republic*, translated by Desmond Lee (New York: Penguin Books, 1987), p. 45. Plato did not endorse this view. For that matter, neither does his character Glaucon. Glaucon is simply adopting the view of Thrasymachus to play devil's advocate against Socrates.

2. For more on Plato and Gyges, see chapter 7, "Plato on Gyges' Ring of Invisibility: The Power of Heroes and the Value of Virtue," by Don Adams, in this volume.

3. Plato, *The Republic*, p. 46.

4. See Thomas Hobbes, *The Leviathan*, edited by J. C. A. Gaskin (Oxford: Oxford University Press, 1996).

5. Ibid., p. 65. Spellings have been modernized in this quotation.

6. Ibid., p. 64.

7. Ibid., p. 63.

8. Of course, later Adam was killed, but it was by someone with powers. Arthur Petrelli took his powers, and Adam's age quickly caught up with him ("Dying of the Light").

9. John Locke, *Second Treatise of Government* (Wheeling, IL: Harlan Davidson, 1982).

10. Ibid., p. 18.

11. Hobbes, *Leviathan*, p. 63; Locke, *Second Treatise of Government*, p. 3. See also Jean-Jacques Rousseau, "On the Social Contract," in *The Basic Political Writings*, translated by Donald A. Cress (Indianapolis, IN: Hackett, 1987), p. 153.

12. One could also try to take away their powers. More on that later.

13. See John Rawls, *A Theory of Justice: Revised Edition* (Cambridge, MA: Harvard University Press, 1999), p. 56.

14. See John Rawls, *Political Liberalism* (expanded edition) (New York: Columbia University Press, 2005), p. 6.

15. Rawls, *Political Liberalism*, pp. 22–28.

16. Rawls, *A Theory of Justice: Revised Edition*, p. 87.

17. Or, of course, one could deal with Sylar by convincing him that he is Nathan, thus causing him to shape shift his body into Nathan's and live out Nathan's life—but that would never work, right?

18. Hobbes, *Leviathan*, pp. 89–90.

19. Technically, Good Samaritan laws are meant to excuse people who try to help others in a crisis from being held liable if their attempt to help fails. So, an off-duty doctor who tries to administer CPR on a car crash victim cannot be held liable under usual professional standards. The purpose of such laws is to encourage people to go beyond the call of duty and help their fellow person. There are no laws in the United States that require people to actively help others in trouble (except perhaps to report a crime in progress). That's the stuff of crime dramas.

20. Claire's moral obligations are a different matter. For more on this and specifically Claire's moral obligations to save others, see chapter 2 of this volume, "Heroes, Obligations, and the Ethics of Saving the World" by J. K. Miles.

TWO

HEROES, OBLIGATIONS, AND THE ETHICS OF SAVING THE WORLD

J. K. Miles

In "The Fix," we find out that Claude Rains has left the Company and is using his power of invisibility to steal money to survive—most people wouldn't call him a hero. Eventually, Peter Petrelli convinces him to help save the world. But what would have been wrong with Claude merely remaining an invisible petty thief? Spider-Man's answer would be "With great power comes great responsibility."

My intuition is that Spider-Man is right; we should not simply hoard our talents and refuse to act, nor should we use our power only for selfish gain. So, Claude should help save the world. But this is *just* my intuition.

Is it really true that extraordinary obligations follow from having extraordinary power? Most people think the answer is yes, and many people choose their jobs based on their talents. Mozart had special skills in music, so he became a professional musician. Politicians (ideally) have a gift for public service, so they work for the public. If someone has a skill, we think they should use that skill for the public good—and we have no problem if their use of that skill becomes their job. But this raises another question. Superheroes often scrounge for money, working at some lame newspaper or hosting a sexy webcam site as Niki Sanders does—and sometimes they even have to give up great opportunities, as Hiro Nakamura did when he passed up the chance to run his family's company. Why can't saving the cheerleader and saving the world be a hero's job? And shouldn't we be paying them for it?

Niki, D.L., and the Nature of Obligations

Do extraordinary obligations follow from having extraordinary power? Well, what do we mean when we say someone has an obligation? An obligation is something we owe to others—analogous to a debt we owe. Normally, a debt is the result of an exchange. If I agree to mow your lawn, I have an obligation to mow it. Some obligations, though, are more general. They are "debts" we owe to any other person we come in contact with. For instance, we have obligations not to lie and not to harm others.

Obligations are not optional. If we don't fulfill our obligations, it isn't simply unfortunate; we are as blameworthy as if we ignored a debt we owed. For example, if D.L. Hawkins can save someone by phasing through a wall, and he chooses not to save that person simply because he doesn't feel like it, he has done something wrong.

But what if our obligations conflict? What if we have an obligation to help someone in need and an obligation to provide for our family, but we can't do both? In Volume 2's "Powerless," Niki has an obligation to rescue Micah's cousin Monica Dawson from the burning building but also an obligation to be a good parent to Micah. These obligations conflict, and you can see it in Niki's face when she runs into the

burning building. Did Niki do wrong by fulfilling her obligation to save Monica while leaving Micah without a mother?[1]

The philosopher Immanuel Kant (1724–1804) might be
able to help us answer this question. He divided obligations
into *perfect* and *imperfect* ones.[2] Kant thought imperfect obligations were those that allow for one to choose among several
possible ways of fulfilling them. For example, I have an obligation to help those in need. To fulfill this obligation, I could,
whenever I see someone in need, help the person if I can. I am
not obligated, however, to spend my life searching out people
in need. I might "help those in need" by giving money to
the poor, if I have it. I might also visit the sick or the elderly.
I get to choose when and how I help. The obligation is to
"help others," not to help any particular person.

By contrast, perfect obligations involve no such choosing.
The obligation to "do no harm" to others is an example of a
perfect obligation. Hiro always has an obligation not to teleport innocent bystanders into traffic. He should always refrain
from doing so; he does not get to pick and choose when or if
he teleports innocent bystanders—he simply shouldn't do it.
Luckily, this obligation is easy to fulfill. All he has to do is walk
around all day not teleporting innocent people into traffic. To
ignore this obligation would be to become, in the words of
Hiro, "a villain."

This kind of obligation is also called a "negative" obligation, because we fulfill it by refraining from an action, rather
than by performing one. Perfect obligations, however, can
also be positive. Kant thought that promise keeping was a
perfect obligation. You don't get to choose which promises
you keep or how you keep them; you are obligated to keep
all of your promises. Because this requires positive action—
yep, you guessed it!—that's why it would also be a positive
obligation.

These are helpful distinctions for our problem of conflicting obligations. Niki has an imperfect obligation to be a good

mother to Micah (she can fulfill it in numerous ways), but she also has a perfect obligation to rescue Monica (there is pretty much only one way to accomplish this). Kant would say that the perfect obligation takes priority over the imperfect one, and thus Niki should rescue Monica. And this is what Niki does. If she dies, she can no longer fulfill her imperfect obligation to Micah. But her final action did fulfill that imperfect obligation to be a good mother, in that she was a good example to him.

These distinctions can cause problems, however. Kant thought that we all have a perfect obligation not to lie. It is also a negative obligation. Just don't lie. See how easy that is? (This is an obligation you are probably fulfilling right now.) Kant also thought that we have an imperfect obligation to protect others and, if we can, prevent them from coming to harm. So far, so good—unless you're one of our heroes.

Noah Bennet, for example, has to lie to his family to protect them from the Company. And in "The Kindness of Strangers" Angela Petrelli lies without hesitation to keep the first-generation heroes' secret, telling the police that she killed Kaito Nakamura. Both Noah and Angela violate their perfect obligation—not to lie—to keep from violating an imperfect obligation to protect (not harm) others. It doesn't seem as though they have done wrong, but Kant would say they have. They shouldn't lie *even if* it would help others, because not lying is a perfect obligation. In fact, if you agree with Kant, you shouldn't even lie to Sylar when he asks whether you have extraordinary abilities! (You don't have to volunteer the information and you could simply change the subject—or run!—but you shouldn't lie.) So, these distinctions can complicate matters.[3]

Claire, Hiro, and Minimal Obligation

Now let's examine the idea of obligation and, as Sylar says, see "how things work." (Fortunately, we won't be opening up your brain—only your mind.) Imagine that you are Micah walking along train tracks and you notice an infant stranded in the path of an oncoming train.[4] All you have to do is use your techopathy (ability to talk to electronic devices) to divert the train down a different track. Contemporary philosopher Peter Singer thinks most reasonable people would say that you are obligated to save the baby. You have the power to rescue the baby and no overriding risk or danger, so this generates the obligation to save the baby. We can call this the principle of minimal obligation: "If you can save a human life without too much cost to yourself, you are obligated to do so."[5]

Now Singer's principle seems right. The only time you would be immune from fulfilling the obligation is when doing so would put you at comparable risk. To illustrate this, imagine now that the baby is in a burning building. Since Micah's powers don't protect him from fire, saving the baby would require significant sacrifice and risk. Is Micah still obligated to save the baby? No. If Micah ran into the burning building at great risk to himself, he would be worthy of praise precisely because he wasn't obligated to do so. The debt he owes to others doesn't include risking his life.

But now suppose you are Claire Bennet. With your regenerative ability, the risk and sacrifice are negligible. What makes Micah immune to the obligation is the fragility of his body. Claire doesn't have this fragility, so she would be in the same state when saving someone from a burning building that Micah would be in by saving an infant simply by switching the tracks.

Another factor might be the distance. Most people would think that if the baby were on the other side of the city, Micah would not be obligated to rescue it. If you don't know about the baby or can't get to it in time, then you are not obligated to save it. You can't be obligated to do what is impossible for you to do. But, Singer said, if you did know about it and somehow could render aid across the distance—for example, if you heard about it on the news and could fly, as

Nathan Petrelli can—then in fact you are obligated to save it. Some people might suggest that the distance plus the fact that you aren't acquainted with the baby or its parents means you aren't obligated to save it (even if you can get there). But acquaintance wasn't morally relevant when Micah was next to the infant on the tracks. (How awful would it be for Micah to stand two feet away from the kid, totally able to save it, and just stand there saying, "But I don't even know this kid.") Why would distance change anything? For Singer, the only thing that is morally relevant is your ability to help. Even if the baby were across the country, if you knew about it and you could get to it in time—if you were Hiro and could teleport three thousand miles and save the baby—the obligation stands.

Singer used this illustration to make a case for providing aid to those on the other side of the world. People are starving all over the world and, like our heroes, we can miraculously cross the miles to save them—not with our actual bodies, but with our money. Singer thought that if we were obligated to save the baby, then we would be just as obligated to save starving people in Third World countries. In both situations, we know about the dying person and we can save him or her without comparable harm to ourselves. Neither our distance from the person nor the fact that we don't know this individual makes any moral difference whatsoever.

Singer even went so far as to suggest that we could be obligated to give starving people up to half of our income. Why? Because only if saving them risks significant harm to ourselves is our obligation to save them lifted, and given that we live in a rich country, with an abundance of money and resources, many of us could give away up to half of our income without really risking any harm to ourselves. (Yes, maybe some discomfort—similar to what Claire felt when she absorbed Ted Sprague's nuclear blast—but not harm.) We should, because we can, save the world just as our heroes do.

Singer's thought experiment is famous for giving a principle for sacrifice and welfare in helping others. If you can save the baby, you are obligated to do so. The same holds true for a world full of poverty. If Singer is right, people with extraordinary abilities do have extraordinary obligations. This means that Claire is obligated to save the baby from the fire. It also means that Peter is obligated to save the cheerleader, and all of the heroes are obligated to save the world. All that matters morally is the principle of minimal obligation.

Peter Petrelli and the Limits of Obligation

But maybe Singer is wrong. Maybe there are some assumptions hidden in Singer's thought experiment that are harder to find than Claude in a glass house.

Obligations take on a whole new dimension when we consider the main story arc in the first volume of *Heroes*: "Save the cheerleader, save the world." Saving the world seems like the most heroic thing anyone could do. And the morality seems simple: those who are gifted with special powers ought to use them to prevent great evil. If they don't, they are not worthy of being called heroes. If Singer is right, heroes are obligated, because it is in their power to save the world, and their sacrifice isn't comparable to the harm that would be suffered by those who need saving. But just as Peter has limits, so do obligations. When he absorbs too many powers, he, well, explodes. Likewise, when we examine the obligations entailed by special powers, the normative force of obligations may explode when it comes to saving the world. In other words, what works on a small scale might not hold up quite as well on a large scale.

That's exactly the objection that another contemporary philosopher, James Fishkin, leveled at Singer.[6] Fishkin said that there are three ways in which the principle of minimal obligation can explode faster than Ted Sprague having a temper tantrum. The three conditions that could lessen our debt to others are:

1. The great number of persons to whom the hero could be obligated.
2. The great number of heroes who could fulfill the obligation.
3. The great number of situations in which the hero must fulfill the obligation.

Consider Fishkin's first way that this obligation might break down. Because people are always putting themselves in danger (especially in the *Heroes* world), a hero's superpowers can make him or her able to help a great number of people. We agreed that Claire would be obligated to save someone from a burning building because doing so poses little risk to her. But suppose Claire lives in a strange world where buildings are burning and collapsing all the time. Maybe she lives in a war zone like Fallujah. Every time she walks out of the house, she is confronted with multiple situations like the burning building example. At any given moment, there are some dozens of people who need saving. Is she obligated to save them all?

Be careful how you answer. Remember that if Claire has an obligation and she doesn't fulfill it, she has done wrong. If it turns out that Claire is obligated to save all of the people, her obligation in each case is perfect (there is no leeway)—if she doesn't save even one person she could save, she has done a moral wrong. But what if she can't get to all of them in time? Even if this is the case, it's still true that for any given person, she could save him or her—she could just get to that person first. So, according to Singer and the minimal obligation criteria, if Claire fails to save one of those people, she has done a moral wrong. But that's ridiculous! She literally couldn't get to them all—and she can't be obligated to do what is impossible for her to do. So it seems that if there is a great number of people to save, the obligation to save any particular one is reduced.

The second way that our normal obligations could break down on a large scale is if there is more than one person who can fulfill the obligation. Remember when all of the heroes start working together in the final episodes of Volume 1? In "How to Stop an Exploding Man," Jessica finally lets Niki have some control. In "Landslide," Matt Parkman and Noah Bennett work together to stop Thompson. They each do their part with their own unique abilities. But suppose there is someone or something that needs saving and there are several heroes who can do the saving. Now saving others looks more like an imperfect obligation. The heroes can choose whom to save, and they are not each obligated to save all of the same people.

Take, for example, the case of some real-life heroes. Suppose that you are a lifeguard, but you're off duty. You see someone in trouble in the water. If no other lifeguards were around, with your special lifeguard training, you would have an obligation to jump into the water and help the drowning person. If you didn't help, you would be blameworthy. If there are several lifeguards on the beach, however, and they see the person in trouble and can get to him or her just as fast (or faster) than you can, then it seems you are not obligated in the same way. The mere fact that you have this great training doesn't necessarily carry with it a great obligation if there are others around with the same skills.

A third way our normal obligations might be affected is if we have numerous chances to fulfill our obligations. We've established that if someone has a special ability or power, it creates obligations that people without those powers don't have. Because of their powers, heroes like Claire, Claude, and Hiro are obligated in ways we are not. But there is more to these obligations than meets the eye.

After all, as *Heroes* makes clear, saving the world takes a lot of time, risk, and sacrifice. Claire misses school; Nathan's campaign suffers; Micah ends up moving a lot. If we had all the powers of Peter Petrelli, we could fight a lot of evil, but because there is so much evil out there, we could end up doing *nothing but* fighting evil. So, are heroes obligated to sacrifice all of their free time to fight evil? Or are they obligated only when it comes to major threats like saving the world? And what if it's not a matter of a lot of obligations at once? What if it's similar obligations over and over? What if the world just happens to need saving over and over again?

Singer would say it doesn't matter; the obligation to save one person when you can should carry over, even if that is all you do and the person needs saving over and over again. All that matters, morally, is your ability to help without comparable sacrifice to yourself. Because no amount of inconvenience will be comparable to the deaths of billions of innocent people, it seems our heroes are always obligated to save the world no matter how many times it needs saving, even at the considerable expense to their lives.

But that doesn't seem right. Think again about Micah and the infant. Suppose we live in a wacky world where babies are constantly crawling onto train tracks. Every time you walk outside, there's another baby to save and you are the only one who can do it. You can't really have a life. You can't graduate from college, get a job, have a family, or do anything because you are the only one who can save those babies and they always need saving. (Some philosophers are gifted with the special power to make up weird thought experiments—a power not even Sylar would want!) Intuitively, it seems that your obligation lessens the more you have to sacrifice. It would be noble of you to take it upon yourself to get up every day and save the babies, but I don't think you would be as obligated as you would be in Singer's single-person scenario.

These fantastic scenarios illustrate that it really isn't as simple as "With great power comes great responsibility." (Ever notice that Spider-Man never seems to graduate from college?) The fact that we would be obligated to save an infant in danger doesn't mean that the same intuitive obligation requires giving away up to half of our income to save thousands of starving people. Likewise, obligations that heroes would have on a small scale might not be strong when we consider saving the world. Heroes certainly would be good people to sacrifice their own pursuits to save the world from major disasters. It would be very heroic. The obligation lessens, however, given the facts that there are numerous heroes to do the saving, that no one individual can save everyone, and that the world needs saving every season finale.

Compensation and Saving the World

Molly: Does that mean you passed your detective's exam?

Matt: With flying colors. Why? You proud of me?

Molly: Mmm, depends. Did you cheat?

Matt: Why would you ask me that?

Molly: Reading the answers out of people's minds, it's unfair.

Matt: No, it is my natural talent. You wouldn't think a baseball player's cheating 'cause he's athletic, would you?

Molly: It's not the same and you know it.

—"Four Months Later"

We could, of course, make things simpler. Our heroes would have a lot more time to save the world if we made it their job—if we paid them for it. But what if, after the first volume, all of our heroes had handed New York City a bill for expenses and time lost. Claire wants compensation for missed school; Nathan wants compensation for the damage to his political career. There's something not quite right about this picture. And so, there is something not quite right about our heroes making "saving the world" their job. Isn't it unheroic to ask for compensation for doing what you are obligated to do?

But that's just it; it's not clear that they were obligated. In light of Fishkin's argument, it seems they were not, if for no other reason than that a number of heroes could have taken on the mantle of saving the world. They were simply the ones who did. They went beyond the call of duty by saving the world; they were not obligated to do so. Thus, it seems that the world actually does owe them a debt. In effect, they are no different from professional lifeguards, soldiers, law enforcement agents, or diplomats. These are all people who have special skills—skills that not all of us have—that allow them to do things to help others. They don't have to do these things because other people also have these skills, but they choose to spend their time and energy using their skills to help others. And we pay them for it. Our heroes simply have another set of skills. Why would that mean that we shouldn't pay them for their services?

Let me put it this way. Molly Walker thinks that Matt cheats when he uses his mind-reading skills to pass his detective exam. But Matt raises a good point when he says that it is simply a skill. Just as someone might be better at baseball because he is athletic, Matt is better at detective work because he can read minds. We don't object to paying the skilled athlete for playing his game. Why should we object to paying Parkman, the especially skilled mind reader, for his criminal interrogation and detective services? We don't object to paying the especially skilled marksman for his military sniper services. Why should we object to paying Peter, the especially skilled world saver, for his world-saving services? And, it seems, if our heroes do have to save the world, again and again—every season finale—we could view this as their job.

Why would it be wrong if our heroes asked to be reimbursed for saving New York City from the exploding man, while trained security agents are paid to prevent just such catastrophes every day? What's the difference, ethically? It seems there is a tension between the sacrificial character we think superheroes ought to have and the intuition that people who save the world professionally deserve compensation. But maybe the answer lies in the difference between TV and real life. In fantasy, we expect our heroes not only to meet their obligations but to go above and beyond the call of duty. The ethics of saving the world may include obligations, but we also want our heroes to be noble and self-sacrificing. The reason we find the idea of compensating comic-book heroes repugnant is that we hold them to a very high standard. But if superheroes actually existed, that standard would probably be unfair and unrealistic.

All in all, heroes have no special obligation just by virtue of their special abilities. Saving the world, whether from hunger or catastrophe, isn't as simple as Spider-Man thinks. It's not necessarily the case that "with great power comes great responsibility."

NOTES

1. For more on the obligations we owe our families, see chapter 17 of this book, "Heroes and Family Obligations" by Ruth Tallman and Jason Southworth.

2. Although Kant was fond of the term *duty*, I'll keep using the term *obligation*.

3. For more on lying, see chapter 18 of this book, "Concealment and Lying: Is That Any Way for a Hero to Act?" by Michael R. Berry.

4. Philosophy has a long tradition of bizarre ethical thought experiments that begin and end with a train or an infant (and usually some Nazis). There is a method to this madness. Intuitively, infants represent innocent parties and trains on tracks are great examples of actions that are determined but alterable with minimal risk. Nazis are just evil and work well as villains in any scenario.

5. This particular formulation is taken from James Fishkin, *The Limits of Obligation* (New Haven, CT: Yale University Press, 1982), p. 3.

6. Ibid., pp. 46ff.

THREE

CORPORATE CAPERS: THE MORAL DIMENSIONS OF WORKING FOR THE COMPANY

Christopher Robichaud

The Company was formed thirty years ago with a group of like-minded individuals, ordinary men and women who were gifted with extraordinary powers. They wanted to help their own—to find them and to protect them. We find people and we make sure they don't become dangerous. Now sometimes that can mean making sure they understand entirely what they're capable of and teaching them to use their abilities for the good of mankind. And sometimes it can mean eliminating them . . . you yourself [Mohinder] tried to put a bullet in the brain of a man named Sylar. . . . You were willing to kill him for the greater good. You acted on a moral imperative to protect your species.

—Bob Bishop, "Four Months Later"

Bob is morally gray at best.

—Mohinder Suresh, "Out of Time"

Something's Rotten at Primatech Paper

The Company was conceived in 1961, after Angela Petrelli, Charles Deveaux, Bobby Bishop, and Daniel Linderman witnessed the massacre at Coyote Sands ("1961"). Angela said that she foresaw that they would form "a group, a company" that would protect those with powers, keep them a secret, and keep anything like the massacre from happening again. The dream was realized in 1977, when this group and eight others (Susan Amman, Harry Fletcher, Paula Gramble, Carlos Mendez, Kaito Nakamura, Maury Parkman, Arthur Petrelli, and Victoria Pratt) founded the Company, with the goal of identifying those with powers, using them if possible, controlling them (taking their powers, locking them up, and so forth) if necessary, but ultimately keeping them and the world safe. The Company was destroyed at the end of Volume 3 and revitalized at the end of Volume 4, but it has always participated in what Angela calls "necessary evil."

It's unclear whether the Company is good or bad. Is it heroic or villainous? It tries to keep people like Ted Sprague (Radioactive Man), who can't control their powers, from becoming a danger to others. That's good. To do so, sometimes it kills them. That's bad. It took away the evil Sylar's powers with a virus it developed. That's good. In developing the virus, it created (and failed to destroy) another virus that, if released, would kill 93 percent of the world's population. That's bad. It tries to save the world. That's good. To do so, it thinks it has to blow up New York City. That's bad. (Can I go now?)[1]

So, is the Company evil? Well, it's not that simple. Like Bob, the Company is morally gray. That's part of the fun of the show. But we don't have to stop our moral evaluation there. For starters, it's worth looking at ways the Company goes morally astray that aren't as obvious as its attempt to nuke a crowded city. For example, it tries to control the evolutionary forces that have given rise to superpowers. Is controlling evolution noble or ignoble? If it is morally wrong, who exactly is responsible for this wrong? Everyone at the Company? Only those at the top? The Company itself? If you work for the Company but determine that it is evil, as Noah Bennet did, what should you do? Quit? Tell the authorities? Try to take it down from the inside and then restart it again with government backing and you in charge? (We could ask the same questions about Pinehearst, but for simplicity we will limit our evaluation to the Company.)

Messin' with Mother Nature

Superpowers in the *Heroes* universe are not explained by enhancement through genetic engineering, by a radioactive asteroid falling to Earth, or by divine intervention. Rather, they are the products of natural evolutionary forces. Whatever the scientific merits of this scenario, we'll take it as given that in the world of *Heroes*, nature itself produces persons with special abilities.[2] To control or master this phenomenon, the Company tracks persons with super-abilities, teaches some how to use their powers, eliminates those it deems too powerful, and develops drugs to dampen the manifestation of powers. Although that mastery might fall short of being able to directly manipulate the processes that are giving rise to superpowerful persons, there's little doubt that doing so is a long-term ambition of the Company. Let's ignore the ways that the Company goes about accomplishing this goal and simply ask, "Is this a bad goal to have?"

Many would say yes. Headlines today steadily scream with news about the increasing knowledge we have of our genetic makeup and the growing ability we have to exploit this knowledge in fascinating ways. Stem cell research, cloning, and genetic engineering are among the hottest issues discussed in bioethics, and there has been much worry expressed over activities carried out with the aim of enhancing human nature. Research programs with this ambition are often labeled *eugenics* programs by their opponents, a description intended to convey all of the negative associations with similar programs of the past, chief among them Adolf Hitler's.

It's not at all obvious, though, that the goal of improving human nature is morally wrong, despite the rhetorical force of pointing out villains who have pursued it. Enhancing the human race through eugenics—by, for example, making the average human smarter and more resistant to disease—could solve a lot of the world's problems: disease, overpopulation, hunger, poverty, war, and so on. The moral theory known as utilitarianism states that the morally best thing to do is that which achieves the greatest good for the greatest number. So according to utilitarianism, if eugenics does these things, pursuing it would be the morally right thing to do.

This is the view that Peter Petrelli seems to endorse, although in the opposite direction. In Volume 3, he objects to using the formula to give others powers but only because he thinks doing so will result in the destruction of the world. If he thought the formula would save it, he wouldn't hesitate. He even used the formula on himself when he thought that was the only way to save his brother, Nathan ("Dual").

But even if eugenics is wrong, the Company may not favor it in the first place. We've already acknowledged that the organization wants to control the natural processes at work in the production of persons with superpowers. Seeking that kind of mastery, however, needn't be done in the service of satisfying some further desire for advancing the human condition.

Indeed, the Company's higher aim seems more likely to be just the opposite. It plausibly seeks to *preserve* the human condition, rather than to promote its enhancement. After all, it wants to *save the world*, and it's hard to imagine doing that without saving the human genome, as it is. Supposing that's right, we can comfortably put aside objections to the Company's activities on the basis of its pursuing the goal of human improvement and, in doing so, avoid a more rigorous evaluation of this challenging aim.

But this hardly puts the Company in the clear, nor does it leave us without work to do. There are potential problems with the desire for mastery itself, regardless of the higher goals that might be motivating it or the specific means that are employed in achieving it. One problem stems from the view that nature is in some sense sacred and therefore not to be tampered with. This idea is often given voice by those who affirm the virtue of "letting nature be" and the vice of "trying to play God." And this objection needn't be inherently religious, either. It's simply the belief that certain natural processes have an intrinsic value, and that this value trumps whatever value might be gained by interfering with them. For those who subscribe to this line of reasoning, the Company's desire to control evolved abilities is morally wrong because holding this attitude fails to respect the value inherent in the natural processes producing and underlying our heroes' powers (such as Matt Parkman's ability to read minds or Niki Sanders's superstrength).

Notice that proponents of this viewpoint endorse *two* claims, as stated previously: First, certain natural processes are valuable, in and of themselves; that is, they're not valuable in virtue of anything else. Second, this intrinsic value outweighs whatever value might be gained by interfering with them. This first claim, though not unimpeachable, is certainly widely held and plausible. The second, however, is not. There are no processes more natural than that of a complex living organism suffering ailments and, eventually, dying.

But we don't find anything problematic about interfering with these processes in numerous ways. For example, we administer CPR to heart-attack victims and provide antibiotics to those with infections, all in order to promote what we take to be a greater good.

Acknowledging this is not to reject the intrinsic value of nature but to reject instead the idea that this value is in some sense absolute. And once that idea is rejected, it's no longer a good argument to oppose the Company's goal of mastery *simply* because this aim promotes values other than those inherent in the evolutionary process. More needs to be said about what these other values are before we can make an appropriate moral evaluation of the Company's attitude.

Eating a Little Humble Pie

A different and potentially more serious problem with the Company's goal of mastery over nature is offered by the contemporary philosopher Michael Sandel, who in his book *The Case against Perfection* argued against the aim of perfection as it appears in the pursuits of parents and scientists to create "perfect" persons.[3] Sandel believes the desire to control nature reveals a dangerous kind of arrogance that will lead to various unpleasant consequences. These include an increase in our moral burdens due to an inflation of our moral responsibility, a decrease in our ability to promote a sense of community and togetherness, and the emergence of a society unable to adjust to the unexpected or disagreeable elements it will face.

Let's apply Sandel's philosophy to the Company. The more the Company tries to achieve its goal of mastery by deciding exactly what the next generation of superpersons will be (the more it involves itself in determining which powers to allow folks to possess, where to allow the evolved to live, when to step in and dampen powers, and so forth), the more it burdens itself with a significant degree of moral responsibility over what individuals choose to do with their superpowers. The more it does that, the more it removes the ability of such persons to form their own supportive communities. The more it does that, the more inflexible it makes itself in dealing with the vagaries that will inevitably come its way. And given what *Heroes* has shown us, it seems quite reasonable that such things are happening and will continue to happen, regardless of whether they are brought about by the Company or not.

So, should we conclude that the Company's goal of mastery is morally wrong? As it stands, no. Let's focus for a moment on the argumentative strategy Sandel used. His objective, like ours, is the moral evaluation of a particular goal. And his tactic in determining what distinguishes good goals from bad ones was to consider the likely consequences that would ensue if that goal were adopted. This is a fine approach as far as it goes, but it opens itself up to the counterargument that the good things likely to result from pursuing the goal have been ignored or at least downplayed. If, instead, they're given their proper due, so the counterargument goes, it'll be seen that they outweigh the bad things that are likely to happen.[4]

When it comes to the Company, this response amounts first to acknowledging the bad things that are likely to result from the Company's efforts to control the emergence of superpowers. But it then goes on to emphasize the good things that will also likely ensue, suggesting that they outweigh the bad. These good things will no doubt include suppressing the powers of folks who have the kind of devastating nuclear abilities of a Ted Sprague or even the dangerous persuasive abilities of an Eden McCain. Such suppression will potentially save millions of lives. And when the good of these saved lives is weighed against the bad of the Company's increased moral responsibility and inflexibility, and even its interference with intrinsically valuable natural processes, it clearly seems that the former trumps the latter. So, eating humble pie might be good for a variety of reasons, but forgoing dessert and keeping a large number of folks around for another day is even better.

Now should we conclude that the Company's goal of mastering evolutionary forces *isn't* morally wrong? That, in fact, it might even be morally right? Believe it or not, the answer again is no. This is because of the inherent limitations on *any* speculation about the consequences of pursuing a specific goal. The problem is that the speculation is, well, speculative. What does this line of thinking amount to? The moral status of some goals is determined by the *actual* (versus the likely) consequences of following the goal. That's all well and good, of course, but it makes evaluating goals *prior* to their adoption difficult and speculative, at best.

Where does this leave us? While some goals might be inherently bad, that is, bad regardless of a consideration of further factors, the goal of mastering nature is not like this. A consideration of the further relevant factors that would help us determine its moral status, however, has proved inconclusive. So on this count, at least, the Company has a get-out-of-jail-free card.

Finding Where the Blame Lies

Even though the Company may not be morally blameworthy for adopting the goal of mastery, it is blameworthy for many of the things it's done. Kidnapping, spying, imprisonment, not to mention the nuclear explosion plot—these activities are villainous by almost all moral standards. Usually, it's unproblematic to determine who's morally responsible for acts of wrongdoing. When Sylar kills the cheerleader Jackie Wilcox in "Homecoming," what he does is wrong, and we need look no further than Sylar to figure out whom to blame and punish. But things get complicated when we consider an *organization,* rather than a single person. Are all members of the Company, or only some, morally accountable for its crimes? Could it be that the Company itself is somehow accountable but not any individual person?

Two issues need to be addressed: first, how to distribute moral blame among the Company's members for its acts of wrongdoing, and second, how to figure out what a member of the Company ought to do if she no longer finds herself in moral agreement with its agenda. Let's begin with the issue of distributing blame, and let's focus on the Company's large-scale operation of kidnapping, tagging, and mind-wiping persons with evolved abilities. Who's to blame for this wrongdoing? Obviously, there are several positions we could adopt.

The first position is that everyone who's a part of the Company or directly related to its activities shares in the moral responsibility for this program. That includes the founding twelve members, as well as Noah Bennet, the Haitian, even Aron Malsky (an accountant of the Linderman Group in "Godsend"), and Hank and Lisa, who presumably help to keep the wheels turning at one of the Company's fronts, Primatech Papers. (You may remember them as the couple who pretended to be Claire's parents in "Better Halves.") The problem with this option is that it places blame on too many people. Given the presumably large size of the Company and its affiliates, there are, no doubt, many people who are a part of it and yet know absolutely nothing about its bag-and-tag program. And this ignorance, if nothing else, would seem to pardon them from being morally responsible for it.

The second position we could adopt is that only the persons "on top" are to be held morally responsible for the Company's tracking program. This means that blame falls on the twelve founding members, who seem to be the ones calling all the shots. The problem with this option is the opposite of the first: it doesn't hold enough people morally responsible.

Perhaps the ones on top are to blame, but when it comes to the tracking program, so, too, are Bennet and the Haitian, as well as Thompson, their immediate superior.

A third position would be to hold the Company itself responsible, but not any particular person who's a part of it. But this is also an unsatisfying option, for the same reason the second approach is. Once more, blame falls in too few places. Surely, there is individual responsibility in addition to the Company's overall responsibility, even if the Company is distinct from the people who compose it. It's not as if it exists and acts in complete independence. Individual persons make decisions on its behalf.

This leaves us with the last and most promising possible position, which is holding some but not all members of the Company morally responsible. Attractive as this option is, it obviously invites the problem of determining just who to blame. If it's not everyone but it's also not only the folks on top, who is it? The contemporary philosopher Dennis Thompson, in his book *Political Ethics and Public Office*, pointed to one answer.[5] He argued that we should distribute praise or blame for a particular policy of an organization to all persons whose actions are causally responsible for that policy's adoption and execution, as long as those persons act freely and knowingly.

When it comes to the Company's tracking program, this gives us the result we're looking for. The founding members are morally responsible because they presumably pushed for this agenda (this "pushing" helped cause the program to be created) and did so freely (they acted noncoercively) and knowing what it involved. Bennet and the Haitian are also morally responsible, because they enacted the program (satisfying the condition of causal responsibility) and did so freely (there's no reason to suspect they were forced into kidnapping folks or were brainwashed into doing so), and they also knew full well what the program involved. But it is important to note that accountants such as Aron Malsky aren't found morally responsible in this view. Although he was neck deep in Linderman's affairs, there's no reason to suspect that he was a causal factor in bringing about or enacting the tracking program. The same undoubtedly goes for Hank and Lisa.

Blowing the Whistle on the Bad Guys

To bring down this company, sometimes we have to do bad things. Don't disappoint me, Suresh.

—Noah Bennet, "The Line"

We're now in a position to determine for each act of wrongdoing the Company performs who in the Company shares the blame for doing it. But if anyone is going to be brought to justice for these various acts of wrongdoing—if placing this blame is going to amount to anything—then the Company's actions need to be made public. Since it's a clandestine organization, that's a tall order. To be sure, making the public aware of organizational wrongdoing is difficult even for groups that aren't clandestine. As we've seen time and again with certain groups— one need think only of Enron—the wrongdoing that organizations involve themselves with is often not made known to the public until someone from within the organization brings its crimes to light. This has come to be known as whistle-blowing, but it's a difficult matter to determine when a member of an organization ought to blow the whistle. It neither seems right that one should always make organizational wrongdoing public, nor that one should never do so.

Consider Noah Bennet. He is a company man through and through at the start of the series. But he begins to have a change of heart when, because of his adopted daughter Claire's emerging powers, he recognizes just how destructive some of the Company's policies are. At this stage, one plausible necessary factor that would warrant whistle-blowing seems to have been met: the whistle-blower genuinely believes that the organization is involved in *serious* wrongdoing. When it comes to the Company, this isn't too hard a condition to meet once a person in the organization starts thinking clearly about what's going on.

But although this condition is necessary, it's not sufficient. Other factors are relevant as well. One factor might be whether the whistle-blower herself is morally responsible for the wrongdoing in question. This ties in with our previous considerations. Bennet, for example, is morally responsible for many of the Company's disreputable policies, and this might also be a necessary condition on permitting him to blow the whistle. Then again, perhaps not. If Aron comes to believe that the tracking program is a serious crime, must he somehow be responsible for it in order to blow the whistle on the program? It doesn't seem so. We can agree, though, that even if it isn't a necessary condition on warranting whistle-blowing, being morally responsible for the wrongdoing in question certainly counts in favor of being permitted to bring the wrongdoing to light. Doing so provides some means of atonement.

Other relevant factors in determining whether a person should blow the whistle are determining whether doing so will be effective and evaluating what the costs of doing so will be. The two are obviously connected. If bringing the Company's operations to the press poses a serious threat to Bennet's life— as seems to have been the case with Nathan in "Powerless"— or poses a serious threat to his family, then he may not be obligated to blow the whistle. This is true, even if doing so would result in stopping the Company from continuing its programs. Moreover, he certainly isn't obligated to whistle-blow if there's little chance of the Company's activities ceasing.

This leads to a further concern. Suppose a person genuinely believes that whistle-blowing won't be effective. What, then, should she do? Resign? Perhaps, but it might also be permissible to seek out other means of holding the organization accountable. This has to stop short of engaging in criminal behavior, though; two wrongs don't make a right. And this is precisely why Bennet's scheme of bringing the Company down from within became morally impermissible the minute he started murdering and attempting to murder Company members (that is, when he started doing "bad things").

We're left, then, with a helpful but incomplete set of criteria for determining when a member of the Company ought to whistle-blow. If she believes that the Company is involved in serious wrongdoing and that bringing this wrongdoing to light will be effective in stopping it and that she is not significantly compromising her own well-being or the well-being of those closest to her, then she has good reason to whistle-blow. She has a better reason if, in addition to this, she is partially responsible for the wrongdoing. If these conditions aren't met, then she has good reason not to whistle-blow. But if they are, it's unclear whether she should resign or pursue some other means of stopping the Company from doing its dastardly deeds.

The means our heroes pursued took down the Company by the end of Volume 3. But by the end of Volume 4, the Company was reinstated, this time with government backing. Our heroes realized that as bad as the Company was, it is needed to keep those with powers under control, a secret, and protected from the public. No doubt, there are many more questions to ask about the Company (both old and new) and its various enterprises. And these questions will provide us with more grist for the mill of moral reflection. For now, we leave the Company in some sense exonerated for its goal of mastering the evolutionary forces at work in the *Heroes* universe but nevertheless morally culpable for many of its programs. This culpability falls on the heads of various persons throughout the Company. But we should hope that the new Company is able to stay out of the morally gray area, at least a little more often than the old one did. After all, that is part of what being a hero is all about: doing the morally right thing but finding a way to do it in the morally right way.

NOTES

1. Sorry for the Simpsons reference. (See *The Simpsons*, "Treehouse of Horror III: Clown without Pity.") It was my editor's idea.

2. To be accurate, evolution isn't really compatible with the events of *Heroes*. If Tim Kring, the creator, doesn't want to ignore such problems, he may have to appeal to divine intervention to make sense of the story. See chapter 11 of this book, "The Science of *Heroes:* Flying Men, Immortal Samurai, and Destroying the Space-Time Continuum," by Andrew Zimmerman Jones.

3. Harvard University Press, 2007.

4. This is precisely the response that bioethicist Frances Kamm adopted in responding to Sandel in her paper "What Is and Is Not Wrong with Enhancement" (Faculty Research Working Paper, John F. Kennedy School of Government at Harvard University). Interestingly, Sandel denied that his evaluation is primarily of a consequentialist variety, although it's difficult, then, to figure out what else it's supposed to be.

5. Harvard University Press, 1987.

FOUR

WITH GREAT CREATIVITY COMES GREAT IMITATION: PROBLEMS OF PLAGIARISM AND KNOWLEDGE

Jason Southworth

Heroes is wildly popular with mainstream audiences, and you might expect it to be even more popular with comic book fans. But, actually, many of them actively dislike *Heroes;* their posts on comic blogs and message boards have made this abundantly clear. Chief among their complaints is that the show too closely resembles characters and stories that have already appeared in comic books. These similarities, in fact, have led some to accuse Tim Kring, the creator, producer, and chief writer of *Heroes*, of plagiarism. "He's just copying the ideas of others and passing them off as his own," comic fans say. Could this be? Could so many people's favorite show simply be the result of petty "intellectual thievery"?

"Cautionary Tales": The Formal
Charges of Plagiarism

Let's get clear on the charges. The various claims that *Heroes* contains instances of plagiarism can be divided into two classes. First and most common is the charge that numerous characters in *Heroes* have the powers of preexisting comic book characters, especially from the X-Men. Claire Bennet's ability to heal is like Wolverine's healing factor; both of them are able to heal from any injury they incur. Sylar and Peter's abilities work like Rogue's mutant power. Like Sylar, Rogue steals the powers of others rendering them powerless and dead (although, with Rogue, the effect is not always permanent and lethal). Rogue acquires the abilities of others by touch, like Peter does in Volume 4. Even Isaac Mendez's power to paint the future predates him in a character from the X-verse—Nemesio from *District X*.

The second charge of plagiarism suggests that the general story of *Heroes* and a few of the character arcs too closely resemble the stories of several comic books. The best example of this is J. Michael Straczynski's *Rising Stars* (1999). Following the trend begun by Frank Miller's *Dark Knight Returns* (1986), *Rising Stars* depicts superheroes in the real world. In Straczynski's story, just as in *Heroes*, people are born with superhuman abilities, and the story follows the lives of these individuals as they come to learn about their powers and decide how best to use them. And again, as in *Heroes*, the primary threat for these superhumans is that one of them is killing the others in an attempt to gain their powers. Even the narrative structure is the same; *Rising Stars*, like *Heroes*, has a nonlinear narrative with various scenes taking place at different points in time. If *Rising Stars* were coming out now, we would clearly say it was copying from *Heroes*, but it came out seven years prior to the premiere of *Heroes*!

With these claims out in the open, we are now on our way to determining whether plagiarism accusations are warranted. But how should we evaluate these accusations? In philosophy, before we address a question like this, we first get clear on the terminology we are using. So, we must first establish what plagiarism is.

"The Line": What Is Plagiarism and Has It Occurred?

The *Merriam-Webster Online Dictionary* gives four definitions of plagiarism. These are "(1) to steal and pass off (the ideas or words of another) as one's own; (2) to use (another's production) without crediting the source; (3) to commit literary theft; and (4) to present as new and original an idea or product derived from an existing source."[1] Given the two classes of plagiarism accusations presented at the start of this chapter, we can quickly conclude that no plagiarism has occurred under definition 3. Definition 3, taken in the broadest sense, expresses a common view of plagiarism that a literary work or a substantial portion of one must be taken and represented as one's own. The claims of plagiarism surrounding *Heroes*, however, are more subtle. They accuse Kring and the other writers of taking character ideas and story ideas, not whole works.

Some people would want to reject any claims of plagiarism under definition 3 for an additional reason—the works that the creators of *Heroes* potentially "borrowed from" are not *literary* works. An objection of this type is misguided, however. Despite popular opinion, comic books and other forms of sequential art are indeed literary works. They are able to present the same concepts and ideas that traditional literature does, and they do so using written words on paper: the tools used in literary works. The argument that comic books are not literary works is usually motivated by their use of illustrations in conjunction with written words. This is a weak reason, committing those who present it to the distasteful position that certain books that are generally recognized as literary works, such as Lewis Carroll's *Alice's Adventures in Wonderland* and Kurt Vonnegut's *Breakfast of Champions*, are not literary works because they contain illustrations.[2]

We can also quickly reject the plagiarism claims made under definition 2, which suggests that plagiarism occurs when another product is being used without citation. This type of plagiarism is most likely to occur in academic works where sections of one text are inserted into another without any recognition of the actual author of the passage. For this type of plagiarism to have occurred in the case of *Heroes*, the show would have to contain a character or a story arc created by someone not on the *Heroes* staff. Again, the claims of plagiarism made against the show are more subtle than this. What is claimed is that character traits and story points in *Heroes resemble* those of other works, while not being identical.[3]

Let's deal with definitions 1 and 4 at the same time. Each of these definitions involves the subtle form of plagiarism, which is our present concern. There are two things common between these definitions, and they will need to be present for something to be called plagiarism: (1) the ideas or content of one work must appear in another, and (2) the ideas or content must be used in the second work with the intention of deceiving others about the origin of the material.

It is clear, given the examples offered by those who claim there is plagiarism in the show, that at least the first criterion is met. For example, all of the powers possessed by characters in *Heroes* are present in other works of superhero fiction. These include the cases mentioned from the beginning of this chapter but extend even to the characters who appear in the show for only a scene or an episode. (For example, the super-hearing of Dale Smither, the female mechanic, is just like Superman's.) In addition, the story similarities between *Heroes* and *Rising Stars* are undeniable, and many of the character arcs and story concepts from the show are hardly new. Consider the number of stories where an individual chooses to keep his powers a secret even from his family, as Claire does, or the number of stories where there are secret organizations tracking and investigating individuals with powers. But this isn't that surprising. The genre of superhero fiction has been around since at least 1938 (with *Action Comics* #1—even earlier, if you count pulp heroes like the Shadow). Completely original superhuman powers, stories, and plot devices come few and far between at this point.

The trouble in making a charge of plagiarism stick is the second condition: that there was an intention on the part of the creators to present these aspects of the show as original when they knew they were not. Unless we develop powers like those of Matt Parkman, we will never have access to the actual intentions of Kring and the other writers, because their intentions exist in their minds. What will count as good reason, then, will be something less than certainty. But the standard I suggest is a strong one: if Kring knew about it, he must have copied it. If there is any evidence that Kring had knowledge of other characters with the powers he gave his heroes, we will assume that his use of them was intentional, unless we have evidence to the contrary. In the case of the similarities between *Heroes* and *Rising Stars*, if Kring has read the comic book, then we will assume that his use of similar story points was intentional.

To discover whether he did have such knowledge, we'll consider interviews with both Kring and producer-writer Jeph Loeb. Let's begin by addressing the story similarities between *Heroes* and *Rising Stars*. In an interview with Damon Lindelof (the creator of *Lost*), Kring explicitly addressed the question of whether he had read *Rising Stars*. In response to the question, Kring said,

> I'm intrigued by this question because obviously some-
> thing I've done with *Heroes* proves to you that I didn't
> read it. The problem is, since I didn't read it, I don't
> know what that is. Did I miss something I should
> have stolen? Did I steal something and don't know it?
> I fear the latter from the tone of your question. But
> the truth is I didn't read it for a couple reasons. First
> and foremost, because this show deals in the arena of
> the superhero and comic book world, I didn't want to
> be tempted or discouraged by other ideas out there.
> Very early on in the process, I went to see my friend
> Jeph Loeb for just this reason. I told him I was not
> well versed in this world and wanted him to steer me
> away from anything that was derivative or just out and
> out stealing. Unfortunately, *everything* I pitched to him
> had not only been done once, but many times in many
> ways. I literally went home that night convinced that
> I couldn't touch this subject without reinventing the
> wheel at best, and outright plagiarism at worst. I finally
> decided, maybe foolishly so, not to read anything. In
> this way, at least my conscience is clear.[4]

This quotation seems to put to rest the issue of plagiarism
from *Rising Stars*. If Kring has never read the story, then
there is no way that he could have taken ideas or story content from it.

We can find further evidence of Kring's ignorance about
superheroes and their powers—and put to rest any worries of
intentional copying—in an interview with Loeb, on the comic
book podcast *Wordballoon*. In response to a question from the
host, John Siuntres, about how Loeb became involved with
the show, Loeb described his first meeting with Kring about
Heroes. In this discussion, Loeb explained that Kring had
wanted to include in the show a character with the ability to
control metal objects. The opening scene for the character

was that a car would be coming down the road and almost hit him, but instead the character is able to flip the car over in the air. Loeb claimed that his response to this description was to ask, "Like Magneto?" and that Kring replied, "Who's Magneto?"[5] For those who, like Kring, don't know Magneto, he is one of the most famous villains in comics. He is the primary enemy of the X-Men and has appeared in hundreds of comics, all three X-Men films (played by Sir Ian McKellen, no less), and the animated series. So, if Kring does not know who this fairly popular character is, then it seems clear that he does not know very much about super-heroes at all.

"Unexpected": Accidental Plagiarism and the Case against It

There is one more type of plagiarism we must address: accidental plagiarism. As we have already discussed, ordinary plagiarism requires an intention on the part of an individual to represent the work of another individual as his own. With accidental plagiarism, this intention no longer needs to be shown. As the name implies, accidental plagiarism occurs when an individual presents the work of another as his own by accident. This can occur when an individual internalizes a preexisting idea or concept and at the time of creation does not realize the material is actually the product of the work of another person.

A classic example from the history of superhero fiction is Steve Gerber and his creation *Howard the Duck*. Some might remember Howard as the subject of a terrible movie produced by the most overrated director in the history of American cinema, George Lucas (that's right—I went there). For those who don't know, Howard is a three-foot-tall, ill-tempered, cigar-smoking duck that exists in the world of Marvel comics. Howard's comic was an adult satire dealing with both social issues of the day and popular concepts in comic book history. At first pass, this may seem interesting and original, but it is also obvious that any new talking ducks will invite comparisons to the most successful of all talking waterfowl, Donald Duck. As a result, the Walt Disney Corporation sued Marvel comics over copyright infringement (an issue related to plagiarism). Marvel settled out of court, agreeing to make several changes to Howard's character (for instance, he would have to start wearing pants). While it is clear Gerber did not intend to imitate the Disney character, it also seems clear that he had let the character in some way influence Howard. This is what motivated Marvel to agree to the changes, rather than go to court.[6]

So, maybe Kring, in creating *Heroes*, committed an act of accidental plagiarism. Maybe. But this still doesn't seem likely. By his own admission and based on the anecdote from Loeb, we can see that Kring knew little to nothing about the genre of superhero fiction when he created the show. This is a significant difference between Kring and Gerber in the case of Howard the Duck. Gerber was fully aware of Donald Duck, and even though he was not thinking of him at the time of Howard's creation, character traits were able to assert themselves subconsciously (or so the claim from Marvel and Disney said). This could not be the case with Kring, however. He knew so little about superheroes that he did not even know the powers of the most popular X-Men. Although Kring has not explained which superpowered characters he has knowledge of and which he does not, if we take him at his word, he knows very little. It is plausible to assume that he knows about Superman, Batman, and Spider-Man, given the success of their film and animation projects, but at present, there have been no characters in *Heroes* who come close to resembling these icons, so that is not a worry. (Taking Kring at his word, though, we must also assume that he missed the highly successful X-Men films.)[7]

"Truth and Consequences": So, What Has Kring Done Wrong?

Now that we have concluded that Kring has not committed plagiarism, overt or otherwise, there will be some who would like to end the discussion. I, on the other hand, think that this is premature. Even if Kring has not plagiarized, it still seems that he has done something wrong. The reason for this stems from Kring's ignorance and his apparent pride in being ignorant. I am fairly certain I am not alone in wanting to say that Kring *should* have known about the genre of superhero fiction, in order to avoid similarities to other works, and that to the extent to which he does not know about the genre, he has done something wrong.

There is a philosophical concept that captures this sense of wrongdoing: epistemic responsibility. Editors and readers alike should not be afraid of this term. *Epistemic* is simply a ten-buck word for "having to do with knowledge." So, when we talk about epistemic responsibilities, we are talking about the things that we are responsible for knowing, or things we have a duty to know. According to contemporary philosopher James Montmarquet, to be epistemically responsible a person must have a desire for truth and for the avoidance of error.[8] This responsibility extends only to the areas in life that you care about and only to the degree to which you care about them.[9] So, Hiro Nakamura has an epistemic responsibility concerning Takezo Kensei because the stories about Kensei are very important to him. Likewise, Hiro has an epistemic responsibility concerning his powers, as they are also quite important to him.

With responsibility comes the potential for blame. If an individual has a responsibility but fails to meet that responsibility, he has done something wrong and is deserving of blame. If there is no obligation, however, there can be no blame. So, Hiro had no epistemic responsibility to learn how to drive a car, because he was never called on to drive in Japan. This lack of responsibility explains why we do not blame Hiro for not knowing how to drive a car when he has the opportunity to drive in the United States ("Hiros").

We are responsible for knowing about the things that affect the things we care about, to the degree that we care about them. So, Niki Sanders has an obligation to learn as much as she can about Jessica, even though she may not care about Jessica. After all, Jessica affects Niki's health and safety, and the health and safety of her son—two things Niki cares a great deal about. To the extent that Niki does not try to learn about Jessica when she can, as she fails to do at the beginning of the first volume, she is to be blamed.[10]

In addition to the concept of epistemic responsibility, Montmarquet identified three other separate and distinct epistemic criteria for evaluating an individual: impartiality, sobriety, and courage. By impartiality, Montmarquet meant "an openness to the ideas of others, the willingness to exchange ideas with and learn from them, the lack of jealousy and personal bias directed at their ideas and the lively sense of one's own fallibility."[11] We can understand this concept best by reflecting on Mohinder Suresh. Every time Mohinder refuses to consider the research of his father *because* his father is the laughingstock of the university (and because Mohinder's involvement in his father's work will cause Mohinder to lose his job), he is exhibiting a lack of epistemic impartiality.[12] He is letting his personal biases about his father and his fear of embarrassment affect his judgment of his father's research.

We can contrast "sobriety" with unwarranted enthusiasm: the actions of a person who, out of excitement and love of new ideas, believes things that are not warranted, and who does not consider the limits of his own evidence. In the flashback scene when Mohinder criticizes his father for wanting to go to America to study human genetic mutations, he is accusing his father of lacking epistemic sobriety. Mohinder thinks his father is so excited by his theory that he is neglecting evidence that runs counter to the theory: the findings of traditional biology.[13]

Finally, "courage" is a willingness to consider alternatives to popularly held beliefs and is the ability to continue an investigation in the face of opposition from others.[14] For example, Mohinder lacks epistemic courage when he, as a young academic, criticizes his father for pursuing research that other academics reject out of hand. But later in life, when he reconsiders his father's research in the face of blind criticism from his colleague Nirand, Mohinder shows that he has developed epistemic courage ("Homecoming").

We now have the tools to explain the intuition that Kring has done something wrong with his work on *Heroes*. In addition, we have the tools to assess the level of Kring's blameworthiness. The first thing we must do is establish that he cares about *Heroes*—which is pretty obvious. He has invested a great deal of time in the show, his livelihood and reputation are tied to the success of the show, and he has had to sacrifice other things he seems to care about (such as his job writing for the series *Crossing Jordan*) in order to be so involved with *Heroes*.

Given that Kring cares about *Heroes*, we can now ask what he ought to know. These things include facts about the show and the production of the show, but they also include several broader issues concerning how the show fits in with the medium and the genre in which it participates. This is because the success of the show is in part tied to whether it is original, and, at the very least, critical acclaim is contingent on creativity and originality. So, it seems that for those who care about *Heroes* in the way that Kring does, there is an obligation to know whether the show is creative or original. To know this, however, requires knowing both about the medium in which the show is presented (television) and about the genre in which it participates (superhero fiction). It seems clear that

Kring knows about the medium, but it seems equally clear that Kring knows very little about the genre.

The best and only reliable way that Kring can come to this knowledge about the genre is to research it. This research should at the very least involve reading any story that someone warns him *Heroes* resembles. Kring did not do this, however. In the interview with Lindelof we saw that although Kring even had a copy of *Rising Stars* (given to him by Lindelof), he did not bother to read it. Similarly with the Loeb anecdote, Loeb told Kring that one of his character concepts was remarkably similar to an X-Men villain. Rather than investigate the X-Men, Kring simply refrained from using that character as a major character and moved on.[15] So, it seems that Kring failed to be epistemically responsible. Strike one, Kring.

Now let's consider epistemic impartiality. There are several elements needed to make a person epistemically impartial. The most important are openness to the ideas of others, willingness to exchange ideas with others and learn from them, and a lack of personal biases. Given the quote from Kring, we can see that he is not sufficiently open to the ideas of others, nor is he willing to exchange ideas with or learn from the ideas of others. In fact, he pointed out that he is quite the opposite. Recall that Kring said, "I finally decided, maybe foolishly so, not to read anything. In this way, at least my conscience is clear."[16] It seems evident from this quote that his concern is to have a conscience free from guilt about plagiarism, at the expense of knowing anything about superhero fiction. It is worth pointing out that if Kring were willing to investigate superhero fiction, he would be able to improve *Heroes* as well. This is because he would be able to learn from the storytelling mistakes of others. Strike two.

What of epistemic sobriety? It seems that like Chandra Suresh, Kring lacks epistemic sobriety. There were, by Kring's own admission, several warning signs that *Heroes* might at best be similar, and at worst be trite imitation, of other super-hero works. As he said in the previous quote, regarding his discussion of the show with Loeb, "Unfortunately, *everything* I pitched to him had not only been done once, but many times in many ways."[17] Despite this fact, Kring went ahead with his plans for the show without doing any research about superheroes. The reason seems to be that he, like Chandra, was so excited by his initial idea that he failed to investigate superhero fiction further. This point was solidified later in the interview between Lindelof and Kring when Kring said, in response to a question about whether he would start reading superhero comics, "I am a little afraid of knowing too much. I guess my fear is that I could get too invested in the 'powers' and lose sight of what attracted me to these characters."[18] Kring is blameworthy once again.

Some might object that the obligation Kring has to know what has come earlier in the genre should be waived because it is impossible to be original in this genre. The problem with this objection is that the history of superhero fiction is full of examples of original and creative works. It was original for Spider-Man to have the problems of a normal teenager, rather than be depicted as a god among men, like previous superheroes. It was original when Dennis O'Neil wrote stories where superpowered beings had to deal with contemporary social issues ranging from racism to drug addiction in *Green Lantern/Green Arrow*. It was original when Alan Moore and Dave Gibbons produced *Watchmen* and brought post-modernity to the sequential arts with the inclusion of written works from their fictional universe in the body of the story. Granted, these are high-water marks for the genre, but there are plenty of less impressive, yet highly original, stories and plot points in the genre. Among these is Grant Morrison's reimagination of the villainous machines, the sentinels, in *New X-Men*. Morrison made these machines, which previously have been many stories tall, so small that they move in the bloodstream of mutants. So, it seems that the genre does not preclude originality.

This leaves us with only epistemic courage. It seems that on this ground, we can't actually evaluate Kring because establishing whether someone has epistemic courage requires that he be pursuing an epistemic investigation. Kring, of course, has refused to participate in one. As a result, we may quickly conclude that there is no praise or blame to award regarding this point.

"The Hard Part"

Although there is no plagiarism in *Heroes*, Tim Kring has failed to meet his epistemic responsibility. But let's not be too quick to throw stones. We all fail to meet our epistemic responsibility from time to time. While it is useful to have a standard that allows us to judge others, it is more important for us to ensure that we do not fail to meet an obligation. This type of self-reflection is the most important element of philosophy.[19]

NOTES

1. I obtained this information from plagiarism.org, www.plagiarism.org/learning_center/what_is_plagiarism.html. Notice that I cited the material that led me to the actual source of the material. It's called intellectual honesty and not being a hypocrite.

2. Due to space considerations, I will not labor on this point and merely recommend that anyone who is still not convinced should read Scott McCloud, *Understanding Comics* (New York: Harper Paperbacks, 1994). This book has a section offering a more detailed argument than the one I have just given, along with a thorough descriptive and psychological explanation of how the art form works.

3. You might think that my reading of definitions 2 and 3 is too broad, and this might be the case. I have interpreted the sentences in the way that I have because they are the type of answers people often give when pressed to explain what plagiarism is. This still leaves us with definitions 1 and 4, which I will interpret in a far more nuanced way further on, so even if I was too general in my treatment of definitions 2 and 3, a subtle reading of them will be covered by my reading of the other two.

4. Untitled interview, www.nbc.com/Heroes/interviews/tim_kring.shtml.

5. "Riding Shotgun with Jeph Loeb in the Valley" aired on *Wordballoon*, in 2007. See http://wordballoon.blogspot.com/2005/11/riding-shotgun-with-jeph-loeb-in.html.

6. See Tom Field, *Secrets in the Shadow: The Art and Life of Gene Colan* (New York: Two Morrows Publishing, 2005), p. 114.

7. For those interested in reading more on plagiarism, and I am sure you all are, I recommend Richard A. Posner, *The Little Book of Plagiarism* (New York: Pantheon Books, 2007).

8. Although the term *epistemic responsibility* was originally coined by Lorraine Code, I will be relying on Montmarquet's analysis of the concept.

9. James Montmarquet, *Epistemic Virtue and Doxastic Responsibility* (Lanham, MD: Rowman and Littlefield, 1993), p. 21.

10. Ibid., p. 21.

11. Ibid., p. 22.

12. We see this very clearly in the dream sequence in "7 Minutes to Midnight."

13. Ibid.

14. Montmarquet, *Epistemic Virtue and Doxastic Responsibility*, pp. 21–23.

15. The character called "the German" (first introduced in the graphic novel, in the chapter titled "Berlin, Part I") had magnetism as a power, as Magneto does. But he was a fairly minor character, appearing briefly in Volume 3, only to be killed off by Knox (Benjamin "Knox" Washington) in "One of Us, One of Them."

16. Untitled interview.

17. Ibid.

18. Ibid.

19. I would like to thank Ruth Tallman for all of her helpful comments on previous drafts of this chapter.

PART TWO

SUPERMEN, SAMURAI, AND INVISIBLE MEN

FIVE

TIME AND THE MEANING OF LIFE IN *HEROES* AND NIETZSCHE

Tyler Shores

You do not choose your destiny. It chooses you.
—Mohinder Suresh, "Nothing to Hide"

Questions and issues of choice and destiny drive the plot of *Heroes.* Consider, for example, Mr. Linderman's explanation of the choice between happiness and meaning:

Linderman: You see, I think there comes a time when a man has to ask himself whether he wants a life of happiness or a life of meaning.

Nathan: I'd like to have both.

Linderman: It can't be done. Two very different paths. I mean, to be truly happy a man must live absolutely in the present, and with no thought of what's gone before, and no thought of what lies ahead. But a life of meaning, a man is condemned to wallow in the past, and obsess about the future.

—*"Parasite"*

Is it truly an either/or situation, as Linderman describes it? Must a life of meaning come at the expense of a life of happiness, and vice versa? This concern with past, present, and future is one of the main themes throughout the first volume of the series and provides us with a perfect jumping-off point for examining the philosophy of Friedrich Nietzsche (1844–1900) and his idea of eternal recurrence.

Nietzsche: "We Are Unknown to Ourselves"

Although self-knowledge is a crucial component of our internal lives, Nietzsche believed it was lacking in far too many of us.

> We are unknown to ourselves. We are deaf to the sounds we hear around us, including the sounds and echoes of our own being. We exist in an absent-minded manner and are like someone sunk deep in their own thoughts who upon hearing the twelve strokes of midday, wakes up with a start and wonders, what hour has just struck? Only afterwards, upon the delay of time, do we rub our ears and ask, just what did we experience then? And who am I in fact?[1]

Sleepwalking through our daily existence, distracted by day-to-day events and routines, we forget to ask ourselves the most important questions of all: "Where am I going?" and "How did I get to where I am?" The "twelve strokes of midday" remind us that if we're not careful, we could live most of our lives having never realized why we do the things that we do because we have never figured out who we are.

Fittingly, the first volume of *Heroes* follows different characters as they discover their powers and confront the question "Who am I?" In "Genesis," Hiro Nakamura says, "People think of time as a straight line . . . but time is actually more like [a circle]." In one of Nietzsche's greatest works, *Thus Spoke Zarathustra*, the protagonist and prophet Zarathustra confronts a dwarfish figure who mutters a similar sentiment: "All that is straight lies . . . all truth is crooked; time itself is a circle."[2] This reconsideration of time introduces us to one of Nietzsche's most complicated but arguably most important ideas: the eternal recurrence. The idea of eternal recurrence, as described by Nietzsche, holds that everything that has happened, is happening, and will happen has already happened and will happen again, an infinite number of times in exactly the same way.

Nietzsche offered the eternal recurrence not as a scientific theory but as a thought experiment to better understand one's self. In no uncertain terms, Nietzsche wanted the reader to realize how truly unsettling such a thought would be: "Let us think this thought in its most terrible form: existence as it is, without meaning or aim, yet recurring inevitably without any finale of nothingness: 'the eternal return.'"[3]

We as readers might rightfully ask ourselves, "What's so bad about the eternal recurrence?" Nietzsche answered this question by pointing out that every fact could become dreadful if everything repeated infinitely. Consider Volume 2's main villain, Adam Monroe, and the poetic justice with which Hiro temporarily dispatched Adam, by placing him in a coffin. Since Adam could not die of old age, starvation, or any other natural causes, if he had been left there, he would have been doomed to experience the same thing, the inside of the coffin, over and over—forever.[4] Could there be a worse fate than living out eternity in an unending state of living death? This is the eternal recurrence in its "most terrible form." The ominous implications of the eternal recurrence are even more vividly described when Adam (in a monologue that follows the time-honored tradition of the supervillain revealing his plan just before it is thwarted) rationalizes his unleashing the Shanti virus that will decimate the world's population:

> Wars, famine, disease. Four hundred years later, nothing has changed. When God wasn't happy with what he'd created, he made it rain for forty days and forty nights. He just washed it all away. He had the right idea. Because when this virus is released, those of us who are left will be granted a second chance. And I'll be their hero.
>
> *—"Powerless"*

From Adam's perspective, nothing has changed. His response is to create a new future—one that diverges from the eternally recurring pattern—regardless of the consequences.

When Peter Petrelli gains Hiro's time-jumping ability, he witnesses firsthand the postapocalyptic future that results from the virus and travels back in time to prevent that future from ever happening. The prevention of the repetition of events is also very much the driving motivation of the show's first volume. "Save the cheerleader, save the world," is the cryptic message Future Hiro delivers to his past self: the future mustn't be repeated in the past. Granted, there are a number of very good reasons Peter and Hiro would want to prevent that particular future from ever occurring, but Nietzsche's philosophy probes the basis for *why* we would want to change the future—or anything else, for that matter. What is it about our worldview that would compel us to want to change things from how they already are? Nietzsche presented the eternal recurrence as a hypothetical, a "what if?"

> What if some day or night a demon were to steal after you into your loneliest loneliness and say to you: "This life as you now live it and have lived it, you will have to

live once more and innumerable times more; and there will be nothing new in it, but every pain and every joy and every thought and sigh and everything unutterably small or great in your life will have to return to you, all in the same succession and sequence."

Sounds pretty bleak, doesn't it? Yet this isn't simply a depressing mental exercise, but rather a challenge:

Would you not throw yourself down and gnash your teeth and curse the demon who spoke thus? Or have you once experienced a tremendous moment when you would have answered him: "You are a god and never have I heard anything more divine." If this thought gained possession of you, it would change you as you are or perhaps crush you. The question in each and every thing, "Do you desire this once more and innumerable times more?"[5]

Nietzsche unequivocally believed that an understanding of this idea was crucial to finding and accepting meaning in our lives. The eternal recurrence is a test—a *self*-test. What attitude toward ourselves and our actions would we need to have in order to accept reliving the same events—the most mundane as well as the most extraordinary, the most wonderful as well as the most terrible—over and over again? Nietzsche asked, "[H]ow well disposed would you have to become to yourself and to life *to crave nothing more fervently* than this ultimate eternal confirmation and seal?"[6] The attitude you're able to bring toward the eternal recurrence can be taken as a reflection of your attitude toward yourself.

In the New York of five years to come, the future selves of Mohinder Suresh and Matt Parkman have a conversation in the spirit of Nietzsche's eternal recurrence challenge:

Future Mohinder: Haven't you ever wished you could change the past? Set your life down a different path?

Future Matt: I used to be that guy. Wishing it and making it happen are two different things.
                                    —*"Five Years Gone"*

Future Matt's rather stoic response here reflects Nietzsche's sentiment. The eternal recurrence becomes a personal test of affirmation to not only accept things, but to never want things to change. For Nietzsche, the choice of which path we take ultimately burdens every choice and decision we confront: "The question in everything that you will: 'am I certain I want to do it an infinite number of times?' will become for you the heaviest weight."[7]

A Tale of Two Paths

Keep in mind Future Mohinder's wish for a "different path." Nietzsche likewise described the eternal recurrence not as one path, but two: "Two paths meet here; no one has yet followed either to its end. This long lane stretches back for an eternity. And the long lane out there, that is another eternity."[8] In *Thus Spoke Zarathustra*, the image of two paths that run endlessly from each other serves as a simple yet elegant metaphor for the eternal recurrence and the fact that every choice made takes us yet further down a different path.

> "Behold this moment!" I went on. "From this gateway Moment a long, eternal lane runs back: an eternity lies behind us. Must not all things that can run have already run along this lane? Must not all things that can happen have already happened, been done, run past? And are not all things bound fast together in such a way that this moment draws after it all future things? Therefore— draws itself too? . . . And this slow spider that creeps along in the moonlight, and this moonlight itself, and

I and you at this gateway whispering together, whispering of eternal things—must we not all have been here before? . . . [A]nd must we not return and run down that other lane out before us, down that long, terrible lane—must we not return eternally?"[9]

Are there two paths? Or simply two ways of looking at the same path? Nietzsche's description of the eternal recurrence might now cause us to reexamine Linderman's earlier choice between the life of meaning and the life of happiness. If we find "all things bound fast together," perhaps the choice is not quite as simple as Linderman would have it seem.

For Nietzsche, "the moment" is the most fundamental of all measures of time. We find moments valuable and precious precisely because they can be so transient and fleeting. Some people spend their entire lives pursuing a lost moment or perhaps seeking a moment that may never arrive. But what if that one moment were to happen interminably and without end—would it hold the same value? Would we pursue it and esteem it in the same manner? Nietzsche urged us to find the meaning that exists in each single moment, an idea that Mohinder echoes in saying, "In the end, what does it matter when the human heart can only find meaning in the smallest of moments?" ("Genesis").

Heroes provides a twist on valuing single moments because we are able to glimpse how a single moment or event can produce vastly different outcomes. Hiro's power to travel through space and time affords him the possibility of experimenting with different choices and their outcomes. In Nietzsche's eternal recurrence, we non–time travelers are confronted with the reality that our choices are irrevocable, yet we must live our lives as if we would want to repeat those same choices (and mistakes) over and over again. *Heroes* lets us indulge in the fantasy of wondering how things might have turned out if we only had a second chance to choose differently:

Hiro: But what if I'm on the wrong path?

Ando: Maybe we can do it better . . . you can come back and fix things.

Hiro: Like a do-over? A do-over, I like that.
—*"Better Halves"*

Sometimes Hiro tries to choose a different path, only to find that his choice is trumped by forces greater than his own free will. For example, when he tries to prevent the waitress Charlie Andrews from being murdered by Sylar, he discovers that she is destined to die of a blood clot in her brain. Later, when Hiro tries to save his father from being murdered, his father cautions him that there are certain things that we are not meant to decide for ourselves: "We have the power of gods. That does not mean that we can play God" ("Cautionary Tales"). This leads us to another one of the more interesting themes of the show: dealing with fate and destiny.

Nietzsche's Love of Fate

For all his bluster, it is the sad province of man that he cannot choose his triumph. He can only choose how he will stand when the call of destiny comes. We all imagine ourselves the agents of our destiny, capable of determining our own fate. But have we truly any choice in when we rise or when we fall? Or does a force larger than ourselves bid us our direction?

—Mohinder Suresh, "Don't Look Back"

According to Nietzsche, the key to passing the self-test of the eternal recurrence is being able to take possession of one's own fate. Nietzsche called this idea *amor fati*—"the love of fate." The circumstances in which we find ourselves are largely matters of fate, over which we have little or no control. Where free will and fate intersect is in our ability to accept the circumstances that fate lays before us. What distinguishes the heroes of *Heroes* is not the powers they have, but their willingness to make choices despite what fate has seemingly predetermined.

But at the end of Volume 1, Angela Petrelli wants to keep Claire Bennet away from the events that are rapidly converging at Kirby Plaza:

> Angela: It's inevitable, dear. There's nothing anyone can do about it.
>
> Claire: That's insane! Nothing is inevitable. The future is not written in stone.
>
>   —*"How to Stop an Exploding Man"*

Sometimes, being heroic can be as simple as refusing to accept the inevitable. But for Nietzsche, free will may be less about changing events than it is a matter of being able to create meaning out of the events of the past, and subsequently the future: "I taught them to create the future, and to redeem by creating—all that was past."[10] Nietzsche did not want us to passively accept the events of the past, but instead to adopt the attitude that we would not want it any other way. Even if the future were inevitable, we shouldn't want any other future to occur: "To redeem that past of mankind and to transform every 'it was' until the will says, 'but I willed it thus! So shall I will it.' "[11]

It is in this way that Nietzsche's philosophy diverges from *Heroes*. For Nietzsche, the future may be written in stone, but we can make it our destiny in choosing to embrace it as a future we would want to eternally repeat. In the world of *Heroes*, the future is not written in stone and can be reshaped by actions in the present. And the writers of *Heroes* seem to be aware of this divergence. If you watch closely in Volume 3, you'll notice that Arthur Petrelli holds a copy of *Thus Spoke Zarathustra* while he talks to Peter about the consequences of releasing the formula. "We can make sure the future you saw never happens" ("Eris Quod Sum"). Arthur contradicts the central theme of Nietzsche's book while he holds it.

Meaning must be found and created; it cannot be given to us or granted through external means. In order to better know ourselves, we must become better at finding meaning in even the smallest of moments. As Nietzsche repeatedly stated in his works, the ideal life is one in which we can fully accept and desire each and every moment: "My formula for greatness for a human being is *amor fati*: that one wants nothing to be different, not forward, not backward, not in all eternity."[12] The eternal recurrence might thus be seen as a way of reading meaning into our own lives, as what might be described as a "perfect narrative . . . in such a story no detail is inconsequential, nothing is out of place."[13]

"Lives Fixed in Paint": Life Imitates Art or Art Imitates Life?

People think I collect art. What I really collect are lives fixed in paint. A perfect moment capturing an entire existence, made immortal—all perfect moments frozen in time. Alone, each tells a single story. Together they can tell the future.

—Daniel Linderman, ".07%"

. . . every human action, and not only a book, in some way becomes the cause of other actions, decisions, thoughts, that everything that happens is indissolubly tied up with everything that will happen.

—Friedrich Nietzsche, *Human All Too Human*

Both *Heroes* and Nietzsche would have us think of things as being inevitably related: events never occur in a vacuum—instead, they constitute a never-ending series of causes and effects. Linderman's collection of Isaac Mendez's paintings may depict single moments, but the paintings also represent the separate, parallel plotlines that compose the show's overall narrative. In a similar fashion, Nietzsche would have us note that all such moments and actions are in fact connected with what has happened and what will happen.

Nietzsche's eternal recurrence encourages us to cultivate a more artistic outlook toward our actions and our lives. To this, Nietzsche remarked that "We desire endlessly to relive a work of art. One must live one's life so that one feels the same desire toward each of its parts."[14] Every event and detail is necessary and therefore desirable—the extraordinary and the mundane serve to contrast and differentiate each other. We therefore can't have the one without the other.

If we were to think of our lives as a story, then nothing should change, because every detail has a point that is essential to the narrative: "in order to maintain the coherence of the story . . . we would have to make corresponding changes throughout, and we would thus produce an entirely different story; if anything were different, indeed everything would have to be different."[15] Thus, Hiro's future self reasons that saving Claire from Sylar will have a domino effect that will ultimately prevent an entirely different future from coming to pass. To that end, Future Hiro creates a "string map of the past" to determine the precise moment to go back and prevent that future from ever occurring. As he says, "This is a map of time. The events that led up to the bomb. . . . To determine the precise moment to go back in time to change the future" ("Five Years Gone").

For Nietzsche, it was unsettling to realize that every choice we are confronted with would bear an enormous burden of responsibility for every event in the future. We go about our daily lives and make the choices we make or have made for us, more often than not with little insight into the consequences of those choices. Future Hiro's timeline represents a convenient metaphor for Nietzsche's burden of responsibility that he felt that each of us had to accept. Each and every action is in some way connected, even if we are not immediately aware of the connection. Only on reflection might we be fortunate enough to see the effects of our choices and actions. Future Mohinder explains it with Hiro's string map, saying, "Each string represents a person. Every action, every choice. How people came together, how they were torn apart. It's a living map of the past" ("Five Years Gone").

"The Future Is Not Written in Stone"

Nietzsche's outlook can seem pessimistic because of his basic premise that life is necessarily about tragedy as much as it is about comedy. But in fact Nietzsche is optimistic in his affirmation of life. The eternal recurrence calls for us to accept all things as necessary and desirable, to say, "Was that life? Well, then! Once more!"[16]

So, let's return finally to Linderman's two paths and his implication that to have a life that is both meaningful and happy is impossible. In considering Nietzsche's eternal recurrence, we see that a life of meaning is possible once we're able to reconcile ourselves to the fact that we must bear responsibility for everything that has happened and will happen—with every choice that we will make. But a life of meaning *and* happiness is also possible if we can look upon the entirety of our life, and say to ourselves, "Well, then! Once more!" Linderman's error is in setting the past, the present, and the future against one another—as if you must either live life in the present or obsess about the past and the future. But in the self-test of the eternal recurrence, when we consider one we can't help but consider the others. We can never live life absolutely in the present, but rather are always reminded of the past and always thinking ahead to the future.

Nietzsche's philosophy encourages us to realize that we have a choice in how we confront not only our past and present, but the future as well. At the same time, *Heroes* reminds us that for better or for worse, "The future has not happened yet" ("Landslide"). It provides us with a dramatic opportunity to see the role of choice and fate in altering the course of events. As Mohinder suggests, "Of all our abilities, it is free will that truly makes us unique. With it, we have a tiny, but potent, chance to deny fate" ("Six Months Ago").

NOTES

1. Friedrich Nietzsche, *On the Genealogy of Morals*, translated by Walter Kaufman (New York: Vintage Books, 1967), p. 15.

2. Friedrich Nietzsche, *Thus Spoke Zarathustra*, translated by Walter Kaufman (New York: Penguin Books, 1966), p. 158.

3. Friedrich Nietzsche, *Will to Power*, translated by Walter Kaufman (New York: Vintage Books, 1968), p. 35.

4. Of course, he was not left there. Hiro let him out, and then Adam's powers were stolen by Arthur Petrelli. Adam's age immediately caught up with him.

5. Friedrich Nietzsche, *The Gay Science*, translated by Walter Kaufman (New York: Vintage Books, 1974), pp. 234–235.

6. Ibid., p. 274.

7. As translated by Keith Ansell Pearson in "The Eternal Return of the Overhuman: The Weightiest Knowledge and the Abyss of Light" *Journal of Nietzsche Studies* 30 2005: 6.

8. Nietzsche, *Thus Spoke Zarathustra*, pp. 157–158.

9. Ibid., p. 158.

10. Ibid., p. 198.

11. Ibid.

12. Friedrich Nietzsche, *Ecce Homo*, translated by Walter Kaufman (New York: Vintage Books, 1967), p. 258.

13. Alexander Nehamas, *Nietzsche: Life as Literature* (Cambridge, MA: Harvard University Press, 1985), p. 163.

14. As translated by Ned Lukacher in *Time-Fetishes: The Secret History of Eternal Recurrence* (Durham, NC: Duke University Press, 1998).

15. Nehamas, *Nietzsche: Life as Literature*, p. 165.

16. Nietzsche, *Thus Spoke Zarathustra*, p. 318.

SIX

HIRO NAKAMURA, BUSHIDO, AND HERO ARCHETYPES

Erik Daniel Baldwin

> It's no coincidence we named him Hiro . . . he truly is on a hero's quest.
>
> —Tim Kring[1]

Hiro Nakamura sees himself as a superhero as well as a modern-day samurai following Bushido: "The way (*do*) of the warrior (*Bushi*)." But is Hiro's understanding of Bushido historically accurate? Hiro is a superhero, even when he doesn't have his powers, but is he *also* a samurai?

The "Genesis" of the Popular View of Bushido

Like agents from the Company digging up information on people with abilities, we can investigate the history and origin of Bushido. Let's begin with Inazo Nitobe's (1862–1933)

Bushido: Samurai Ethics and the Soul of Japan, one of the most widely read and influential books on Bushido.[2] As the title implies, Nitobe maintained that Bushido, being the soul of Japan, provided not only a moral code of conduct for the samurai, but "an ethical system" that "set a moral standard" for all Japanese people.[3] The Bushido code "permeated all social classes" and was "not only the flower of the nation, but the root as well."[4] Nitobe claimed that Bushido's core virtues are rectitude (or justice), courage, benevolence, politeness, veracity and sincerity, honor, loyalty, and self-control. Of course, as Nitobe recognized, these virtues appear in warrior codes (as well as in systems of ethics) all over the world, such as the European knight's code of chivalry.[5] The upshot is that Nitobe's book helped to form the popular (mis)conception of Bushido as a code of ethics.

Another thing that contributes to the popular conception is our own assumptions. Carl Jung theorized that embedded deep within the human collective unconscious are universal archetypes, powerful symbols that all humans share in common. Jung thought that these archetypes come to us primarily in our dreams and are represented in folktales, art, and epic poems and stories (not to mention TV shows about humans with special abilities). Among these archetypes is "the Hero."[6] Influenced by Jung, Joseph Campbell wrote that a hero is "someone who has given his or her life to something bigger than oneself." He went on to say that "there is a certain typical hero sequence of actions . . . in stories from all over the world. . . . It might even be said that there is but one archetypal mythic hero whose life has been replicated in many lands by many, many people."[7] The idea of "the Hero" is in all of us, and many of us assume that the samurai are simply another example that fits this archetype. That is why we assume that the code that guided the samurai, Bushido, must be an ethical code.

Directors Akira Kurosawa and George Lucas also made significant contributions to the popular view of Bushido.

Kurosawa's films are firmly rooted in Japanese culture, yet they explore certain Western hero ideals and universal hero archetypes. Campbell and Kurosawa are among Lucas's stated influences. And, as many fans know, Kurosawa's *Seven Samurai* and *The Hidden Fortress* inspired many of the characters and situations in the *Star Wars* movies. In an interview with Bill Moyers, Lucas said that *Star Wars* is an old myth told in a new way.[8] Essentially, Lucas created the character of Luke Skywalker in the form of a universal hero archetype. Although not everyone associates *Star Wars* with Bushido, Lucas clearly let his understanding of Bushido (as a moral code) influence Luke's behavior.

But now more questions arise (and I always hear them in Mohinder's voice): "Does Bushido really offer a moral code? Are samurai simply manifestations of the universal hero-archetype, or are they something more?" To get satisfactory answers to these questions, we need to consider the popular view of Bushido, in contrast to the historical view.

Being Willing to Tear Out One's Own Heart; Historical Bushido

Unfortunately, the popular view gets Bushido wrong. To see how, let's consult a classic text on historical Bushido: *The Hagakure* (*The Book of the Samurai*) by Yamamoto Tsunetomo (1659–1719). *The Hagakure* was written around 1700, during the Tokugawa period. Before the Tokugawa period were the Kamakura (1185–1333), Muromachi (1392–1573), and Momoyama (1568–1600) periods. During those times, Japan was war-torn and chaotic, much as the era is depicted in the Hiro, Takezo, and Whitebeard story arc in Volume 2. During this time of war, samurai had neither the time nor the inclination for scholarly pursuits; they were too busy fighting. When samurai of this time did express their code, they did so *very* concisely. For example, Tsukuhara Bokuden (1489–1571) merely said, "The warrior who does not know his business is like a cat that does not know the way of ratting."[9]

During the peaceful Tokugawa period, samurai turned their attention to religious and scholarly pursuits, writing *The Hagakure* and other handbooks, such as *The Book of Five Rings* and *The Code of the Samurai*.[10] True, they grew accustomed to the comforts and luxuries of life during peacetime and ended up lacking discipline and other warrior virtues. (They were like heroes who had forgotten how to use their special abilities.) But they still knew what Bushido was.

One of the first very lines of *The Hagakure* is "The Way of the Samurai is found in death."[11] A samurai is "constantly hardening [his] resolution to die in battle, deliberately becoming as one already dead."[12] A samurai should adopt a noncalculative, nondiscriminative mode of action. Calculative reasoning is detestable because it concerns worry about "loss and gain," things that samurai should not care about.[13] Rather, samurai should "view life as a dream" and "think of death as merely waking up."[14] A samurai should "dash bravely and joyfully into difficult situations" and rush into combat "without any regard for his own life."[15] A samurai is ready to die at any time because "the condition of being a Samurai . . . lies first in seriously devoting one's body and soul to his master."[16] Samurai are "desperate in the way" because "the way of the Samurai is in desperateness."[17] Death is never "a long way off." Rather, "the way of the Samurai is, morning after morning, the practice of death, considering whether it will be here or be there, imagining the most sightly way of dying, and putting one's mind firmly in death."[18] Although these passages seem to have been written with Future Hiro in mind, we don't see much of the popular view of Bushido within them. No justice, benevolence, or politeness here— just be ready to die.

Furthermore, the business of a samurai is to focus on one thing and one thing only: being a samurai. A passage from *The Hagakure* puts this point well:

It is not good to divide your concentration. Seeking only bushido, one should not pursue anything else. Hearing Confucianism or Buddhism and taking it for bushido on the basis that the final character is the same will not lead to the realization of bushido. If one bears this in mind, then even if he studies various schools of thought, he will assuredly realize bushido.[19]

The scholar Robert Ames argued that in the previous passage, Yamamoto drew a distinction between moral codes, which provide the basis for social ethics, and modes of actions—*how* one goes about doing what one does. A social ethic is "a standard or set of standards whereby the [moral] man can guide and evaluate his conduct."[20] This would be what a religion or a philosophy, such as Confucianism or Buddhism, is. But Bushido is a mode of action; it is "mobile and neutral . . . it can be attached to any cause or purpose, no matter how trivial or contrary that might be to the prevailing morality . . . the morality, the cause, the purpose determines the action—bushido simply describes the manner in which that action is carried out."[21]

Because it is merely a mode of action, Bushido neither endorses nor entails a particular social ethic and thus is consistent with whatever code of ethics a superhero (or supervillain, for that matter) might accept.[22] As long as one is devoted to one's master and always ready to die, one could be unjust, mean, and impolite but still practice Bushido. For example, although Takezo Kensei is a villain, he seems to accept and act in accord with *something* like the Bushido code. He is given over to his purpose, and he is not afraid to die (at least not until his final confrontation with Arthur Petrelli!).

Another defining aspect of historical Bushido that sets it apart from the popular view is the state of the historical samurai's mind. The samurai of the Tokugawa period and earlier clearly distinguished between morality and self-interest, and when the two conflicted, they cared nothing for the latter. Because a samurai has died to self-interest, he is "the uninhibited agent of his morality, whatever morality that might be."[23] A samurai lives in the immediate now; he is "no-minded." This state is similar to and consistent with (but not exactly the same as) states of immediate awareness that Buddhists talk about. D. T. Suzuki (1870–1966), well known in the West for his essays and books on Zen Buddhism, commented on what it is for a samurai to live in the immediate now. First, Suzuki considered a quote from *The Hagakure*:

> The Samurai is good for nothing unless he can go beyond life and death. When it is said that all things are of one mind, you may think that there is such a thing as mind. But the fact is that a mind attached to life and death must be abandoned, when you can execute wonderful deeds . . . that is to say, all things are accomplished when one attains a mind of "no-mind-ness" . . . a state of mind which is no more troubled about the questions of death or immortality.[24]

A samurai who masters "no-mind-ness" will "avoid distraction . . . but go on to the extent of living single thought by single thought."[25] This single thought is nothing other than being continually prepared to die a warrior's death.

So it would seem that even Sylar approximates Bushido in his mode of action. On several occasions, Sylar shows that he is not afraid to die. For example, in "The Hard Part," Sylar even dares Hiro to kill him. As with Kensei, certain aspects of Sylar's character are admirable, namely, his tenacity, his determination, and his devotion to his purpose—to survive and develop his special powers to their utmost potential, to embrace his special fate. And yet Sylar is "a very bad man." Although many who follow Bushido are good guys, you don't have to be a good guy to follow Bushido.

I Just Want to Be a Hero

Hiro fancies himself a follower of Bushido, but does that make him a samurai? To answer this question, we first will have to figure out how Hiro views himself. But this won't be easy. We can't read his mind as Matt Parkman can, and Hiro's goals might not even be that clear to himself. Complicating matters, Hiro's notion of "what it is to follow Bushido" evolves over the course of the series. Despite these obstacles, however, we can get a fairly good idea of what Hiro's self-understanding is by constructing it on the basis of what he's revealed through his words and actions during the course of the show.

Throughout the first volume, Hiro is not following the historical Bushido. For one thing, his understanding of Bushido (and what he should do with his powers) seems to be grounded in comic books, video games, and movies. Superman and Spider-Man, but not Kensei, are cited as examples and role models. As a comic fan, Hiro surely knows about Wolverine of the X-Men and his one-time rival, the Silver Samurai, both of whom received formal samurai training.[26] This would (mis)inform his understanding of Bushido. He even seems to cite comic book "principles of conduct" directly. In "Genesis," he says, "A superhero doesn't use his power for personal gain." Later he says, "A hero doesn't run away from his destiny" ("One Giant Leap"), and that "a hero doesn't hide" ("Six Months Ago"), a hero never gives up and cannot be bribed ("The Fix"), and "more than anything, a hero must have hope" ("Run!").[27] Hiro's favorite superheroes include Luke Skywalker, Mr. Spock, Kitty Pryde, Superman, and Spider-Man. After stopping the passage of time on the Tokyo subway train, Hiro writes on his blog (which uses the Stardate system from *Star Trek*) that he wonders whether he is a Jedi, and he even signs off, "May the Force be with you."[28] Hiro compares developing his time-travel and teleportation skills to leveling up a video game character.[29] In "Better Halves," after he discovers that Future Hiro has a sword, Hiro excitedly swings an imaginary light saber while making "whoosh" noises.

In addition, Hiro's actions line up with the popular view of Bushido. Hiro shows beneficence when he saves the schoolgirl ("One Giant Leap") and when he helps D.L. Hawkins save the woman from a burning car ("Nothing to Hide"). He shows determination when attempting to save Charlie Andrews ("Six Months Ago") and courage when he helps to save New York from exploding ("How to Stop an Exploding Man"). But his actions and attitudes do not line up with the historical Bushido. When Hiro wants to go back in time to prevent Charlie's murder, Ando reminds him that their mission is to save the cheerleader. Infatuated with Charlie, Hiro decides to try to save her anyway. Unfortunately, he fails and Sylar succeeds in "cutting off her top." But even if Hiro had been successful, he still seriously jeopardized the success of their mission for the sake of a personal quest. In choosing this course of action, he wasn't being much of a samurai. It seems that Hiro played video games like *The Legend of Zelda* and *Super Mario Brothers* one too many times: "If a girl I like is in danger, I must be like Mario and save the princess!" In a time of trial, Hiro let self-interest and personal feelings get in the way of his mission. *That* is not in accord with genuine, historical Bushido.

Hiro's failure to do what he ought to have done, compounded by his inability to save Charlie's life, causes him to doubt whether he has what it takes to be a hero. His powers progressively weakening as a result, Hiro believes that he needs Kensei's sword to get them back. After Hiro steals the sword from Mr. Linderman's archives ("Parasites"), his powers return. But in his first confrontation with Sylar, Hiro hesitates. Sylar gets the upper hand, defeats Hiro, and breaks his sword. Dejected, Hiro goes with Ando to a swordsmith (you really can find anything in New York!) in order to fix the sword. They are astonished to find Kaito Nakamura, Hiro's father, waiting for him to help give him the training he needs to kill Sylar. Kaito tells Hiro that "the sword is not important. Your journey is what restored your power." Although beset with difficulties, Hiro overcomes them to confront and defeat Sylar.

By the end of Volume 1, although Hiro has made great progress in his Hero Quest, and Kaito's training reaffirmed his power and enabled him to develop his swordsmanship, none of this clearly indicates that Hiro's understanding of Bushido has changed.

You're a Badass

In contrast with Volume 1 Hiro, Future Hiro is confident, acts unflinchingly, and does not allow self-interest to get in the way of his mission. Future Hiro is a "badass" who is not at all afraid of death. His voice, mannerisms, and dress are reminiscent of Kurosawa's famous characters in *Seven Samurai*, *Yojimbo*, and *The Hidden Fortress*. When he dies in "Five Years Gone," he does so boldly and without hesitation. In all likelihood, when Future Hiro studied Battojutsu (a mode of swordplay that focuses on the art of unsheathing one's sword and attacking from a variety of neutral starting positions, such as sitting or standing), he also studied manuals and handbooks on Bushido, such as *The Hagakure*.[30] There is a veritable chasm between happy-go-lucky Hiro and Future Hiro, the samurai badass. Hiro won't even talk to his future self, telling Ando, "I scare me."

Over the course of Volume 2, Hiro becomes more like Future Hiro. Consequently, Hiro's understanding of Bushido grows into something that is much closer to the historical view. Let's consider a few events from Volume 2 that reveal the extent of his growth. First, we need to see the extent of his failures. At the start of Volume 2, we see that Hiro still has a weakness for pretty girls. He falls in love with Kensei's girlfriend, Yaeko, and he *really* messes up when he kisses her. Kensei sees them and is crushed, so much so that he switches allegiances, captures Hiro and the others, and plots to help Whitebeard in his conquest of Japan. Kensei tells Hiro that his betrayal "cut him deeper than any blade possibly could" ("The Line") and vows that "as long as I have breath, anything you love I will lay to waste. I swear. You will suffer" ("Out of Time"). Much later, Kensei makes good on his word. He resurfaces as Adam Monroe and murders most of the founders of the Company, including Kaito, and tries to release the Shanti virus.

After his fallout with Kensei, Hiro must have felt a little bit like Peter Parker did when he decided not to stop that robber when he had the chance. Perhaps he laments, at least occasionally, "If only I tore my heart out *before* kissing Yaeko." But Hiro learns from his mistakes. He always bounces back, in accord with the Japanese proverb "Fall down seven times, get up eight." And each time he gets back up, his understanding of Bushido grows. Even though he at first messes up the timeline, Hiro does his best to fix it. By leaving Yaeko, he tears out his own heart, as Kensei did in the story of Kensei and the dragon.[31] By the end of Volume 2, Hiro resembles Future Hiro more than ever; he toughens up considerably and wouldn't be scared by his future self.

At the least, we can say that at the end of Volume 2, Hiro is much more like the historical samurai. I'll let you decide whether Hiro has become more or less of a historical samurai since Volume 2. (Is his quest to destroy the formula a samurai's quest? How about his quest to get his powers back, or to make Ando a hero? What about when he used his powers to save Noah in "An Invisible Thread," even though he knew that using his powers again might kill him?)

The Wind at the Back of History

Let's suppose that Hiro does fully understand and implement the practices and attitudes of historical Bushido. He doesn't fear death. He is dedicated to this quest to save the world. He studies Battojutsu and reads *The Hagakure*, and the like. Could we then rightly claim that Hiro is a samurai? I think the answer is still no.

To see why, we need to consider a bit of the history. In the Meiji period (1868–1912), Japan sought modernization after almost three hundred years of self-imposed isolation. Prior to this time, Japan was ruled by Daimyo, who held offices similar to barons, dukes, and so on. Each Daimyo swore allegiance to the military and political leader of Japan, the Shogun. For hundreds of years, various clans fought for control of Japan. This state of constant warfare ended when Japan was unified under the Tokugawa Shogunate in 1603.

By 1854, Japan had opened up to the West. The Daimyo saw the technological advances of the *gaijin* (foreigners), and they knew they had to get with the times. Since samurai were in positions of influence and power, they were at the forefront of these social reforms, known as the Meiji Cultural Revolution. One of the most significant reforms was that Daimyo relinquished their lands and power to regional governors in order to form a national Japanese government and military. As a consequence, samurai had no lords to serve and no lands to protect. Already severely marginalized, in 1876 they were forbidden to carry swords in public.

This law effectively outlawed and abolished the samurai warrior class. Many samurai vigorously resisted these changes, resulting in the Satsuma Rebellion led by Saigo Takamori (1828–1877), the *real* "Last Samurai." Eventually, the Japanese National Army decisively defeated the rebel samurai. Those who were not killed fled or blended in with the general population. Others were later captured and either imprisoned, executed, or drafted into the military. Some chose to commit *seppuku* (ritual suicide by disembowelment performed in order to maintain or regain one's honor).

So, unlike the Jedi, the samurai really were wiped out. Thus, for Hiro to claim to be a samurai is anachronistic at best and silly at worst. It would be rather like claiming to be a Medieval knight because one dresses up in a suit of armor and goes to the Renaissance fair. Because the social institutions to which one must belong in order to be a samurai no longer exist, Hiro couldn't possibly be one. So in a crucial way it is actually impossible for Hiro to be a samurai. But given that Hiro knows this, it is highly unlikely that he thinks he is a samurai in that way. What is more likely is that when Hiro says things like "I am a samurai," he is speaking analogically. He is saying that he follows Bushido as samurai understood it and practiced it. If *that* is what he means, he is correct.

So, if Hiro practices Bushido as it is taught in *The Hagakure*, it is correct to say (analogically) that Hiro is a samurai. And since Bushido is not a moral code, Hiro can still look to the moral examples of superheroes such as Spider-Man and Superman when trying to decide how to act. So in the end it is possible for Hiro to be both a superhero and a samurai. And that concludes our voyage for now. May the Force be with you.

NOTES

1. See Alex Wainer, "Hiro's Journey, Our Journey," www.breakpoint.org/listingarticle.asp?ID=6036.

2. Inazo Nitobe, *Bushido: Samurai Ethics and the Soul of Japan* (Mineola, NY: Dover, 2004).

3. Ibid., chaps. 1 and 15, especially pp. 93 and 95.

4. Ibid., pp. 89–91.

5. For example, see the epic poem about Medieval codes of chivalry in France *The Song of Roland*, translated by Dorothy L. Sayers (Penguin Books: New York, 1957).

6. For these and other of Jung's ideas, you may want to refer to *The Basic Writings of C. G. Jung*, edited by V. S. DeLaszlo (New York: The Modern Library, 1993).

7. Joseph Campbell with Bill Moyers, *The Power of Myth* (New York: Doubleday, 1988), pp. 123, 136. To the curious, I recommend "The Making of a Hiro," in *Saving the World: A Guide to Heroes*, edited by Lynnette Porter, David Lavery, and Hillary Robson (Toronto: ECW Press, 2007). The more adventurous readers are encouraged to read Joseph Campbell's *The Hero with a Thousand Faces* (Princeton, NJ: Princeton University Press, 1949).

8. Bill Moyers, "Of Myth and Men," *Time*, April 16, 1999.

9. S. R. Turnbull, *The Samurai: A Military History* (New York: Macmillan, 1977), p. 286.

10. *The Hagakure*, translated by William Scott Wilson (Tokyo: Kodansha International, 1983); *The Code of the Samurai: A Modern Translation of the "Bushido Shoshinshu,"* translated by Thomas Cleary (Boston: Tuttle Publishing, 1999); and Miyamoto Musashi, *The Book of Five Rings*, translated by Thomas Clearly (Boston: Shambhala, 2005).

11. *The Hagakure*, p. 17.

12. Ibid., p. 33.

13. Ibid., p. 44.

14. Ibid., p. 82.

15. Ibid., p. 45.

16. Ibid., p. 66.

17. Ibid., p. 45.

18. Ibid., p. 73.

19. From the *Hagakure*, as quoted in Robert Ames's "Bushido: Mode or Ethic?" *Japanese Aesthetics and Culture: A Reader*, edited by Nancy G. Hume (Albany: State University of New York, 1995), p. 282.

20. Ibid.

21. Ibid., pp. 285–286.

22. Ibid., p. 282. Ames's conclusion is borne out if one considers the fact that in Kaiten Nukariya's classic, *The Religion of the Samurai* (Stepney, Australia: Axiom Publishing, 2006), one finds almost nothing on Bushido but a great deal on Zen, the religion that most samurai accepted. This wouldn't make much sense at all if Bushido *was* an ethic or a religion, as it is often mistaken to be.

23. Ibid., p. 287.

24. D. T. Suzuki, *Zen and Japanese Culture* (Princeton, NJ: Princeton University Press, 1971), p. 74.

25. Ibid., p. 69.

26. Tim Kring wouldn't know this, but Wolverine has a healing power much like Claire Bennet's. His bones, including his foot-long retractable claws, are laced with adamantium. He trained under the samurai mutant Ogun, settled in the Japanese village of Bando Saburo, married, and had a son. The Silver Samurai is a Japanese mutant trained in the samurai arts who has the power to channel energy into his sword so that it can cut through virtually anything—except adamantium. See *New Avengers* #11–13, *Daredevil* #111, and *Wolverine* (vol. 3) #40. See also chapter 4 in this book, "With Great

Creativity Comes Great Imitation: Problems of Plagiarism and Knowledge" by Jason Southworth, which discusses Kring's willful ignorance of *X-Men*.

27. I have benefited here from a discussion about Hiro's "code for modern heroes" in "The Making of Hiro," from *Saving the World*, pp. 122–125.

28. "Hiro's Blog," Captain's Log: Stardate, 1742.5. "Strange Day," http://blogs.nbcuni .com/hiro_blog/2006/09/captains_log_stardate_17425.html.

29. "Hiro's Blog," Captain's Log: Stardate, 1758.5. "Let it Ride," http://blogs.nbcuni .com/hiro_blog/2006/10/let_it_ride.html.

30. See Oscar Ratti and Adele Westbrook, *Secrets of the Samurai: A Survey of the Martial Arts of Feudal Japan* (Edison, NJ: Castle Books, 1999).

31. In "Landslide," Kaito reads a version of Kensei and the dragon to young Hiro. The story is also told in the documentary *Takezo Kensei: Sword Saint*. See www.yamagatofellowship .org/videoPlayer.shtml?mea=157365.

SEVEN

PLATO ON GYGES' RING OF INVISIBILITY: THE POWER OF HEROES AND THE VALUE OF VIRTUE

Don Adams

In the *Heroes* universe, evolution has given select individuals special powers. But it is up to those select individuals to decide how to use them. Many have opted to use them for good, but Sylar is not the only exception to that rule. Daphne Millbrook, the blond Speedy Gonzales, opts to use her super-speed for super-theft, hiring herself out to Pinehearst, because no one can ever catch her moving that fast. Micah steals money from an ATM ("The Fix") and even steals pay-per-view wrestling ("The Kindness of Strangers") and doesn't get caught. (How could he? He can always tell whatever security system he is up against to "look the other way.") In Vegas, Hiro Nakamura freezes time to cheat at roulette and poker ("Hiros"). Although his opponents eventually catch on, if he had been more careful—if he had pulled cards only out of the untouched deck instead of his opponent's hand— they wouldn't have noticed. And Noah Bennet continually commits atrocities and uses the Haitian to erase everyone's memories of them. All of our heroes could do something similar—commit atrocities and never get caught.

The stories of our heroes aren't new, nor are the questions about them. They go back at least as far as Plato (c. 429–347 BCE), who considered the tale of Gyges, a man who finds an invisibility ring. Gyges uses the ring to viciously, but secretly, depose the king and take his wife. No one is ever the wiser; he is invisible while he does it. Such stories raise the question: do such "superpowered" individuals have good reason to be virtuous, even though they can get away with being immoral? Or maybe their actions aren't even immoral? After all, isn't it "only natural" for people to use their own powers to their own advantage? But is that an excuse? Is human nature really that selfish, or is there a part of us that doesn't want to take advantage of others for our own aims, but instead wants to join with and help others? Do we want to be villains or heroes?

Plato argued that our nature is to be heroes and that there is good reason to be a hero. But to understand his argument, we have to understand what, for Plato, it meant to be virtuous and why virtue was so important.

Claire's Thumos Saved the World

According to Plato, being virtuous is important, because if you are not careful to develop the core virtues, then you will be doomed to suffer from their opposed vices. No superpower can free you from this dilemma. In fact, Plato would argue that the virtues become more and more important the more powerful you become. The more you suffer from the vices, the more your life begins to spin out of control. So if you have superpowers, your vices are super-vices and will make your life spin "super" out of control.

To see what it means to be virtuous for Plato, let's begin with one of the characters in *Heroes* whom Plato would admire: Claire Bennet. Think about one of the most important choices Claire ever made. In "One Giant Leap," the local police chief asks which cheerleader performed the daring fire rescue a day earlier. Even though he indicates that Claire looks like the hero, she chooses not to take credit. Good thing! The cheerleader who steps forward to take credit catches Sylar's attention and is eventually murdered for "her" powers. Claire's choice not to receive the accolades and glory for a heroic feat saves her life (and of course, since the cheerleader was saved, so was the world).

It's easy to understand why Claire might want to take credit for her heroic act: she did something noble and deserves to be honored for it. Plato would say that this desire comes from her *thumos* (thoo-MOSS).[1] Thumos is not a part of your brain (that's your "thalamus"); thumos is a part of the soul. There really is no good translation of the Greek word *thumos*, but look at Claire's face when Jackie Wilcox, the cheerleader standing next to her, takes credit for the rescue and you'll see the face of thumos.[2] Claire is surprised but also indignant and even a little angry. Jackie has done something shameful, and Claire thinks less of her for doing it. Our thumos reacts when we sense an insult to our dignity, our worth, and our honor. That is why Plato associates thumos with anger. When someone insults you unjustly, you get angry, and out of that righteous anger you might hurl an insult or even throw a punch at the person who offended you.

Thumos and the acts it inspires are not necessarily bad, according to Plato; in fact, they can be very good. Thumos can help you develop the virtue of courage. A strong sense of dignity and personal honor guided by courage can protect you from people who try to take advantage of you and can also help you set the bar high for yourself. Expect more of yourself, and you might be surprised by how capable you are. But your thumos can also get you into trouble. If you throw a punch every time you think someone has insulted you, you are indulging the vice of recklessness, and you will get into more trouble than you bargained for.

Claire Is Logical; Spock Is Not

We need to be thumotic, but, more important, like Claire, we need to be *logistikos* (log-IST-i-KOS) to develop the virtue of wisdom.[3] The English words *logic* and *logistics* derive from the Greek adjective *logistikos*, and both are involved in its fundamental meaning. So let's call this the "logistical" part of the soul. Claire has thought logically about her situation. She concludes that if anyone finds out about her ability, it will ruin her life. She will either be a freak or a lab rat. All things considered, thinking coolly and calmly, rationally and strategically, it is best for her long-term good if the number of people who know about her special ability is very, very small.

> Zach: All right, besides the fact that it was so gross I almost fudged myself, this is the single coolest thing to happen to this town in, like, a hundred years.
>
> Claire: Not if nobody finds out, it's not.
>
> —*"Genesis"*

But for Plato, being logistical doesn't necessarily contradict being thumotic. Today we often think that logic and emotion are opposed to each other. Perhaps we are too influenced by Mr. Spock and the Vulcans from *Star Trek*. But for Plato, anger and logistical thinking can go together perfectly and can even help each other. Long-term calculations for your best interest can include so much more if you have a passion for your own dignity and honor. Without a strong sense of self-worth, the logistical part of your soul might sell you short; after all, logistically speaking, it is easier to create a plan to accomplish something small than something great. Ando keeps urging Hiro to set his sights lower—on objectives that are more easily accomplished—but Hiro insists on accomplishing the daunting but truly great task of saving the world. If your thumos is strong, then you won't settle for less than you deserve; you will set the bar high for yourself and will have the driving passion to go for it.

But sometimes your thumos can become too strong and will start running your life. Claire has a strong thumos, but she doesn't let it control her. Even when she takes revenge on Brody Mitchum, the quarterback who tried to rape her ("One Giant Leap"), she doesn't simply lash out at him in anger. She carefully calculates what to do. She thinks logically and logistically about the situation and creates a good plan of action and executes it well.

This, in fact, is how Plato defines the virtue of courage and why he thinks the virtues of courage and wisdom go together. A courageous person is someone whose thumos is strong and daring but who is responsive to reason. Imagine a member of the cavalry charging to meet the enemy. His horse must be high-spirited and willing to face danger, but it must also be well-trained to respond to its rider's lead. If it gets too spirited and unruly, all may be lost. The same is true for your thumos: a courageous person is daring and willing to face danger, but only when led by reason, logic, and good logistical calculation. If you simply run into danger without thinking, you are not courageous but reckless; you are a fool, a danger to yourself and others. Wisdom and courage go together because a truly courageous person consults wisdom when deciding whether to attack or hold back, and a truly wise person knows when to stand up for oneself and boldly attack one's enemies.

If Claire has a moral problem in Plato's eyes, it is simply that she is young and her wisdom is not yet fully developed.

Probably it was a mistake to get back at Brody in the way she did. But Plato would admire her because she has, to the extent possible for someone so young, two of the four core virtues: wisdom and courage.

The Virtue That Sylar Lacks

To understand Plato's third virtue, temperance, we will need to understand the third part of human nature recognized by Plato: *epithumetikon* (epi-thoom-AY-tee-KON).[4] When you drink simply because you feel like drinking, that comes from epithumetikon; the same is true when you eat simply because you feel like eating or scratch an itch simply because you feel like scratching. So we can call this part of your soul "appetite." Your appetite doesn't have to bother your *logistikon*; doing something you feel like doing simply because you feel like doing it doesn't have to involve a whole lot of logistical planning (it doesn't take a lot of thought to get up and get a drink when you are thirsty). But it can. And just as the thumos can be good when it is responsive and obedient to the logistical part of the soul, but it can be bad when it begins to take over and rule your soul, so, too, is the appetite good when it is obedient but bad when it tries to rule. Temperance is the virtue that you exercise when you keep your appetites under control.

The perfect example of intemperance is Sylar. Sylar's special power is intuitive aptitude: he can see how things work, including the special powers of others—if he examines someone's brain, he can see how it works and take the person's power. This, of course, kills those whose power he steals—except Claire ("The Second Coming). As we learned in Volume 3, part of the curse of this power is a seemingly uncontrollable hunger—an appetite—to acquire the powers of others. (This hunger was also passed on to Peter Petrelli when he briefly acquired Sylar's power in "I Am Become

Death" and "Angels and Monsters.") Since Sylar is unable to control this hunger—it rules him—Sylar is intemperate.

Plato argued that intemperance makes one immoral. Sylar, again, is a perfect example. As Arthur Petrelli points out in "It's Coming," Sylar is not simply a mindless killer. "That hunger you've got is not about killing; it's about power." Recall Sylar's disinterest in Peter when he had no powers. "I'm not going to kill you; you don't have anything I need anymore" ("Our Father").[5] Remember also Sylar's lack of interest in killing Claire after he copies her power. Although he couldn't kill her even if he wanted to, he still doesn't want to; he even puts the top of her head back on after he is finished ("The Second Coming"). Sylar does not merely kill for killing's sake. He simply hungers for powers, and examining the brains of those who have them is the easiest way he knows to acquire them— it just happens that most people can't survive the process. So, because Sylar's hunger controls him, he ends up murdering everyone he can find who has powers. It is his intemperance— his inability to control that hunger—that makes him the villain he is. He does succeed in keeping that hunger under control for a while, and in "It's Coming" he learns to acquire abilities through empathy, as Peter did in Volumes 1 and 2.[6] If Sylar had continued down this path, he would have become the temperate heroic family man we saw in the future of "I Am Become Death." That Future Sylar even specifically says that controlling the hunger is what enabled him to turn back into Gabriel. But it is when he gives in to his hunger again—most notably, when he kills Elle Bishop, the girl he supposedly loves ("The Eclipse: Part II"), thus losing his temperance—that he becomes a villain once again.

Just like Sylar, when we are intemperate—when we let our appetites rule our actions—we are immoral (villains) as well and suffer the consequences. As a trivial example, think about not being able to keep your appetite for food under control. If you get used to eating simply because you feel like eating, you can develop some very unhealthy eating habits, health problems, and flabby body parts. As a more extreme example, what would happen if, the next time you got really angry, you lost your ability to control your desire for violence? And how much longer would you be in your current relationship if you lost your ability to keep your appetite for sex under control?

This is not to say that appetites are a bad thing. It's important to enjoy life, and that involves doing things that you feel like doing. Plato's central point is that there has to be balance and order in your soul. When appetite begins to take over and rule your soul, it turns into a kind of tyrant, like a spoiled child demanding whatever it wants. Instead of exercising wisdom and developing temperance by eating healthy, nutritionally balanced meals, people who suffer from the vice of intemperance will wolf down whatever they want, as much as they want, and will be very cranky if they don't get their way. Obviously, letting your appetites rule your actions is a bad way to go. Gluttony, after all, is one of the seven deadly sins.

Superpowers and Super-Vices

For Plato, the virtue of justice is to the human soul what health is to the body: as the various systems in the body need balance and harmony in order for you to thrive biologically, so you also need the various parts of your soul to be in balance and harmony with one another in order for you to thrive psychologically. Your thumos and your appetite should do their jobs, but it is the logistical part of the soul that should be in control. And just as a healthy diet and healthy exercise help to keep your body in good condition, wise, courageous, and temperate actions help to keep your soul in good condition. The more you give in to an unhealthy lifestyle, the worse your health will become; the more you give in to foolishness, intemperance, and cowardly or reckless actions, the more your life will spin out of control. The more unjust you become, the more miserable you will be.

This is why Plato would worry about Micah stealing from the ATM. Forget about the chances of getting caught. What about the consequences for Micah's soul? What if Micah gets used to doing whatever he feels like doing and becomes the sort of person who doesn't think logistically about his actions? Allowing his appetite to take control of his soul and ignoring or even suppressing his logistical planning would make Micah suffer from the vice of intemperance. Plato would say something similar to Daphne about her super-speed thievery.

This is why Plato would disapprove of Hiro's and Ando's behavior in Vegas ("Hiros"). Recall, Ando gambled away all of their money except for one last chip, which he bet on the roulette wheel. Because it was the last of their money, Hiro stopped time and cheated to win. Immediately, his thumos made him feel very ashamed. But Ando had no trouble convincing him that it was okay, so his appetite rejoiced at the opportunity to continue cheating to win. But when the thumos or the appetite gets out of control—when the soul is not balanced or harmonized properly by logistical planning—we are unjust, and bad things happen. Ultimately, Hiro and Ando cheat the wrong person and get beaten up, robbed, and dumped in the desert.

Unless you make choices in a balanced way, develop the wisdom to plan things out so that you enjoy things you feel like doing without becoming ashamed of yourself, and have courage and temperance to be able to stick to your plans, you will be unjust, and your indulgences will tear you apart. An overly thumotic person will become increasingly obsessed with other people's opinions, doing anything to gain acceptance but never getting enough. An overly appetitive person will grow increasingly indulgent; his appetite will grow until no amount of money or superpowers will be able to satisfy him. At first, his thumos will continually make him feel ashamed, but if he practices ignoring the thumos, he may weaken or even kill it off. Then he will be utterly shameless and will have no ambition to amount to anything at all in life. Like a drug addict who cares about only one thing in life—the next fix—the intemperate and unjust person loses all self-respect and no longer strives for anything worthwhile in life.

This is part of Plato's problem with Gyges. Once Gyges gained his superpower, he handed control of his life over to his appetite. He allowed it to boss his logistical part around. The problem is that only the logistical part is good at logic and logistics. Thumos and appetite will inevitably make a mess of things, demanding more and more honors, as well as more and more pleasures. There will be more conflicts among the things he wants, and so there will be more dissatisfaction in his life.

Now we see why Plato thought that "superpowered" individuals do have good reason to be virtuous, even though they can get away with being immoral. To see what this implies about the way we should treat one another, let's turn to Claire.

Why Claire Apologized

In "One Giant Leap," Claire is attacked by Brody, the football quarterback. He tries to rape her but accidentally kills her. Of course, Clair recovers—at least, from her physical injuries. She, however, finds out that Brody has raped another student and seems to have picked yet another victim. He appears to be a budding young serial rapist who is utterly remorseless, and she decides to take action. She gets him to give her a ride home after school, but instead she drives. She finds out from his own mouth that he does indeed seem set on this despicable course. So she steers a course directly for a wall and crashes the car into it, seriously injuring both of them. Of course, Claire recovers.

Surely, there is a bit of revenge in her plan: she's getting back at Brody for what he did to her. But that is not all she is doing.

In fact, it looks as if she might not have done anything if she hadn't discovered his serial rapist tendencies. So, it seems, she is exacting punishment on behalf of his other victim and trying to stop him from hurting anyone else. Who knows? Maybe part of him does feel bad about what he's done, and a serious injury will help wake him up and change his mind. Perhaps Claire was right to do this; perhaps not. But to discover Plato's fourth virtue, we need to focus on what Claire does afterward in the hospital.

Claire goes into the quarterback's room and apologizes to him. She says that what she did was wrong. But why does she think she was wrong and why does she apologize? She doesn't have time to explain herself because she is interrupted by the cheerleading squad chanting, "Brody, Brody, Brody," coming in to cheer him up. So we have to speculate. To do so, let's talk about Plato again. Before Plato brought up the idea of Gyges' superpower of invisibility, he discussed a principle widely accepted by the Greeks. We might call it the "Pagan Golden Rule": help your friends and harm your enemies.[7]

Unlike the Christian Golden Rule, which tells us to treat everyone according to the same benevolent standard, the Pagan Golden Rule advises us to use two different standards: one for our friends and one for our enemies. Obviously, you shouldn't treat friends as if they were enemies; they deserve better than that. And you shouldn't treat enemies as if they were friends; they will take advantage of you and perhaps even destroy you.

Plato pointed out that we need to be careful not to misinterpret the "Pagan Golden Rule." It is not a license to attack your enemies or to show indiscriminate favoritism to your friends. The Greek tragedian Sophocles wrote what could be considered a footnote to the Pagan Golden Rule when he had the mighty hero Ajax say, "I have learned that my enemy is to be hated only so much, since he may soon be my friend; and the friend I help, I will help only so much since he may not always remain my friend."[8] This fits Plato's view of interpersonal justice in *The Republic*, and it also fits much of what we see in *Heroes*.

It may sound sad to think of dealing with your friends in the realization that they may not remain your friends for very long, but it is good advice. Claire's father (by adoption), Noah Bennet, realized it was good advice when he emphasized to her the importance of being careful after he saw that she was interested in Brody. When someone is friendly to you, as Brody was to Claire before he tried to rape her, it doesn't mean that you can trust this person. This is even clearer in the case of Noah himself. Claire loves and trusts him as a father, but he is an employee of the Company, and his loyalties to it might possibly lead him to do something that would not be in Claire's best interest. Of course, ultimately, Noah proves loyal to Claire—but even with her most trusted ally, caution is needed.

Yet perhaps an even more important part of the requirement to exercise caution with our friends is what Matt Parkman learns. In "Hiros," after he has been reading his wife's mind and working to fix their relationship, Matt points out to her that they have been taking each other for granted and living together more as roommates than as husband and wife. We need to treat our friends with caution in the realization that they might not be our friends for long, but if we start taking them for granted, we might lose their friendship. Friends and allies are so important in life that we need to live every day realizing how fortunate we are to have them and make sure that we don't start to ignore them or assume that they will always be around and always support us. We need to keep the lines of communication open, we need to touch base with our friends and be sure that our aims and goals are still compatible with theirs. People grow and change, and often a healthy friendship needs to be renegotiated in some ways so that we continue to be good for one another.

There is a similar profound truth about enemies. Yes, you need to protect yourself and your friends against your enemies. When Plato developed his ideal form of government, the military played a crucial role. We need to protect ourselves from danger. But we also need to remind ourselves that even enemies can become allies or friends. In "Hiros," when Isaac Mendez and Peter realize that they need to work together to prevent the bomb from destroying New York City, they are able to set aside their hostility over Simone Deveaux, Isaac's former girlfriend and Peter's current love interest. Isaac was treating Peter as a total enemy, but when he saw that Peter would make a powerful ally in working toward a vitally important goal the two of them shared, he was able to set aside his anger and work with Peter.

It is a strategic mistake to treat an enemy as a *complete* enemy. We always need to be on the lookout for objectives we might share with our enemies, because people who work together for shared objectives are teammates, and teammates are allies. Yes, Brody deserved what he got, and perhaps Claire has no moral obligation to apologize. But it's better to try to mend the relationship so that Brody may one day be an ally again. To not apologize is to guarantee that he will always be an enemy, and Claire may want (or need) him as a friend someday.

But Isn't It Only Natural?

You are virtuous when you do justice to yourself as a human being; when you enjoy life and do things you feel like doing (you satisfy your appetite); when you don't sell yourself short but live up to your full potential (you satisfy your thumos); and most of all when you actively think about your life, planning things out logically and logistically, restraining your ambition and your appetites wisely. And don't forget to keep in mind that enemies can become friends if you are smart, and friends can become enemies if you take them for granted or treat them badly. Just as a healthy body is natural to us, so also a virtuous soul is natural to us.

This identifies our fundamental mistake when we think that it is only natural for someone with a superpower to take advantage of it to hoard the good things life has to offer. The core virtues of justice, wisdom, courage, and temperance are of value, according to Plato, because they are essential to living our lives as successful human beings. If virtue is to the soul what health is to the body, then virtues are not mere tools that we can use when they suit our purposes and ignore when they don't help us get what we want. Virtues are not merely instrumentally good because of what they can do; the virtues are intrinsically good because of what they are: healthy states of our soul that allow us to live our lives as human beings. Virtue is its own reward.

Plato gave the analogy of sheepdogs bred to protect flocks of sheep.[9] It would be unnatural and monstrous if dogs bred to protect the flock instead ripped the sheep apart. If virtue really is a crucial part of a healthy human soul, then it is horrendously unnatural and monstrous to turn on a friend and an ally, as Brody did to Claire. Instead of using his physical strength and athletic prowess to harm enemies (defeat rival football teams) and to help friends (enhance the reputation of the school), he perverted his special talents to harm an ally and a friend.

Still more degenerate is Sylar's treatment of his own (adoptive) mother, Virginia Gray, in "The Hard Part."[10] To show her how special he is, he uses a kitchen hose, his freezing power, and his telekinesis to turn her apartment into a big snow globe. She is frightened, and her grip on reality is questionable, but her subsequent refusal to accept that Sylar is truly her son, Gabriel, is based on a profound realization: the quest for power has destroyed Gabriel, leaving only Sylar. After killing Virginia—the only woman who ever loved him—with a pair of scissors, Sylar calmly paints the future with her blood. Nothing could be more contrary to human nature.

Heroes like Claire, Matt, Hiro, and Peter are able to form alliances and friendships with one another. Being a team player is not about mere conformity. From the perspective of simple conformity, you are foolish if you try to change things and ridiculous if you don't fit in. That's not the case with true heroes. Matt wants to change things because he wants to help others and make the world a better place. Peter has tremendous empathy for others and looks for opportunities to use his remarkable powers to help in ways he never could before.[11] Hiro is a freak because of his unusual ability, but that doesn't make him embarrassed about not being like others; instead, it gives him a profound sense of responsibility. His ability brings something very powerful to the alliance. Our common aims can bring us together, and our distinctive differences enhance our capabilities as a united team.

These remarkable heroes face a choice that all of us unremarkable, ordinary people face. The core virtues of justice, wisdom, courage, and temperance are not simply a matter of "fitting in" or conforming to society's expectations. Rather, they allow you to help your friends and harm your enemies. They give you the intelligence to find common objectives that can turn enemies into allies and give you the insight to cultivate your friendships and not take them for granted. Mere conformity will make you try to hide what makes you unique and prevent you from rocking the boat or trying to change things. Virtue shows that what makes you unique can make you a great asset to the community and that your attempts to change things for the better can make a difference. Whether we have spectacular powers like the characters in *Heroes* or only the ordinary abilities of a normal human being, we all face the same choice: what will we do with what has been given to us? Regardless of what physical abilities you have or lack, you can still choose to be a hero. After all, it's only natural.

NOTES

1. See Plato, *The Republic*, 4.439e–441c. All translations are made by the author.

2. The closest translations would be "heart" or "spirit," but both of those have very different connotations in English from what *thumos* has in Greek. "Heart" is too romantic, and "spirit" is too spiritual.

3. See Plato, *The Republic*, 4.440ab.

4. Ibid., 4.439d.

5. Not to mention the poor scared kid in the elevator after Sylar acquired his ability to detect lies ("Our Father").

6. Arthur explicitly referred to empathy when he spoke of teaching Sylar to acquire his powers a different way ("It's Coming"). For more on Peter and how he acquires his abilities through empathy, see chapter 15, "Peter Petrelli: The Power of Empathy" by Andrew Terjesen in this volume.

7. See Plato, *The Republic*, 1.332a–335e.

8. Sophocles, *Ajax*, 678–682 (author's translation).

9. See Plato, *The Republic*, 3.416ab.

10. Of course, Sylar's biological mother was killed by his biological father, Samson Gray ("Exposed").

11. In fact, Peter's power may simply be empathy. For more on this, see chapter 15, "Peter Petrelli: The Power of Empathy" by Andrew Terjesen.

PART THREE

METAPHYSICS, REGULAR PHYSICS, AND HEROIC TIME TRAVEL

EIGHT

THE FOREKNOWLEDGE OF A PAINTER, THE FATE OF A HIRO

David Kyle Johnson

> We all imagine ourselves the agents of our destiny, capable of determining our own fate. But have we truly any choice in when we rise or when we fall? Or does a force larger than ourselves bid us our direction?
>
> —Mohinder Suresh, "Don't Look Back"

Although he is now dead and not the only fortune teller, Isaac Mendez has played a major role in the *Heroes* story. His paintings and comics could supposedly foretell the future, and the information his paintings suggested was viewed by most as priceless. But it's not clear how "fated" his paintings and comics actually were. Isaac painted the explosion of New York City, but, as we all know, that wasn't fated—it was prevented. And many of his paintings were merely self-fulfilling prophecies. The people in the paintings—usually in an atte-mpt to prevent the prophecies—made them come true.

So, is fate actually at work in the *Heroes* universe? By answering this question, maybe we can learn a little about how (or whether) fate works in our universe.

What Is Fate?

You do not choose your destiny. It chooses you. And those who knew you before fate took you by the hand cannot understand the depth of the changes inside.

—Mohinder Suresh, "Nothing to Hide"

An event is fated only if it cannot be prevented. Like Matt Parkman with Daphne Millbrook, people often believe they meet and marry their spouses by fate, other people think we are destined to die at a certain time, and many religious people believe the end of the world is fated to occur on a specific date.

But belief in fate stands in the way of free will. You can freely choose to perform an action only if you can also refrain from performing that action. If you can't refrain from doing something, you don't really have a choice, and so you can't do it freely. But if you are fated to perform an action, such as meet and fall in love with your future spouse, then you can't do otherwise. And if you can't do otherwise, you are not free—even if it seems or feels as if you are.

There are a number of reasons for thinking that an event is fated. Maybe you live in ancient Greece and believe in the Moirae ("the fates") and think they have preordained certain events. Maybe you are alive today, believe in God, and, as Nathan did for a while, think God has preordained certain events. Maybe you think the superpower to paint the future really exists and the events so painted are fated to occur. But quite often, people really haven't thought about it.

The Truth about Fate

My destiny is not to shoot you. The universe cannot
be that lame.

—Claire Bennet, "The Hard Part"

But philosophers have thought about it and found some
genuine reasons for thinking that events are fated. Aristotle,
for example, considered the proposition "There will be a sea
battle tomorrow." If all propositions are either true or false,
then so is that one. But, Aristotle argued, that means whether
there will be a sea battle tomorrow is already determined.
Why? Because if it's already true that there will be a sea battle tomorrow, if one doesn't occur, then it wasn't already true;
and if it's already false that there will be a sea battle tomorrow, if one does occur, then it wasn't already false. Either way,
you have a contradiction, and contradictions cannot be true.
So, regardless of whether the proposition is true or false, the
event that the truth or the falsity of it entails must occur; it's
fated. And it's not only sea battles. Take any future event you
like: for example, "Peter Petrelli will lie, bloody, underneath
the homecoming banner at Odessa, Texas, at 10:34 the night
of Odessa's homecoming." The proposition that expressed
that event's occurrence was true, even before that event happened, thus the event is fated. And because every event that
ever occurred was, at some point, a future event—and the
proposition that expressed that event's occurrence was true
before the event occurred—every event is fated.

"But that's just it," you might say, "Isaac's paintings aren't
true when they are painted—they 'come true.'"[1] In the same
way, propositions about the future aren't true—they "become
true." The problem with this reply is that it defies one of
the fundamental laws of logic, *bivalence*, according to which
every proposition is either true or false. What the objection
suggests is that a proposition about a future event isn't true or

false until the event occurs. But if so, that proposition doesn't have a truth value—contrary to the law of bivalence.

One might also object, "But I know that Isaac's paintings are true. I don't know which propositions about the future are true." This doesn't matter, though. Ignorance is no excuse. Think about a huge art gallery where Isaac has painted every event that will occur. Each of those events is fated, right? But suppose someone has also painted everything that won't occur and hung his or her paintings in the gallery. You walk through the gallery, unable to tell the difference between them. Does this mean that the events depicted in Isaac's paintings aren't fated? No. It simply means that you can't tell which ones are fated. Your ignorance doesn't change the fact that the events depicted in Isaac's paintings are inevitable. The same is true of propositions.

Maybe the easiest way to think about it is in terms of Hiro Nakamura. True propositions are true for a reason: they match up to the way the world is. If it's true that "A book is on the table," it's because, out in the world, there really is a book on the table. Philosophers call this the "correspondence theory of truth." In the same way, if "New York City will explode on November 8, 2006," is true, it's because that is the way the world is: that event is already "written on the timeline." If Hiro travels to that place on the timeline, he will see New York City explode (as he did in "One Giant Leap"). But you can't unwrite the timeline. "The past," as Mohinder says, is "written in stone" ("6 Months Ago"). Once the milk is spilled, you can't unspill it. If something has already happened—if it is already written on the timeline of the past—it cannot be undone. The same would be true of the future; if something is already written on the timeline of the future, it cannot be unwritten. So, we could say, the truth of propositions about the future entails universal fatalism because it entails that the future timeline is already written.

The Foreknowledge of Hiro

The earth is large. Large enough that you think you
can hide from anything—from fate, from God. If
only you found a place far enough away. So you run. . . .
You can run far. You can take your small precautions.
But have you really gotten away? Can you ever escape?
Or is the truth that you do not have the strength or
cunning to hide from destiny—[that] the world is not
small, you are, and fate can find you anywhere?

—Mohinder Suresh, "Seven Minutes to Midnight"

Some people believe that God predestines certain events
to occur. For example, Maya Herrera believed that God
"delivered" Gabriel Gray (Sylar) to her and her brother,
Alejandro, to lead them to Dr. Suresh ("The Line"). The
Haitian believed that God punished him with sickness for
abusing his power and that God sent Mohinder to cure him
("Lizards"). All of these events would be, according to them,
"fated by God."

But if a fated event depends on a human decision, that
human decision cannot be free. For example, if God fated
Mohinder to go to Haiti and cure the Haitian, Mohinder
could have done nothing else but decide to go to Haiti. Yet if
he can't refrain from making that decision, the decision is not
free. This is why most philosophers don't believe that God
predestines specific events to occur.[2]

Another way God's existence hinders free will is by God
having infallible prior knowledge regarding the events of
the future—that is, by having "infallible foreknowledge."
Philosophers ask, "What if God doesn't make you do what you
do, but he still knew what you were going to do before you did
it. Could you be free?" You may think the answer is obviously
yes, but things are not so simple. We can envision this problem in terms of Future Hiro's time travel. Future Hiro travels
into the future to see Sylar blow up New York City. Of course,

Future Hiro travels back in time to try to prevent it and eventually does prevent it. But what if Future Hiro's visions of the future are infallible and unchangeable—whatever he sees is exactly what will happen and there is no chance for change or error?[3] If so, given Future Hiro's vision, the event of Sylar blowing up New York City is inevitable—it is fated. If Hiro's vision is both unchangeable and infallible, then it will be impossible for Sylar not to blow up New York City. Thus, Sylar won't have any free choice in the matter; he can't do otherwise.

Philosophers have argued the same regarding God. God doesn't need to travel to the future to see what will happen—he simply knows. But God is infallible. He can't be wrong. And once he believes something, it can't be unbelieved. As Mohinder points out earlier, the past is "written in stone" ("6 Months Ago"). So if God believed something yesterday, the fact of his belief cannot be changed.[4] If God believed yesterday that Sylar will blow up New York City on November 8, then Sylar can't do anything but exactly that. If he does anything besides exactly what God believed he would do, he would either be changing God's past belief or making it false—and he can do neither. Of course, this doesn't mean that God makes him do it, but it does mean that Sylar can't do otherwise. And if he can't do otherwise, he can't be free. And because God, as traditionally conceived, has infallible unchangeable beliefs about all of everyone's actions—he knows everything—it seems that God's foreknowledge is incompatible with everyone's free will.

One attempt to solve this problem, inspired by the philosopher Boethius (c. 480–c. 525), would be to say that God doesn't believe anything about Sylar *yesterday*. God is timeless—outside space and time viewing all of the timeline simultaneously—and believes things timelessly, not at specific moments in time. But this solution fails for the simple fact that timeless beliefs are just as unchangeable and infallible as ordinary beliefs. For example, if instead of traveling into the future, Hiro travels outside of space-time and knows the future by "looking down" on the timeline, what he sees is unchangeable and infallible, even if it is from a timeless perspective.

Wanting to continue to believe in free will and in God, some philosophers, called "open theists," suggest that God does not have foreknowledge. "But," you might ask, "doesn't God have to be all knowing? Isn't he perfect? Otherwise, he wouldn't be God, right?" Right. But lacking foreknowledge doesn't necessarily prevent him from being all knowing. To be all knowing, one must simply know everything it is possible to know. (For example, God doesn't know what a square circle looks like, because square circles are impossible.) But, open theists argue, the future isn't knowable; it hasn't happened yet, so there is nothing *true* about it to know. So, God's not knowing the future doesn't prevent God from being "all-knowing." They might say, "You can't be nonperfect for not knowing *what the future holds* if the future doesn't hold anything." Many open theists even argue that this is the biblical view of God.[5]

Unfortunately, as you may have realized, open theists have to believe that propositions about the future aren't true or false; thus, they must deny the fundamental logical law of bivalence. So, to be an open theist, you have to rewrite logic itself. This is a daunting task, to be sure, but good work on nonbivalent logics is already being done.[6]

A Loose Sense of Fate

Angela: It's inevitable, dear. There's nothing anyone can do about it.

Claire: That's insane! Nothing is inevitable. The future is not written in stone.

—"How to Stop an Exploding Man"

The *Heroes* universe is not really one of universal fatalism. For one thing, the future timeline doesn't seem to be written in stone. Peter travels to the future to see the Shanti virus plague but prevents it ("Powerless").[7] In Volume 3, he sees a future where everyone has powers, but that doesn't happen either. And, as previously mentioned, not even all of Isaac's paintings come true; New York City never explodes, despite the fact that Isaac painted it.

But we can make sense of this by understanding fate in a "looser" way—in terms of "high probability." Maybe Hiro and Peter don't see the *future*; they see the *likely future*. Whether what they see will actually happen is still up in the air, to a degree. This is why Peter and Hiro can prevent what they see. In the same way, maybe Isaac doesn't paint what *will* happen but what is *likely* to happen. Of course, because the events are quite likely, most of the time Isaac gets it right. But once in a while he gets it wrong—especially if people with superpowers set out to prevent the events he paints.

Some philosophers have suggested that this is how God knows the future. Because we have free will, he can't know *for sure* what we will do, but he can be fairly sure; he knows what we are likely to do. The problem with this, however, is that such knowledge is practically useless. To illustrate why, a lesson in probability is in order. If some event's probability is 1, its occurrence is certain. If its probability is 0, it's certain that it will not occur. The chance of heads on a coin flip is 0.5 (50 percent). If you want to know the probability of two things occurring sequentially, you multiply their probability. The probability of getting two heads in a row on two consecutive coin tosses is 0.25 ($0.5 \times 0.5 = 0.25$). The probability goes down the more events you consider.

Now, let's say that God knows Ando pretty well. As Ando sits in the Burnt Toast Diner ("Seven Minutes to Midnight"), God knows that he is 90 percent likely to order waffles instead of fries.[8] God might also know that Ando is 90 percent likely to order maple, instead of strawberry, syrup if he orders waffles. But this means God is only 81 percent sure that Ando will have waffles with maple syrup ($0.9 \times 0.9 = 0.81$). Even if Ando is likely to add sausage, an egg, grapefruit, and a glass of milk (each with a 90 percent probability), the most likely meal scenario for Ando is only 53 percent likely ($0.9\char94 5) = 0.53$). That is as sure as God can be about Ando's meal choice, and that is hardly better than a coin toss. And if God wants to know how Ando's whole day will go, we have to factor in all of the decisions Ando makes in a day. If he makes only 50 decisions a day, even if each of them is 90 percent likely, at the beginning of the day God can only be less than 1 percent ($.014$) sure what Ando will do that day.[9]

A Looser Sense of Fate

My father sacrificed himself so that I could have a life, not a destiny.

—Claire Bennet, "The Hard Part"

But there is another way to think of fate. Maybe certain propositions about certain events are true, but the specifics of how we get there and what exactly happens when we do are left to us. For example, maybe, as depicted in the seventh of Isaac's eight paintings from the second volume, the proposition "Mohinder will fire a Company gun with his right hand and a bandage on his nose" is fated to be true. But the proposition could be true in a number of ways. Maybe he misses; maybe there are blanks in the gun. Maybe Noah Bennet avoids the bullet; maybe Mohinder shoots Bob Bishop instead. And there are a number of ways to get to that point. Maybe Mohinder is given the gun by the Company; maybe he stole it from someone. Maybe Niki Sanders broke his nose; maybe he fell down some stairs.

This seems to be the kind of fate involved in the classic story of Oedipus, who, as a child, is said by the Oracle at Delphi to be fated to marry his mother and kill his father.

His parents, in an effort to avoid this catastrophe, try to kill him but fail. When Oedipus is an adult, he accidentally finds his way back to them and, not knowing who they are, kills his father and marries his mother. But "kill your father and marry your mother" is quite vague. This could have happened many different ways, and any number of things could have happened between the prediction and its coming true. Maybe his parents keep him, maybe not. Maybe he kills his father by sending him to battle; maybe he kills his father in battle. There are a number of different scenarios consistent with the prediction.

In any case, if this is the sense of fate at work in *Heroes*, there is plenty of room for free will. Certain vague propositions might be fated to be true, but our characters get to choose how they become true. And there is evidence that this is how things work in the *Heroes* universe. "New York City will explode" is not fated to be true, but it seems that "Someone blows up near New York City" is fated to be true. Maybe it's Ted Sprague, maybe it's Sylar, maybe it's Peter; whoever it is may or may not blow up the city. If so, even though there is something fated, there is still room for free will.

Self-Fulfilling Prophecy

> For all his bluster, it is the sad province of man that he cannot choose his triumph. He can only choose how he will stand when the call of destiny comes.
>
> —Mohinder Suresh, "Don't Look Back"

When it comes to Isaac's paintings and comics, however, there is another way to think about it. They may not be real prophecy at all. They may simply be self-fulfilling predictions. Think about when Hiro finds a copy of *9th Wonders!* the comic drawn by Isaac that depicts Hiro's actions, past, present, and future. Much of what Hiro does after that point—saves the girl with the red bow, takes Ando to America, rents the Nissan Versa—are all done because the comic says he will do them. "The comic book says we fly together, so we fly together" ("One Giant Leap"). This trend continues all the way into Volume 3. When Hiro loses his memory, he and his friends turn to Isaac's last published comic to figure out how they will get it back. But this makes Isaac's predictions far less impressive. They aren't predictions as much as they are instructions.

Many of Isaac's paintings have a similar effect but in the opposite way. The events shown in some of Isaac's paintings are brought about by the people depicted when they try to prevent the events. In the second volume, for example, Noah tries to prevent the eighth painting in Isaac's last series—the one that portrays Noah being shot in the eye—from coming true. He forbids Claire to date, he tries to move the family away. But he merely ends up making the prediction come true ("Cautionary Tales"). In the graphic novel chapter titled "Isaac's First Time," Isaac is displaying his art in the Deveaux Gallery, and his painting of a woman getting hit by a bus is seen by the woman herself. She runs out of the gallery, upset by the painting, and—you guessed it—gets hit by a bus.

Isaac wonders, What have I done? He fears that he didn't predict the event; he caused it. If this is true of all his paintings, he doesn't have the gift of prophecy at all. His gift is more like those of Eden McCain or Matt Parkman, who can make people do things by suggesting them. Isaac simply suggests in a different way: by painting. If so, it may be that his power interferes with free will after all. I wouldn't call actions that people perform at the suggestion of Eden or Matt "free actions." Did the woman freely jump in front of that bus or was it all Isaac's doing? It depends on whether she could have done otherwise. I'll leave that up to you.

All in all, if every event is fated, we clearly are not free. But maybe it is the mere fact that we are free that entails that universal fatalism isn't true. And that is what makes us so special; we can deny fate. As Mohinder says,

> Was the die cast from the very beginning or is it in our own hands to alter the course of destiny? Of all our abilities, it is free will that truly makes us unique. With it, we have a tiny, but potent, chance to deny fate. And only with it can we find our way back to being human.
> —"6 Months Ago."

But, of course, our believing that we have free will is not enough to give it to us. There are plenty more arguments that suggest we aren't free. I'll let you do your own research.[10] Strangely enough, it may reveal that we are *destined* to believe that we are free, even though we are not.

NOTES

1. Isaac uses this phrase to describe his paintings in "One Giant Leap." Noah Bennet does, too, in "Lizards."

2. For more on this topic, see my chapter "'A Story That Is Told, Again, and Again, and Again': Recurrence, Providence, and Freedom," in *Battlestar Galactica and Philosophy*, edited by Jason T. Eberl (Malden, MA: Wiley-Blackwell, 2008).

3. This is actually the most accurate description of Hiro's power. Hiro cannot change what he sees. He can only create an alternate universe where that event doesn't occur. See chapter 9, "Time to Be a Hero: Branching Time and Changing the Future," by Morgan Luck.

4. Philosophers usually believe that God is immutable (unchangeable). So, his beliefs might also be unchangeable for that reason. At least in my experience, however, not many people take God's having this property that seriously anymore; for example, some think only his character is unchangeable but that other parts of him, such as what beliefs he holds, might be changeable.

5. See Clark Pinnock, et al., *The Openness of God* (Downers Grove, IL: InterVarsity Press, 1994).

6. For an example, see Craig Bourne, "Future Contingents, Non-Contradiction and the Law of Excluded Middle Muddle," *Analysis* 64, no. 2. (2004).

7. This actually doesn't make sense; he prevented the events that caused him to want to prevent them. By preventing them, he caused the future timeline not to contain these actions. But if it doesn't, then where did he go when he traveled "into the future" to see them? Such problems are reason for thinking that any event written on the timeline is written in stone. For more on the possibility of time travel (and where Hiro and Peter

went on their excursions to "the future"), see chapter 9, "Time to Be a Hero: Branching Time and Changing the Future," by Morgan Luck.

8. According to Ando, this is all there is to eat in America.

9. Maybe you think that 90 percent is too low a number; maybe we are 99.9 percent likely to perform the actions we do. But even then, when you multiply the probability of all of our actions together, the probabilities are still too low to be useful. Only if each of our actions is nearly inevitable—99.9 with a billion 9's after it—are you going to start getting useful numbers. But if our performance of an action is *that* likely—so likely that we would have a better chance of winning the lottery a hundred times in a row than we would have at not performing the action—it seems that we could have no free will. My thanks to Mark Gutel for inspiring arguments in this section.

10. A great place to start is Timothy O'Connor, "Free Will," in *The Stanford Encyclopedia of Philosophy*, Fall 2008 Edition, edited by Edward N. Zalta, http://plato .stanford.edu/archives/fall2008/entries/freewill/.

NINE

TIME TO BE A HERO: BRANCHING TIME AND CHANGING THE FUTURE

Morgan Luck

Backward time travel seems like the best thing since (and perhaps even before) sliced bread. It makes Hiro Nakamura seem nearly unstoppable (at least when he has his powers). Think about it: Rather than going toe-to-toe with Sylar, Hiro can simply travel back in time and defeat him while he's still in diapers. Rather than endlessly worrying about whether Ando will become a "bad guy," Hiro can just wait to see whether he does and, if he does, go back in time and prevent whatever event pushed Ando over the edge. Any time Hiro doesn't quite manage to save the day, he can just travel back and try again. What superpower could be more useful to a hero?

Well, unfortunately for Hiro, when you stop to examine the concept of backward time travel logically, it turns out that it is not as useful as it seems. In fact, the ability to travel back in time is perhaps one of the most ineffectual superpowers a hero could have.

The Problem with Time Travel

Some physicists believe that the theory of relativity allows for the possibility of backward time travel.[1] Yet certain philosophers have argued that the ability to travel backward in time is logically impossible. Not even God could do it because the concept itself is incoherent. To understand why, let's begin by examining an incident that occurs in the episode "Cautionary Tales."

In this episode Hiro discovers that his father, Kaito, has been murdered. As a result, he sets out to travel back in time and save his father. If Hiro were to succeed in his mission, however, a paradox would ensue. Think of it this way: Hiro decides to go back in time to prevent his father's death only because he heard about his father's death. But he heard about his father's death because his father died. If he succeeds in preventing his father's death, his father won't die, and if he doesn't die, Hiro will never hear about his father's death. But if he never hears about his father's death, he will never decide to go back and prevent it in the first place. But if he doesn't do that, his father won't be saved and Hiro will go back and prevent it, which means he won't go back and prevent it, and . . .

You get the idea. Because Hiro, by traveling back to save his father, would be preventing the very thing that caused him to prevent it, a logical paradox arises: if he prevents his father's death he doesn't, and if he doesn't, he does. And that's simply nonsense.

This type of paradox is commonly referred to by philosophers as a "grandfather paradox." The name comes from the most well-known example of time-travel absurdity: If you could travel into the past, you could kill your own grandfather at a time before your father's conception, which would prevent your own birth. This in turn would prevent you from time traveling and killing your grandfather before your father's conception.[2] It is because of such paradoxes that some have argued against the very possibility of time travel.[3] This argument can be stated as follows.

1. Backward time travel would make paradoxes possible.
2. Paradoxes are impossible.
3. Therefore, backward time travel is impossible.

Before we advise Hiro to hang up his sword, however—not everyone agrees that backward time travel would give rise to paradoxes.[4] Proponents of time travel quite rightly point out that if Hiro went back in time but didn't save his father (which is what his father actually convinced him to do), no paradox would arise. It is not traveling back to the past that gives rise to paradoxes; it is altering the past. So it *is* possible for Hiro to travel to the past, provided that while he is there, it is impossible for him to change past events. But how could changing past events be impossible? Let's look at two theories of time travel that suggest it is.

Linear Time Travel

The first theory of time travel we'll examine is linear time travel. According to this theory, all past events are laid out on a single timeline and that timeline is fixed; once an event has occurred, it is set in stone.[5] According to this theory, if Hiro were to decide to go back in time and kill Sylar as a child, to stop his murder spree before it begins, Hiro would not succeed. Although this plan seems well within Hiro's power to carry out, according to the theory of linear time travel, he must fail. Because Sylar's survival of childhood is in the past and the past can't be changed, nothing Hiro does will be able to alter this fact. So, even if Hiro does travel back in time to kill baby Sylar, he will, necessarily, fail to do so.

Now, this theory doesn't say why Hiro will fail; it only promises us that he will. Perhaps it is because he cannot bear to kill a child, or perhaps he makes a mistake in his spatial coordinates and ends up killing another child altogether.[6] Who knows? But even though the reasons for Hiro's failure are uncertain, according to linear time travel, we can be certain that *he will* fail.

If the linear time-travel theory is correct, Hiro's backward time-traveling powers are fairly useless. If he goes to the future and sees something happen—such as a nuked New York—he can't go back and prevent it.[7] Once it has occurred, it is written on the timeline and thus becomes an unchangeable fact. If he tries to prevent it, he must fail. When he hears about his father's death, he can't go back and save his father's life. He can go back and see who did it, but he can't prevent it. If he tries, he *will* fail.

At first glance, it might seem that time travel within the *Heroes* universe does operate according to the theory of linear time travel. For example, within the episode "Cautionary Tales," despite Hiro's intention to save his father, Kaito is still murdered. In the episode "Six Months Ago," despite Hiro's attempts to save Charlie Andrews from Sylar, she is still killed. And in the episode "Fallout," despite Hiro warning Isaac Mendez of Sylar's attack, Isaac is still found dead. These instances seem to support the notion that, try as he may, Hiro is unable to alter past events.

But although on these occasions the *Heroes* universe seems to operate according to linear time travel, there are plenty of other instances where it plainly doesn't. The episode "Don't Look Back" features one of Hiro's first trips through time and space. On this occasion he travels from Tokyo on the second of October 2006, to New York on the eighth of November 2006. In New York, before witnessing its destruction, Hiro makes a phone call to his friend Ando back in Tokyo. Ando states that Hiro has been missing for five weeks. If this were the case, then according to the theory of linear time travel, Hiro would be completely unable to meet up with Ando within the five weeks that he was missing. Hiro's absence during those weeks has already occurred. Yet in the episode "One Giant Leap," Hiro does exactly this, arriving back in Tokyo and meeting Ando on the fourth of October. The fact that linear time travel can't account for Hiro's actions is spelled out later in this episode, when he and Ando have the following conversation:

Ando: I'm confused. You said you called me when you went in the future.

Hiro: Yeah. So?

Ando: So, shouldn't I be at home, waiting for your call?

Hiro: We're changing the future.

What's more, if linear time travel is in operation, the destruction of New York witnessed by Hiro in the future should have occurred despite his actions to prevent it. Yet in the episode "How to Stop an Exploding Man," New York is spared this fate. The failure of linear time travel to account for this change is again spelled out for us when, just before the explosion is averted, Nathan Petrelli assures his brother, Peter, that "the future isn't written in stone." Both Hiro's phone call to Ando and New York's destruction are not, according to the linear theory, potential events that may or may not occur in some possible future. Rather, they are events that have already occurred and thus must occur. Because they did fail to occur, it seems that the events within the *Heroes* universe are not consistent with the theory of linear time travel. There is, however, another theory of time travel that is better able to account for the events within *Heroes*.

Branching Time Travel

The second and arguably the only other coherent theory of time travel is branching time travel.[8] Because of the problems that arise from the grandfather paradox, branching time travel theory also claims that Hiro cannot change the past. To be more accurate, it says that he cannot change the past of *his own universe*. Other universes, on the other hand, are fair game. To better understand this theory, you'll need to start considering *alternate universes*.

Have you heard of alternate-history fiction? People write stories about what the world would have been like if Hitler had won World War II or if we had discovered life on Mars in the nineties. Imagine a universe where such a thing did happen; that is an "alternate universe." Alternate universes have pasts identical to ours up until a point where there is a difference. Maybe that is the only difference; everything else is the same. But maybe one small difference makes a universe's timeline entirely different from ours from that point on. For example, it is often said that the random killing of a single bug in the distant past could have prevented the evolution of human beings.

According to this theory, when time travelers go back in time, they don't travel into the past of *their* universe. How could they? Their universe's past doesn't contain the actions they are about to perform. When they travel back, they create a new universe: one whose past does contain those actions. This universe is just like theirs, up to the time when they arrive in the past, but from then on it is different—it "branches off" from the original (hence the name "branching time travel"). And if they time travel again, this time forward, it won't be to their original universe's future. It will be to the future of this new alternate universe, which contains the effects of all of their actions.

If a time traveler goes to the distant past and prevents human evolution by stepping on a bug, he could not have traveled into the past of his own universe. If he prevents human evolution in his universe, he wouldn't exist to step on the bug and prevent it (another grandfather paradox!). According to the branching theory of time travel, by traveling back, he creates a different, alternate universe: one where he steps on a bug and prevents human evolution. If he were to again travel in time—as far forward as he did backward—he would travel into the future of this new universe and find himself to be the only human.

Think about Hiro's trip back to 1671 Japan. Hiro grew up hearing how Kensei saved the village of Otsu. But when Hiro travels back in time and interferes with Kensei's affairs, he prevents Kensei from saving the village of Otsu. That being so, the past of the universe that Hiro has traveled back to can't be the past of *his* universe—"Universe-1," we will call it. In Hiro's universe, Kensei saved Otsu. Hiro hasn't changed the past. All Hiro has really done is created a new, alternate universe—Universe-2—one in which Kensei didn't save Otsu. And when Hiro travels ahead into the future, he will travel into the future of the new universe he created—a future where it is not true that Kensei saved Otsu.

Branching time travel nicely evades the grandfather paradox by denying time travelers the ability to change the past. I can't go back in time and kill my grandfather (Grandfather-1). I can only go back in time and kill the grandfather of some other version of myself in an alternate universe—Grandfather-2. Of course, this means that the alternate version of myself (me-2) will never exist, but what do I care? That's not me. In the same way, Hiro-1 can't travel into the past and save *his* father, Kaito-1, so that he never hears of Kaito-1's death and never travels back to save him. If he travels into the past, he travels to Universe-2's past and would save Kaito-2.

Because it is hearing of Kaito-1's death (not Kaito-2's) that makes Hiro want to travel back in the first place, if he saves Kaito-2, there is no problem. No harm, no foul, no paradox.

But this also demonstrates why Hiro's time-traveling powers are fairly useless. Rather than altering the past in his universe, Hiro is able to shape the future only in other universes.

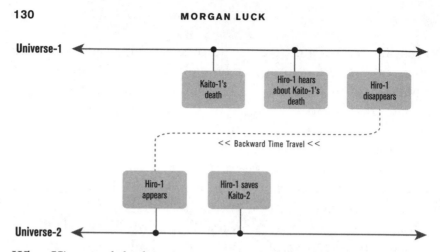

Universe-1

| Kaito-1's death | Hiro-1 hears about Kaito-1's death | Hiro-1 disappears |

<< Backward Time Travel <<

| Hiro-1 appears | Hiro-1 saves Kaito-2 |

Universe-2

When Hiro travels back in time to save his father, he will create a different universe with an alternate timeline. This prevents him from generating a paradox.

Think about the episode "Don't Look Back," where Hiro first travels backward in time, from November 8, New York City (where he witnesses the city's destruction), to October 4, Tokyo, with the intention of saving New York City. According to the branching theory, when Hiro travels into the *future* to see New York destroyed, he is still in his original universe, Universe-1. No big deal. But when he travels back to save New York City, he creates a different universe—Universe-2— one in which he attempts to save New York City.[9]

But even if Hiro succeeds, he will only be saving the New York City of Universe-2. New York City-1 still explodes. No matter what Hiro-1 does, Hiro-1 can't get to the past of Universe-1 to prevent the explosion; any time he travels back, he will merely create a different universe. So Hiro-1 can never do what he set out to do: save New York City–1!

Branching time travel is consistent with the story of *Heroes* and, like linear time travel, it shows that the ability to travel backward in time is a fairly useless power. But at least we have a consistent story—which is a hard thing to get with

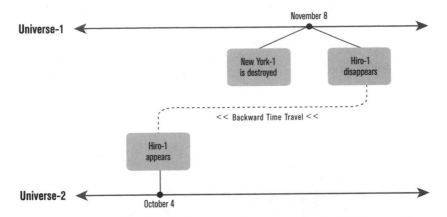

Hiro's time travel powers are useless. After seeing New York City explode, he travels back in time to prevent it. But by traveling back, he creates a new universe with a new timeline containing a new New York City. He might save the new one, but the original New York City he saw explode still explodes on the original timeline.

time-travel stories. This, however, also raises some interesting questions. Both Universe-1 and Universe-2 have identical histories up until October 4, the moment Hiro-1 arrives in Universe-2. Of course, from this point on the universes are different. Universe-1 is the universe where Ando-1 does not hear from Hiro for five weeks. Universe-2 is the universe where Ando-2 does not hear from Hiro for two days. But, presumably, there is a Hiro-2 who travels into the future of Universe-2 whom Ando-2 is waiting to hear back from, before Hiro-1 finds him. But what does Hiro-2 see when he gets to the future?

And what about Future Hiro—the one with the ponytail and the sword who, in "Hiros," finds Peter in the subway and tells him to save the cheerleader? Where did Future Hiro come from? I'm sure you can think of a few more questions. Let's see whether we can't have some philosophical fun by creating a consistent universe-branching story out of the first volume of *Heroes* to answer some of these questions. It might get a little complicated, but I'm sure you can

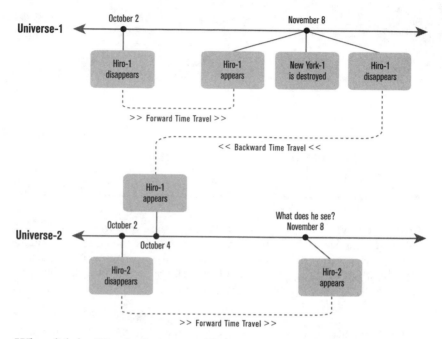

What did the Hiro indigenous to Universe-2 see when he went into the future?

handle it. Just take it one step at a time. Let's explore the *Heroes* multiverse.

The *Heroes* Multiverse

A multiverse is a collection of universes, and that is exactly what Hiro's time travel in Volume 1 gets us. As we discussed earlier, when Hiro travels back in time the first time—after seeing New York City–1 destroyed—he created a branching universe, Universe-2. But he doesn't stay there for long. When Charlie—the cute red-haired waitress in Midland, Texas, with enhanced memory—is murdered by Sylar in "Seven Minutes to Midnight," Hiro travels back yet again ("Six Months Ago") to try to save her. This creates Universe-3. At this time, our focus is shifted to Ando-3, who (unlike Ando-2) exists in a universe where Charlie knew Hiro and even took a photo with him on her last birthday.[10] When Hiro travels forward in time again, he meets up with Ando-3 (in Universe-3). They eventually travel into the future again ("Five Years Gone")—the future of Universe-3—to discover that New York City is still destroyed. They travel back yet again to try to save it yet again. This creates Universe-4. They don't travel backward again, so it is this universe's New York City that is actually saved in "How to Stop an Exploding Man"—by Hiro-1, Ando-3, and the rest of the heroes of Universe-4.

Now I think we can answer our questions. What does Hiro-2 see when he travels to the future of Universe-2? Well, because Hiro-1 doesn't really do anything significant in Universe-2 to differentiate it from Universe-1, Hiro-2 probably also sees a destroyed New York City in the future of Universe-2. Perhaps the small differences between Universe-1 and Universe-2 are enough to prevent the explosion, but because Universe-3 is even more different than Universe-2— in Universe-3 the cheerleader is saved—and yet New York City–3 is still destroyed, that seems unlikely. Of course, this raises the question of where Hiro-2 goes after he sees the destruction of New York City–2. Fortunately, the answer is simple: to yet another universe about which we know nothing.

But what about Future Hiro—where does he come from? Well, in the episode "Five Years Gone," we learn that Future Hiro is from a universe where (he believes) Sylar explodes and destroys New York. In order to save New York, Hiro attempts to kill Sylar by stabbing him. In this universe, however, Sylar kills Claire and takes her power of regeneration. So Future Hiro's attempt to kill Sylar fails, and New York is still destroyed. So, presumably, Future Hiro is like Hiro-1. He exists in some universe, call it Universe-A, and he travels into his own future to see New York City–A destroyed. He travels back to prevent it, creating a different universe

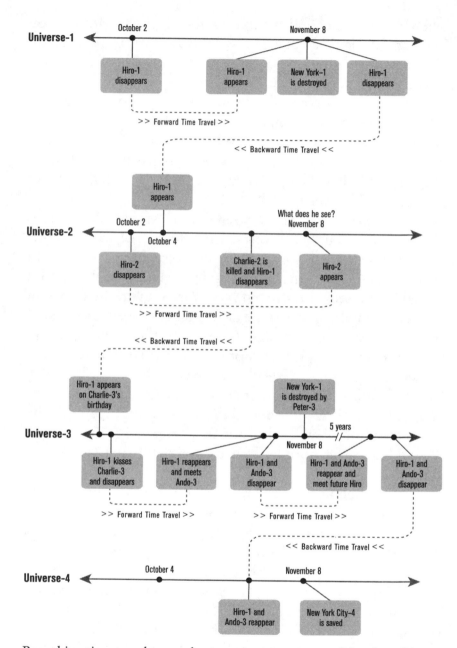

Branching time travel can make a consistent story out of the plot of Volume 1, but as you can see it's a bit complicated.

(Universe-B). He somehow comes to believe that Sylar is the one who did it but fails to stop him from destroying New York City–B.

Hiro-A (Future Hiro) then reasons that if he travels back in time and takes steps to save Claire, he can then travel forward again to a future where Sylar doesn't survive the stabbing and New York is not destroyed. So Future Hiro travels back in time to contact Peter and tell him to save the cheerleader to save the world.

We see Future Hiro do this in "Collision," while we are observing Universe-2, so you might think that the next step in our explanation is to suggest that after Future Hiro fails to save Universe-B and travels back to try again, he lands in Universe-2 and tells Peter-2 how to save the world. But this would not be entirely accurate. Branching time travel does not allow time travelers from the same or separate universes to both travel

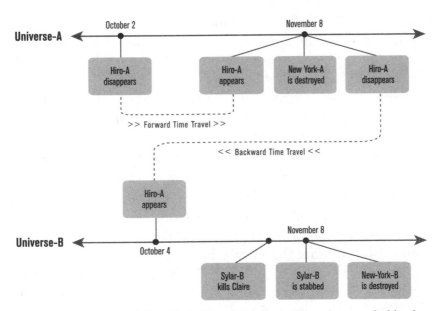

Future Hiro also saw New York City destroyed. When he traveled back in time to prevent it, he also created an alternate timeline.

to the same alternative universe.[11] Since Hiro-1 "created" Universe-2 by traveling back to it from Universe-1, Future Hiro can't also create it by traveling to it from Universe-B. But if Future Hiro can't travel to Universe-2, how does he get there to deliver his message to Peter-2? The answer relies on a deeper understanding of branching time travel.

When a time traveler "creates" a new branched universe by traveling back in time, his appearance in that new universe becomes a "brute fact" of that universe—it is what causes that new branched universe to exist. If another time traveler in that new universe travels back, causing another *newer* universe to "branch off" from the new one, the newer universe will also contain the brute fact of the original time traveler's appearance. Essentially, because the newer universe is (roughly) a copy of the universe it branches from, a copy of the original time traveler will be in that newer universe.

So, we can make sense of Future Hiro's appearance in Universe-2 by supposing that after he fails to save New York City–B and travels back in time to talk to Peter to prevent it, by doing so he creates Universe-1. By doing this, he makes his appearance to Peter in Universe-1 a brute fact of Universe-1. Then when Hiro-1 travels back in time, thus creating Universe-2, because Universe-2 branches off from Universe-1, it also contains the brute fact of Future Hiro's appearance to Peter. So, when we get to that point on Universe-2's timeline, a "copy" of Future Hiro appears to Peter and tells him, "Save the cheerleader, save the world."

That was a bit complicated, but I don't think we need another diagram. (Don't feel bad if you have to read it a few more times. It took the editor a while to get it, too.) We could also ask about the Future Hiro in Universe-3 whom we see at the end of episode ".07%." The answer will be similar; he is a copy of the original Future Hiro from Universe-A, too. But I'll let *you* work out the details (and do your own diagram).

With Coherence Comes a Price

Of course, this is only Volume 1. The time traveling that takes place in subsequent volumes makes things even more complicated. But because the branching time-travel theory is able to avoid paradoxes, we could construct a coherent (but complicated) story out of *Heroes*. Coherence comes at a price, though. We must resign ourselves to the fact that the plot spans numerous universes. Thus, with each act of backward time travel, we abandon old characters for their counterparts.

The *Heroes* plot of Volume 1 is intricately linked to Hiro-1. This is because Hiro-1 is the only character who appears consistently throughout the first volume. As we have seen, on each occasion when Hiro-1 travels back in time, the characters whom Hiro-1 interacts with are from a different universe. For example, the Ando-1 we meet in the episodes "Genesis" and "Don't Look Back" is never seen again after Hiro-1's first trip back in time. Presumably, Ando-1 is still working in Tokyo-1, mourning the destruction of New York-1 and his friend Hiro-1, with no clue that Hiro-1 escaped to another universe. For the next six episodes, it is Ando-2 whom we get to know. Yet when Hiro again travels back in time to save Charlie at the end of the episode "Seven Minutes to Midnight," Ando-2 is forever left behind and our focus is shifted to Ando-3. Hiro-1 and Ando-3 do travel together to the future and eventually save New York City (in Universe-4), but not even they stay with us forever. In the episode "Out of Time," Peter also travels backward in time to a different universe, and thus we are introduced to another set of new characters, including a new Hiro and a new Ando.

But I guess that is okay. We love our heroes, no matter what universe they belong to.[12]

NOTES

1. M. Alcubierre, "The Warp Drive: Hyper-Fast Travel within General Relativity," *Classical and Quantum Gravity* 11, no. 5 (1994): 73–77; A. E. Everett, "Warp Drive and Causality," *Physical Review* 53, no. 12 (1996): 7365–7368; J. R. Gott, "Closed Timelike Curves Produced by Pairs of Moving Cosmic Strings: Exact Solutions," *Physical Review Letters* 66, no. 9 (1991): 1126–1129; M. S. Morris, K. S. Thorne, and U. Yurtsever, "Wormholes, Time Machines, and the Weak Energy Condition," *Physical Review Letters* 61, no. 13 (1988): 1446–1449; A. Ori, "Must Time-Machine Construction Violate the Weak Energy Condition?" *Physical Review Letters* 71, no. 16 (1993): 2517–2520.

2. A really fun take on the grandfather paradox comes from the TV show *Futurama*'s episode "Roswell That Ends Well." The character Fry travels back to 1947, kills a man he thinks is his grandfather, but ends up becoming his own grandfather by unwittingly sleeping with his grandmother. This, it turns out, explains why Fry is so stupid.

3. A good example of this type of argument can be found in the work of David Hugh Mellor. See David Hugh Mellor, *Real Time II* (Cambridge, UK: Cambridge University Press, 1998), p. 135.

4. Interestingly, the physicist Carl Sagan also seems to doubt premise 2, stating that "inconsistencies might very well be consistent within the universe." See Carl Sagan, "Sagan on Time Travel," *Time Travel*, on *Nova*, PBS, October 12, 1999.

5. This theory of time travel is championed by David Lewis. See David Lewis, "The Paradoxes of Time Travel," *American Philosophical Quarterly* 13 (1976): 150. Lewis's approach is also supported by Brown and Vihvalen. See Bryson Brown, "Defending Backwards Causation," *Canadian Journal of Philosophy* 22 (1992): 429–444; and Kadri Vihvelin, "What Time Travelers Cannot Do," *Philosophical Studies* 81 (1996): 315–330.

6. It is because Hiro seems completely unable to kill Sylar that Deutsch and Lockwood have argued that linear time travel invalidates the principle of autonomy. According to this principle, it should be "possible to create in our immediate environment any configuration of matter that the laws of physics permit locally, without reference to what the rest of the universe may be doing." See David Deutsch and Michael Lockwood, "The Quantum Physics of Time Travel," *Scientific American* (March 1994): 71.

7. Try saying "a nuked New York" three times fast.

8. It is of interest to note that scholars such as Belnap and Deutsch advocate branching time, not least of all because of its supposed consistency with our current understanding of quantum mechanics. See Nuel Belnap, "Branching Space-Times," *Synthese* 92 (1992): 385–434; and D. Deutsch, "Time Travel," in *The Fabric of Reality* (London: Penguin, 1997), pp. 289–320.

9. Actually, he doesn't save New York City–2, either. He saves New York City–4. We'll get to that in a moment, but I think you can get the idea here.

10. The fact that Ando-2 wasn't in a universe where Hiro knew Charlie is evidenced by the fact that Charlie does not recognize Hiro when they are first introduced in Universe-2.

11. Of course, this is not to say that if two people traveled backward *together*, as Ando-3 and Hiro-1 do at the end of the episode "Five Years Gone," they can't arrive in the same alternative universe.

12. My special thanks to David Kyle Johnson and Daniel Cohen for all of their considerable help with this chapter.

TEN

HEROES AND THE ETHICS OF TIME TRAVEL: DOES THE PRESENT MATTER?

David Faraci

In the blink of an eye (well, both eyes, really), Hiro Nakamura finds himself standing in the middle of Times Square. Soon Hiro will discover that he has traveled not only through space, but through time; he is five weeks in the future. Just moments after Hiro makes this discovery, New York City suffers a nuclear blast from which Hiro narrowly escapes by transporting himself back to his original time. From there, much of the rest of the first volume of *Heroes* centers on the main characters' attempts to avert this looming disaster. Luckily, they succeed.

Fast forward to the second volume. In the episode "Cautionary Tales," Hiro has just returned from his time spent in feudal Japan only to discover that his father, Kaito, has been murdered. Hiro decides to travel back in time to save him. He succeeds in traveling to the right moment, but when he arrives, his father refuses his help. Kaito tells Hiro (a lesson Hiro accepts later in the episode) that he should not "play God" with his powers:

> Hiro: Later. Right now, we must leave. You are going to die! Here! Tonight!
>
> Kaito: How do you know this?
>
> Hiro: I've just come from your funeral.
>
> Kaito: My funeral? (Hiro nods.) This is my fate then.
>
> Hiro: It doesn't have to be . . .
>
> Kaito: We have the power of gods. That does not mean we can play God.

There are a great number of philosophical issues surrounding time travel of any form; Hiro's experiences throughout the stories of *Heroes* are no exception. There are any number of questions about the methods and possibility of time travel; some of these questions are even dealt with in other chapters of this book.[1] These are *metaphysical* issues: issues dealt with by the branch of philosophy called metaphysics, which addresses questions about what exists and what is possible (that is, questions about how to best understand the nature of reality). These sorts of questions are not my main concern. Rather, I am concerned with an *ethical* or *moral* question, one that would be dealt with by another branch of philosophy: normative ethics.

"Out of Time"

One thing that normative ethics does is to consider situations— whether in real life or in fiction—and ask what moral issues are raised by those situations and how those situations should be seen from a moral standpoint. In particular, normative ethics uncovers the factors influencing moral decisions in any given situation and determines which of those factors are relevant to moral action.

In the two previous scenarios from *Heroes*, there is something interesting going on morally. Hiro sees nothing wrong with trying to prevent the nuclear blast that he has seen in his travels to the future, yet he ultimately decides that it would be wrong to save his father in the past. If Hiro is correct about the rightness and wrongness of these acts, respectively, then there must be some morally relevant difference between them.

Let's take a look at the form of these two actions. In both cases, Hiro wants to take an action in order to prevent a later event from happening. In the first case, he wants to save the cheerleader to prevent the blast that destroys New York City. In the second case, Hiro wants to get to his father before the murderer does, to prevent his father's death. So, we must ask ourselves, what (if anything) makes these two cases different? What makes it the case, at least from Hiro's point of view, that it is permissible (or maybe even obligatory) for him to prevent the nuclear blast, whereas it would be wrong for him to prevent his father's death?

Of course, there are many, many differences between the two cases. For example, the first case involves an explosion, while the second involves a single murder. But assuming that we agree that both of these events are bad, it doesn't seem that this could be relevant to the moral difference between them. There seem to be only two differences that are good candidates for moral relevance: first, one event is large-scale, whereas the other is personal; and second, the first event takes place in Hiro's future, while the other takes place in his past.

" . . . the Tools to Fight the Battles Ahead."

One way that normative ethics tries to determine what is or is not relevant to a moral question is by using *thought experiments*.

Thought experiments are simply little stories that you tell in order to try to get at a particular aspect of a moral question. For example, you might tell a story that is less complicated than what really happened so that you can pin down whether one particular aspect of the real event mattered morally. In other cases, the best thing to do is to vary the case with respect to a possibly relevant factor; that way, you can see whether that factor matters to your *moral intuitions*—your moral reactions to the thought experiment.

For a very simple example, suppose I ask you to imagine that a man is lighting a cat on fire just for fun and then ask you for your moral reaction. You say (I feel safe assuming) that this is a bad situation: "What the man is doing is wrong!" This is your intuition about whether this situation is morally right or wrong, good or bad, or whatever. Suppose I then say, "I agree, but why is this your intuition?" and you say that what matters to your intuition here is that it is, specifically, a *cat* being tortured. To test this, I ask, "Imagine that the man then lights a manatee on fire for fun, instead of a cat. Is that wrong, too?" If that also seems wrong to you, then it would seem that the wrongness of burning a cat for fun stems from something more than just the mere fact that a *cat*, specifically, is being burned. Perhaps what makes both actions wrong is the fact that it is wrong to burn animals (not only cats) for fun, and both the cat and the manatee are animals. We can then offer further thought experiments and ask further questions to determine what our full theory should be.

What sort of thought experiment would be useful in the previously mentioned Hiro case? Because we are trying to decide which of the two proposed factors is morally relevant, we should try altering the scenario with respect to these factors and see whether it makes a difference. Imagine that in the first volume, Hiro travels into the future and finds out that his father is going to be killed in five weeks (rather than his finding out that there will be a nuclear blast). Is it okay for him, once he returns to the present, to try to prevent his father's death? My intuitions tell me that it is. If your intuitions line up with mine, then we likely agree: the fact that Hiro's father's death is a *personal event* isn't relevant to whether it is okay to save him. What is relevant, it seems, is whether the event takes place in Hiro's past or Hiro's future. Trying to prevent something you see in the future is okay, but traveling back to prevent something bad in the past is akin to "playing God." Indeed, in "Cautionary Tales," Hiro comes to realize this himself through discussion with his younger self:

Young Hiro: My father's going to die, too?

Hiro: Not for a long time.

Young Hiro: No! I must stop it. I am a hero!

Hiro: Some things even Takezo Kensei cannot change. We cannot play God.

Young Hiro: But I must honor him.

Hiro: Listen to him. Learn from his lessons. Strength . . . Responsibility . . . and justice.

Hiro: You were right, father. I was being childish. I'm sorry.

We appear to have found the relevant moral intuition. There seems to be an asymmetry in the ethics of time travel; although averting future catastrophes is morally permissible or obligatory, it is wrong to change the past. Now that we have the intuition, we have to ask whether it's a good one; we can't simply assume that our moral intuitions are capturing what we should really believe, morally. Maybe we just haven't thought about the case enough. Perhaps we will discover that our intuitions in this case contradict something else that we take to be even more important.

So, what we want to know is this: Does whether something happened in the past or the future really matter, morally? Is an event's place in time relevant to whether Hiro should try to prevent it? The way we answer these questions is partly through discovering *why* this thing *seems* to matter and then determining whether that reason is a good one. What would make it wrong to change the past but not the future?

"Some Things Even Takezo Kensei Cannot Change."

Perhaps not, but Kensei can certainly try, as can Hiro. So, what would make it *wrong* for Hiro to change the past? One initially plausible answer to this question is that in our experience, a person *can* change only the future. No one can change the past. This might be relevant. Perhaps what is right or wrong has something to do with what we are "naturally" able to do. Our lives are lived in a linear fashion, from the past to the future, and we have an obligation to work within those confines.

But what could justify this sort of principle? Of course, it's a truth of my existence that I can affect only my future, never my past. But does that mean that if I were suddenly able to affect my past, it would be wrong to do so? Natural law theorists, such as St. Thomas Aquinas (c. 1225–1274), might think so. They argue that we can tell what is right or wrong simply by looking at the facts of nature. But what exactly does this mean? Maybe it means that if something is physically possible, then it is morally permissible. But this is far too narrow an understanding of morality. I can do all sorts of things, physically, that we think are wrong. No, natural law theory means something broader than this; it means that as rational beings, we are able to look at our nature as humans and the role that we play in the natural world to determine what is good and thus what it is moral to pursue.

To take an easy example, Aquinas believed that we can clearly see that the killing of innocent people is wrong because we can see that life itself is good. Thus, we should never seek something detrimental to life as our goal, unless it is toward some greater good. Killing innocent people is detrimental to life but doesn't accomplish a greater good; thus, it is immoral. In the same way, we might think that because the role we "naturally" play in the world is to move from past to present to future, it would be wrong of us to violate that role by altering the past.

But traveling back in time to watch Hiro's father's murder is just as unnatural as preventing it would be. So, if we think that it is unnatural—and therefore wrong—for Hiro to save his father, then we would have to think it equally wrong for Hiro to simply travel back in time. But that just doesn't sound right. As long as there aren't any negative consequences, does it seem wrong to go back to the past? What if we are going only for the sake of knowledge? Think of all that we could learn about history! In fact, look at how much Hiro learns of history merely from his brief time spent in the past with Takezo Kensei.

We might go the other way and say that Hiro's time travel is perfectly natural; after all, his ability is part of his genetic code. But then, if the travel itself is natural, why would what he can do in that travel (alter the past) be considered unnatural? It appears as if the natural law theorist would have to either permit or condemn both time travel and the alteration of the past; they cannot be addressed separately. So, it doesn't look as though natural law is going to get us very far.

Here's another suggestion: perhaps we have a responsibility to keep our timeline intact. This seems plausible; we might think that changing our timeline in some way violates the proper order of things. But now we have a new problem: if altering our timeline is immoral, it wouldn't be okay for Hiro to change the future, either. It's not as if he wants to stop New York City from exploding because someone tells him it might happen. Hiro travels to the future; he is actually at that point on the timeline and sees it happen. So, in essence, traveling back from the future in order to prevent a future event is just the same as traveling into the past to prevent a present event because both events are already "on the timeline."

To see why this is true, we must get out of the habit of thinking of the future as somehow unsettled. Again, the future that Hiro travels to is just as real as the present he comes from or the past to which he travels. Imagine if Hiro were to travel into the future and then suddenly lose his time-traveling abilities. It's not as if he would somehow be trapped in some strange world where things would constantly alter around him as people back in the "true" present went about their lives affecting things. No, the future that Hiro would be in would be as real as the present he came from; only another time traveler could alter the timeline.

Through our discussion, then, we have discovered a new problem: the difference between the two actions in question—saving New York City and saving Kaito—cannot simply be a matter of changing the "past" versus changing the "future." These terms are meaningless unless they are taken as relative to a point of reference: a particular *present*. How do we determine when that is? Well, presumably, the relevant present is *Hiro's* present. His present is the relevant one, because our question is about which points on the timeline count, morally, as settled or unsettled from Hiro's perspective. We want to know which parts of the timeline are *morally* open to his influence: which parts he *may* influence. Presumably, those will be the events that are in *his* unsettled future.

For most of us, determining when our present is isn't a problem; because we have never traveled in time, our present is simply *now*. But what about Hiro? What determines which point in time is Hiro's present?

Finding Hiro's Present

The branches of philosophy cannot operate completely independently of one another. The question of what counts as someone's present is a metaphysical question, not a moral one. Yet answering this question is essential to answering our moral question about the rightness or wrongness of changing the past versus changing the future. How can we know whether Hiro is doing something right or wrong if we do not really understand what counts as his past and what counts as his future? In order to answer that question, we must know *when* his present lies.

This is not an easy question to answer, especially given Hiro's time-traveling exploits. We can assume first, I think, that Hiro's present began as the rest of ours did; that is, his present was simple to determine up until he first used his time-altering powers. But we have to be careful. Is it only time *travel* that affects Hiro's present? Or is it all types of time manipulation? For example, Hiro has the power to stop the flow of time. When he does this, time continues to flow *for him*. So, when Hiro starts time up again, is he still in his present? Arguably, we could say that if he stopped time for exactly one minute, then his present is one minute in the future because had he flowed along with time normally—instead of stopping it—that's *when* he'd be.[2]

This seems overly complicated, though. I think it is best to assume that when Hiro stops time, his present "waits" for him through the stoppage. Once he starts things up again, he is still "in the present" just as he was before. For the sake of consistency, we might try to extend this to his time travel. We could say that when Hiro travels through time, his present "waits for him" until he gets back to that moment. So, if on the evening of November 8, 2006, Hiro travels back to 1671 to spend some time in feudal Japan, his present would remain in 2006 until he returns to the evening of November 8, 2006, and continues forward "normally."

We now have our first attempt at a theory of Hiro's present. Hiro's present continues on as would any normal person's but is interrupted by any use of his time-altering powers. Whether Hiro travels through time or merely stops it, his present remains at the point where he used his powers. Not until he returns to normal—starts time again or returns to the moment he left—does his present continue to "move" through time.

This theory might seem plausible, but, unfortunately, it doesn't fit with the facts of Hiro's story. In "How to Stop an Exploding Man," Hiro travels from November 8, 2006, back to 1671, where he has his adventures with Kensei throughout the first half of the second volume. But when Hiro "returns" from that trip, he does not return to the point from whence he left. Instead, he returns to the time where all the other characters are in the story, well after New York has been saved. This means that—with this theory—in Volume 2, Hiro returns to a moment that is in his future. Why? Recall the moment on November 8, 2006, right after Sylar throws Hiro into the air, when Hiro travels back to 1671. According to this theory, that moment is and will continue to be Hiro's present until he returns to that moment. Because the time to which he really returns from the past in Volume 2 is *after* that moment, he returns to his future. In fact, since his father's death occurs at a time later than November 8, 2006, which would still be *the present*, his father's death would be in the future, too. If so, and we hold fast to the theory that it is wrong to change the past but not the future, our intuition that Hiro would be wrong to save his father would be unsatisfied. This view of Hiro's present fails if we wish to retain this intuition.

So, are there any other plausible views? We got the current view by extrapolating from the case of time-stoppage. But, of course, it could be that Hiro's present is not measured in the same way when he stops time as when he travels in time. Because, when he time travels, he is interacting with the timeline in a way that he is not when he stops time, we might think that when Hiro time travels, his present is simply whatever point in time he is experiencing. But this view won't help us at all; as soon as Hiro travels back to try to save his father, his father's death would be in the future, and there would be nothing wrong with preventing it.

So, here's another suggestion: When Hiro travels through time, his present is the moment of departure from his previous present *plus* the amount of time he spends at another point on the timeline. So, for example, if Hiro leaves on November 8, 2006, and spends exactly two months in 1671, we might say that his real present is January 8, 2007.

This theory would probably align with our intuition that Hiro shouldn't save his father. The time span between November 8 and Kaito's death is probably shorter than the time span Hiro spent in Japan, so Kaito's death is probably in Hiro's past. Unfortunately, *Heroes* never tells us exactly how much time Hiro spends in 1671, so we don't know for sure. In fact, because we don't know for sure, we don't know how well this theory fits the story. We don't really have any reason to think that Hiro's return to the "real present" (that is, the present for all of the non-time-traveling characters) is in accordance with this theory. In fact, we know that Hiro's time-traveling abilities tend to be somewhat unruly; he cannot always control exactly where or when he ends up. He even asks Ando how long he has been gone when he first returns from 1671. Given this, it seems somewhat implausible to think that things perfectly line up so that Hiro's activities will always fit this theory of his present.

So, what are we to think? Truthfully, I don't think there are really any other plausible candidates for a theory of how to calculate Hiro's present. But we could go with one that's not really a calculus: Hiro determines his own present. When he arrives at a time that "feels" like his own, that *is* Hiro's present. This may not be a very pleasing or exact answer, but it seems to be the best one available. After all, what else could determine a correct answer? If there was a definite time that counted as Hiro's present, completely independently of his own experiences, then Hiro would always have to worry that he was just a bit off. And how much of a time difference would really matter? What if he returns a minute early or a minute late? What if Hiro returns, not weeks after his father's death, but the next day or the next hour? Would we have to do some sort of careful calculation to make sure that he hasn't "missed" his present on the return trip to see whether it would be okay for him to save his father?

It seems more sensible, I think, for us to say that Hiro's present is, at least to some extent, *subjective*. This means that what time counts as Hiro's present is, at least in part, up to Hiro. But it does not have to be entirely up to Hiro. We might think that there are certain constraints on what time can count as his present. For example, one might argue that Hiro's present can never be earlier than any of his "previous" presents. So although Hiro might be able to miss a few weeks while he's gone and then return to identify with a new time, he cannot travel back to 1671 and call that his present; it is linked in too obvious a way with events that are clearly in Hiro's past (such as the tales of Kensei and Yaeko).

Of course, we might also just say that the present is entirely subjective and that Hiro can identify with any time he pleases. But the point is, it seems most plausible to say that Hiro's present has at least *something* to do with his attitude toward a particular time and not as much to do with how far it is from the time he called the "present" before his last trip.

Should We Stop a Time-Traveling Man?

We can now return to the question of whether our intuition concerning the ethics of time travel was a good one. I have argued that what makes a particular time present for

Hiro is subjective; there is no set metaphysical answer as to what counts as Hiro's present. But if Hiro has no set present, what could justify our moral intuition that it is wrong for him to change the past?

I already hinted at an explanation for the intuition when I talked about natural law. In our daily lives, because of how we experience the passage of time, we tend to think the future is unsettled and open to our influence but the past is not. This might lead us to assume that there is something *wrong* with traveling back to alter the past, because the past is already "written," and it is not our place to do any editing. This seems like a plausible *explanation* for why we have that intuition, but it is not a *justification* for it. Because Hiro can travel in time, the past is no more or less settled than the future is, so why should altering one be any different from altering the other? Hiro is not bound by time in the same way that we are; every moment along the entirety of the timeline is open to his influence.

One might object here that because Hiro's present is subjective, he will still experience the future as less real than his past; thus, affecting the future is permissible, whereas altering the past is not. Remember, though, that while the present may *seem* less real to Hiro, metaphysically speaking it is not. The moments that Hiro experiences when he is in the "future" are as real as those of the present or the past. Hiro might feel differently about them, but it would seem strange if his personal attachment to a particular time really made a moral difference.

So, it seems that there is no good reason to endorse an asymmetry in the ethics of time travel. For a time traveler, all moments in time are equally unsettled and changeable, and it is largely (if not completely) that person's attitude toward the time he is in that determines when his present lies and thus seems to determine what he is morally permitted to change. One might simply say that for Hiro, the present really *is* simply whatever time he happens to be in, and it is his attitude toward certain times (seeing them as settled or unsettled) that tricks him into believing that there is a moral difference between them (one is alterable, whereas the other is not), when in fact there is no difference.

Perhaps Hiro was not being childish in his desire to save his father; maybe that desire was no less mature than the wish to save New York City from a nuclear blast. Of course, because most philosophers believe that altering a single timeline is impossible (again, something addressed elsewhere in this book), this argument is largely specious.[3] But I have not been trying to get you to think about how you should behave if you wake up tomorrow with Hiro's powers. Rather, I was demonstrating how normative ethics often approaches these sorts of moral issues: a moral judgment is recognized and, through the use of thought experiments and reasoning, that judgment—that intuition—is evaluated.

You might be asking why we should care about our moral intuitions at all, why we should think that they tell us anything about what's right or wrong. If you *are* asking that, then you're thinking like a philosopher. That's a good question, and it's one that many moral philosophers are struggling with at this very moment. Unfortunately, though, it's one that will have to be left for another time. Of course, if any of you manage to find a shortcut to that time, please let me know how to get there. I'll bring back the philosophical masterpiece I'll have written by then, and I'll have an answer for you.

NOTES

1. See chapter 9, "Time to Be a Hero: Branching Time and Changing the Future," by Morgan Luck.

2. Technically, Hiro does not *stop* time; he merely slows its passage to a nearly imperceptible rate. In "The Second Coming," for example, Daphne Millbrook (the speedster) is still able to move normally when Hiro has "frozen" time. Because time is passing so slowly, however, this will make little to no difference concerning our determination of Hiro's present. For instance, in the case where Hiro freezes time for a minute

(as he experiences it), it might turn out that his future, once time flows normally again, would be about .996 minutes rather than one minute in the future, because a quarter of a second actually passed (very slowly) during the minute Hiro experienced. Because these differences will always be small enough that they won't importantly affect what events count as being in the future, I will continue to speak as though Hiro can actually stop time.

3. See chapter 9, "Time to Be a Hero: Branching Time and Changing the Future," by Morgan Luck.

ELEVEN

THE SCIENCE OF *HEROES*: FLYING MEN, IMMORTAL SAMURAI, AND DESTROYING THE SPACE-TIME CONTINUUM

Andrew Zimmerman Jones

Science fiction ranges from outlandish space operas to strict scientific extrapolations. So, where does *Heroes* fall in this range? Does *Heroes* make scientific sense? How do the powers work? Is the very premise of the show inherently flawed? To what degree have the creators of the show sacrificed scientific accuracy for dramatic purposes?

Healing, Longevity, and Adam Monroe

One of the most scientifically plausible powers on the show is Claire Bennet's and Adam Monroe's rapid cell regeneration. If we are cut, we bleed, but the blood clots and the wound eventually heals. The human liver, in fact, not only regenerates but, when transplanted, can grow or shrink as needed to match the size of the new body.[1] All biological functions are facilitated by the genetic instructions contained in the deoxyribonucleic acid (DNA) that inhabits every single cell of a living body. So, it seems within the bounds of reason to accept that a specific mutation of DNA could cause drastic alterations to these biological functions, making them speed up. As we learned in "Lizards," some creatures can regenerate body parts, so perhaps with the right DNA mutations Claire could regenerate a lost toe.

The problem with this scenario is that healing takes a lot of time. A lizard regrows its tail over a span of months, not moments, because the process requires a great amount of energy and a lot of extra raw material—far more than the body has readily available. So, although "regeneration" is a power that all of us have to a degree, and limb regrowth is a trait that humans could evolve (maybe, as West Rosen suggests, we'll cross-breed with lizards), it's impossible for such things to happen as fast as they happen to Claire.

In the second volume, an intriguing new twist on the power is revealed when we learn that Adam has been alive for nearly four hundred years without aging (since age forty-two), due to his healing powers.[2] How is this possible?

Aging is ultimately a consequence of the body's inability to replicate its cells properly. When cells replicate, they begin by copying the genetic material in the cellular nucleus. As a person ages and more cells replicate, eventually replication is more likely to produce errors. Why? Each time that DNA is replicated to create new cells, it is essentially deconstructed and reassembled. The telomere—the chemical string at the end of the DNA molecule—shortens with each of these replications. (It can be said to "absorb" the flaws in the replication process as atoms fall off the end of the chromosome, so that the flaws don't get to the important part of the chromosome.) But when the telomere shortens too much, errors are introduced into the genetic material of the cell. The sum total of all of these (and other) replication errors results in the signs of aging, such as wrinkles, metabolic shift, and age-related illness.

In the words of Dr. Aubrey de Grey, the founder of the Methuselah Foundation, our genes "exist to postpone aging, not to cause it, and we only age because those life-preserving genetic pathways are not comprehensive."[3] Thus, it is theoretically possible for there to be someone, such as Adam, who does not suffer from this problem and as a result will not show signs of aging. Such a person's cells would be more robust; his or her life-preserving genetic pathways would be comprehensive enough not to fail. Perhaps the individual's telomeres are fully retained during replication. Someone like Adam would not only generate new cells quickly, but would also generate them without error.

This would be a very fortunate genetic heritage to have (unless one is placed in an eternal prison, as happens to Adam in "Powerless"). In the case of Claire, this gift is attributable in part to her biological father, Nathan Petrelli, whose power of flight demands our attention.

Gravity, Motion, and Nathan Petrelli

From the standpoint of physics, superhero flight is always hard to justify. Clearly, Nathan's flight is not based on any known principles of aerodynamics; he does not generate lift and drag through wings, either stationary (as with airplanes) or moving (as with birds, helicopters, or bees). Instead, Nathan simply seems to move about in the air as he pleases.

To be realistic, Nathan's flight must not violate Sir Isaac Newton's (1642–1727) laws of motion. Newton's first law of motion, sometimes called the law of inertia, states that for an object's motion to change (for example, from being at rest to being in motion), a force must act on the object.[4] Newton's second law, $\Sigma F = ma$, says that the net force (ΣF) being applied to an object can be determined by multiplying its mass (m) by its acceleration (a). Gravity is a force that takes any two objects with mass and pulls them toward each other—for example, the Earth pulls Nathan's body toward it. Newton's first law tells us that force must be applied to Nathan's body in order to counteract Earth's gravity and make him fly. Newton's second law can tell us exactly how much force is required.

As suggested by the episode "Hiros," perhaps Nathan flies using a rocketlike propellant. When captured by Noah Bennet and the Haitian (who apparently forgot to activate his power-negation ability), Nathan takes off into the air to escape, leaving a very clear contrail, like the vapor trail that follows a jet. And we have seen this almost every other time that Nathan flies.

If Nathan does fly by using a propellant, the force generated by the propellant needs to overcome gravity. Assuming that Nathan weighs 778.4 newtons (175 pounds), if he accelerates upward at a rate of five meters per second squared (approximately half the rate at which you would accelerate in gravitational free fall), the power would have to generate 1,176 newtons (264 pounds) of force—even more when Nathan gives Matt Parkman a lift to the Primatech Paper Company in Odessa, Texas ("Powerless").

This is a lot to ask. Nathan's body would have to store highly reactive chemicals, which, when expelled from his body, would exert an equal and opposite force (à la Newton's third law) on the rest of his body, allowing him to fly. But how this could happen is unclear. It's not as if he has an Iron Man suit. Where would the exhaust be expelled? From his sweat glands? If so, it could be only a select few of them (such as those on his feet), to ensure that he goes in the right direction. (If the propellant came from all of his sweat glands, the forces they exerted would essentially cancel one another out.) It also seems unlikely that enough energy could be generated; sweat glands are pretty small. This explanation also fails logistically, because any time that Nathan was wearing shoes (not a problem in the "Hiros" episode, where he was dressed only in pajama bottoms), they would get blown off his feet! So, a chemical propellant must be discarded as a viable theory.

Maybe Nathan's powers are electromagnetic in nature; perhaps he can somehow counteract Earth's natural magnetic field. In principle, this is a perfectly plausible means of nonmechanical flight, and, in fact, numerous Internet videos feature grasshoppers, frogs, and other small creatures being levitated in the presence of potent magnetic fields.[5] But levitating a single drop of water requires a magnetic field on an order of ten tesla, which is about ten thousand times more powerful than the typical magnet you put on your refrigerator. Given how many drops of water the human body is equivalent to, it would take an incredibly intense magnetic field to levitate a human: one capable of generating fifteen million tesla.[6] (That's one big refrigerator magnet.) The ability to manipulate magnetic fields on this level would be distinctly noticeable any time Nathan flew, with metal debris being pulled along in his wake. In any event, his body could not produce that much energy. So, electromagnetism is out.

Finally, perhaps Nathan's power is the ability to directly manipulate the gravitational field in his immediate vicinity. I have no idea how that could be accomplished, but I cannot rule it out. So, perhaps, that is our best answer. Due to Nathan's manipulation, gravitational force itself ceases to exist, and the rules of special relativity take over—rules that Nathan's fanboy friend Hiro Nakamura knows quite well.

Relativity, Quantum Physics, and Hiro Nakamura

Before their rise to greatness, Albert Einstein (1879–1955) and Hiro Nakamura languished as office laborers. And, coincidentally, Hiro's power—the ability to manipulate the "space-time continuum"—was hardly imaginable before Einstein. In addition to teleporting vast distances, Hiro can slow down, speed up, stop, or travel through time. But what is this "space-time continuum" that Hiro is manipulating?

The space-time continuum is part of Einstein's theory of relativity, which is based on two simple postulates. The first postulate, the principle of relativity, states that the laws of physics do not change merely because an observer is moving uniformly (with no acceleration or deceleration). In other words, the same fundamental physical laws apply to both Hiro and Ando, even if Hiro is moving so fast that Ando cannot see him stealing Kensei's katana ("Godsend"). The second postulate was based on observations over the last few decades of the nineteenth century: the speed of light in a vacuum is constant. No matter how fast the emitting body or the observer is going, light will always be measured to be going at the same speed, exactly 299,792,458 meters per second.[7]

From these two postulates, Einstein and others eventually worked out the relationship between physical properties in different frames of reference. (Frame of reference? Think about two people who are each moving with respect to each other; each one is in a different frame of reference.)[8] According to relativity, one's observations of time and even of space are different, depending on one's frame of reference. Literally, objects will be shorter or longer and time will pass faster or slower, depending on how fast you are traveling. And it doesn't simply appear this way; it *is* this way. Time really does slow down the faster you travel. (Of course, if you are the one traveling fast, you won't notice—but everyone you left behind will.)[9]

Hermann Minkowski (1864–1909)—one of Einstein's professors, who had actually declined hiring him as a teaching assistant—eventually developed geometric tools for analyzing all of this. They are called Minkowski diagrams, and they look kind of like the old geometric-plane (*x*-axis and *y*-axis) grids you used in geometry. Those represent two dimensions (length and width); a point on them represents a location on, for example, a piece of paper. A full Minkowski diagram represents four dimensions (length, width, height, and time), and a single point on them represents a certain place in the universe at a certain time. A big Minkowski diagram, which has a point for every place at every time, would represent the entire space-time continuum. That is all a bit complicated and hard to draw, so the following example is a little simpler. On it, the x-axis represents a location in length, width, and height (in other words, a location in "space") and the t-axis represents a location in time. A point on it represents a location in time and space: say, your location in time and space when you started this chapter (see diagram 1).

While reading this book you are probably sitting still, so you are occupying only a single location in space; therefore, if I were to graph the location you have occupied for the last

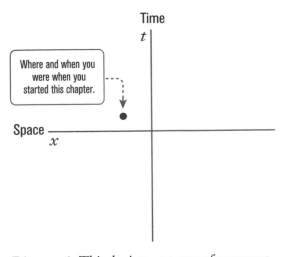

Diagram 1. This depicts one way of representing, with a Minkowski diagram, the space-time location you possessed when you started reading this chapter.

few minutes, your *x*-location would not move. Yet because you are always occupying sequential moments in time—moving forward in time—your *t*-location would move. So I could represent the space-time locations your body has occupied since starting this chapter with a straight line (see diagram 2).

Think about the space-time location of your birth. Using a Minkowski diagram that plots this space-time location, we could trace a line over everywhere you were, are, and will be, to visualize how you have traveled and will travel through time and space during your life. This would be your "world-line." Your worldline would be very squiggly—only if you have never moved since your birth would it be a single vertical straight line—but it would still be a solid line. Because you have never skipped a moment in time, any space-time point you are in is always right next to the last one you were in and the next one you will be in (see diagram 3, page 163).

But because Hiro can travel instantaneously from one location to the next, his worldline is broken. This creates a

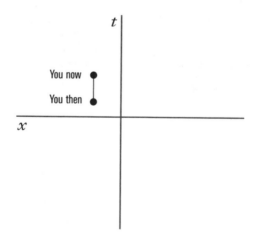

Diagram 2. Assuming you have not moved since starting to read this chapter, we could represent the space-time locations you have occupied since then with a straight vertical line.

problem, because instantaneous travel requires exceeding the speed of light, which Einstein argued is impossible because it would need infinite energy. To demonstrate why it would necessitate exceeding the speed of light, I'll teach you a bit more about Minkowski diagrams.

On a Minkowski diagram, standing still is represented by a vertical line. Movement is represented by a slanted line. If you move slowly, the line will be slanted just slightly past vertical, and the faster you go, the more slanted the line will be. The path of a light beam, which travels as fast as anything can, is represented by a slanted line drawn at 45 degrees. So let's say that when Hiro was born, his mother, Ishi, emitted beams of light from her body (she did contain the catalyst, after all, and it does make you glow). And let's say those beams of light were allowed to travel through space-time unhindered. We could represent the path those light beams would take, as shown in diagram 4 on page 164.

The area between the paths is called a "light cone." Because, according to Einstein, Hiro should not be able to travel faster than the speed of light, the light cone above

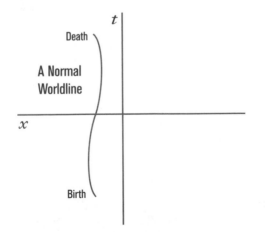

Diagram 3. The worldline of the non–time traveler may squiggle, but it will never be broken.

should define where Hiro can travel during his lifetime. Being anywhere outside the light cone would require him to travel faster than light. And, in fact, for any given location that Hiro is in at a certain time, you can define where he should be able to travel from that point by drawing a light cone from that point.

Understanding this allows us to show why Hiro's teleportation (and time travel) breaks Einstein's law. Think about when Hiro teleported from Sam's Comics in Lawrence, Kansas, to the Bennets' house in Costa Verde, California, to rescue Claire from Sylar and Elle Bishop. Via teleportation, Hiro takes Sylar and Elle to a remote beach and then takes Claire into the past ("The Eclipse: Part II"). If we were to draw a light cone from the space-time location that Hiro was in just before he first teleported, we would define where he would be able to travel from that point without breaking the speed of light. But because Hiro can teleport and time travel,

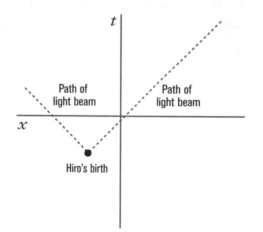

Diagram 4. On a Minkowski diagram, the path of a single particle of light is represented with a straight line drawn at a 45-degree angle from its source. The light emitted from the single space-time point at which Hiro's birth occurred would travel in all directions. If our Minkowski diagram could be drawn in three dimensions, the path of the light would look like a cone. Even though in our two-dimensional diagram it's just two lines at a right angle, it is still called a "light cone."

we see that his broken worldline is all over the place, constantly outside the light cone.

Each time Hiro leaps about throughout the space-time continuum, his line stops and starts again in another place in the diagram. And when he does—especially when he travels vast distances in an instant—his line starts again in a point outside of the light cone of the last point he occupied. Thus, it seems, he is traveling faster than the speed of light (see diagram 5).

One way to solve this problem would be to suggest that Hiro doesn't actually travel faster than the speed of light but instead bends the three-dimensional universe in the fourth dimension, so that he can instantaneously disappear from one location and appear in another through a wormhole. As cool as that sounds (and don't get me wrong, it would be cool), the amount of energy required would be enormous, far more than Hiro's body could produce in a lifetime. And to keep the wormhole open would require "negative energy density"—generated

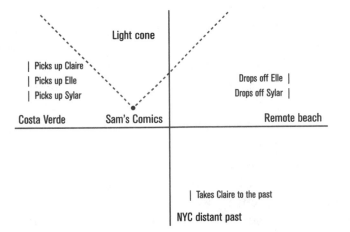

Diagram 5. The light cone defines where Hiro should be able to travel from his location at Sam's Comics (in "The Eclipse: Part II")—if he obeys the laws of physics. Here we see that as Hiro teleports and back and forth among Sam's Comics, Costa Verde, and the remote beach— and finally back in time to New York City—he is far outside the light cone to which the laws of physics would confine him.

by matter that generates negative pressure—and I doubt that Hiro has any available. In addition, the ends of wormholes are unstable, wandering around randomly. So, Hiro would have a hard time getting where he wants to go.

Because Hiro can't use a wormhole, he will have to break the speed of light. And that will take us into the realm of quantum physics. One key concept of quantum physics is the idea that both the wave and the particle interpretations of energy and matter are correct, when properly applied. The reconciliation of this notion came in the form of the quantum wave equation, which defined the different quantum states of a particle in terms of a series of probabilities among all possible states.[10] Light itself is composed of photons, but the probability of discovering a photon in a given location is described by the square of what is called the "wave function" of the particle, which is why light is said to have certain wave-like properties. Once a measurement is made, the probability is irrelevant; observation shows us which state the particle is actually in.

Now let us assume that Hiro is able to somehow manipulate the quantum wave equation at a fundamental level. Could this possibly help him get from point A to point B instantaneously? Unfortunately, it can't. The key to understanding why is this: in certain circumstances, the state of the entire system in the wave equation is determined simultaneously. The particles of the wave equation are "entangled" at the quantum level; when one becomes well-defined, the other does, too. (For example, if one has "spin +," the other will have "spin −.") Until the measurement is made, the system is expressed by the entire wave function containing the probabilities of all possible outcomes for these entangled particles.

This is true no matter how big the system is. The distance between the two particles can be *huge*—even light-years—but when one becomes well-defined, the other will simultaneously be defined. This is why it was once thought that information between the two particles could travel instantaneously, faster than the speed of light. When I measure particle *A* and it takes on a certain property, if you then measure particle *B*, you'll know what property particle *A* took on—even if you are light-years away. So, if we agreed beforehand what different properties "meant," I could communicate to you across vast distances—faster than the speed of light. For example, if *spin+* meant "1," and *spin–* meant "0," we could communicate in binary code.

Or so it seemed. The problem is that I don't get to decide what property particle *A* takes on. So, try as I might to send you the message "1,0,1," what message gets sent will still depend on what properties the particles happen to take on. One might have thought that if such a system became entangled with Hiro himself, there could be a way to transfer the information about the makeup of Hiro's body, instantaneously, to another distant location, thus allowing him to appear there. But, unfortunately, this wouldn't work.

Still, the wave function could offer yet another explanation for Hiro's teleportation. The wave function also represents the location of a particle, such as an atom. Because a distribution of locations occurs in the wave function, there is always a small possibility that for any given atom, it will disappear and instantaneously reappear in a different location. This process is known as "quantum tunneling." An atom could theoretically move five feet through quantum tunneling, but such an event is highly unlikely. To see every atom in Hiro's body simultaneously tunnel in this manner, we would have to sit and watch him for a time that is exponentially longer than the age of the universe. So, again, Hiro's traveling in this way would be a highly unlikely occurrence.

If, however, Hiro had willful control over the space-time continuum and the quantum mechanical wave equation, he could make systems take on the exact properties that he wanted (thus, he would be able to send information over long distances) or will all of his atoms to quantum tunnel to whatever location he wished. Then, by some combination of manipulating these two fundamental components of modern physics, he would be able to perform his feats without directly violating the laws of energy conservation on which physics so strongly depends. I have no idea how he could have such willful control, but if he did, he would have performed a feat beyond anything that modern physicists have accomplished: reconciling general relativity and quantum physics. The search for such a unified theory of everything occupied the latter half of Albert Einstein's life, and many people believe that such reconciliation will be the next great, and possibly the final, revolution in physics.

The Evolution Revolution

From early in the first episode of the series ("Genesis"), it is clear that Dr. Suresh's theory postulates a coming "evolutionary jump." But in order to comprehend what this means, we must clearly understand what evolutionary theory states. Charles Darwin's (1809–1882) theory of evolution by natural selection has been clarified over the years, but its central core has remained unchanged.

In its simplest form, evolutionary theory can be deduced from the following observations:

1. Living creatures pass their traits on to their offspring.
2. They do so imperfectly, allowing for changes in these traits.
3. Traits that confer an advantage to survival will thrive over time (due to step 1).
4. Traits that confer a disadvantage to survival will (literally) die out over time.

In short, if an organism in a population has a new inheritable trait that makes it more likely than others to survive and reproduce, it will (more likely than others) pass on that trait to its offspring, and so will they (and so on), until every organism in the population has that trait. The "fit trait" will have "worked to fixation." Multiple fit traits working to fixation could completely transform a species.

But how do new traits simply "appear" and how are they passed on? The most detailed answer was given by the Nobel Prize–winning work of James Watson (1928–) and Francis Crick (1916–2004), who discovered the double-helix structure of DNA molecules.[11] Though relatively inert, the DNA molecule has the powerful ability to encode a large amount of information. Each triplet of nucleotide base pairs (called a codon) encodes for a specific amino acid, and a strand of DNA contains many codons. The combinations of these amino acids in the forms of proteins, enzymes, hormones, antibodies, and other structural elements give the organism its traits. The random combination of these acids in sexual reproduction allows for new, unique traits to emerge and be passed on to offspring.

Not surprisingly, then, the single helix shows up frequently in *Heroes*, from Jessica Sanders's tattoo to Kensei's sigil, to the Company's and Pinehearst's logos. In the show, the single helix represents "Godsend," but in biology it represents the genetically encoded strand of DNA passed from one generation to the next, the transmission of biological heritage through the ages, such as the genes passed from Nathan to Claire. And that is how the story is supposed to work. Somewhere along the line, a random mutation gave an offspring a special ability—a "superpower"—that made him more likely than his fellow humans to survive and reproduce. He passed that gene along, and, after a while, you've got a whole bunch of people with a whole bunch of powers, ready to spread their DNA throughout all of humanity, pushing it up the evolutionary ladder.

In fact, although not specifically stated, it seems that *Heroes* suggests such a story. Adam (aka Takezo Kensei) has DNA that gives him the ability to heal from (almost) any wound and never age. What trait would allow one to survive and reproduce better—what trait could be more "fit"—than that? According to chapter 66 ("The Ten Brides of Takezo Kensei") of the graphic novel, during his roughly four-hundred-year life, Adam married women and sired children all over the globe. Could this be how so many different super-abilities developed all over the world so quickly? Did Kensei rename himself "Adam" for that reason?

This seems to be the intended story. But, as cool as it sounds, scientifically it doesn't work. It might work a little better if everyone had Adam's ability: rapid cell regeneration. But somehow, the DNA that gives rise to that ability in Adam, has—as it was passed on through generations—mutated so that it gives rise to other abilities (time-space travel, flight, and so on). There are such changes that occur "suddenly" in the fossil record, but they are sudden only in "geological time": hundreds of thousands or millions of years. There is no indication of such changes happening in a few hundred years.

Of course, maybe Adam passes on the same gene, but that same gene manifests different powers in different people.[12] Something like that seems to be the suggestion in Volume 3. Mohinder discovers that a commonality among everyone with powers is that the power is brought about by a rush of adrenaline, but the adrenaline makes different powers emerge in different people. Could this explain the variety of powers? In the field of epigenetics it is being discovered that outside factors can influence how genes express themselves. Twins with identical genetic codes could have very different epigenetic codes because their body chemistry over their lifetime has caused different aspects of the genetic code to manifest in different ways. This is why one twin may get cancer while another does not.

Maybe a similar explanation could be given for why the same adrenaline gives Maya Herrera "poison/disease emission" but gives Mohinder "super-strength." Even if a similar explanation could be given (which would seriously stress the variability allowed by epigenetic factors), the story still wouldn't work. Adam's "adrenaline gene" has not had enough time to spread through the population; if Adam is the father of everyone with powers, after only four hundred years, there would be far fewer people with powers than are depicted in the show. According to the graphic novel's chapter 71, "The History of a Secret," such abilities date back to the ancient Egyptian pharaohs. But even that will not give us enough time to account for all of the people with abilities whom we see. Even rapid evolutionary jumps take millions, not thousands, of years.

Still, maybe multiple people with the "adrenaline gene" have been popping up independently for quite some time, and the gene has become widespread that way. If we buy the "adrenaline gene generates different powers in different people" theory, this could work. The problem is, the same gene popping up independently throughout a population is highly unlikely. The occurrence of a random DNA mutation that leads to a fit trait is rare indeed; most mutations are either neutral (they have no advantage) or unfit (they make one less likely to survive). That is why it takes so long for one species to evolve into another. The chance of multiple random mutations of DNA, all producing fit traits, happening within a few thousand years is quite astronomical. The chance that multiple random mutations of DNA are all producing the *same* adrenaline gene is just flipping crazy.

Intelligently Designed Heroes?

So, unless the vast majority of powers are brought about artificially, by use of "the formula," as they were in Nathan and the triplets (Niki, Tracy, and Barbara), the large number of

powers depicted in the show cannot have a scientific explanation; scientifically, the *Heroes* story doesn't quite work out.
But *Heroes* has a certain mystical element, implying that connections among these individuals are more than mere coincidence. The hand of destiny, the symbol of "Godsend,"
resonates throughout the series. Perhaps God, aliens, or time
travelers from the future are orchestrating events by plant-
ing the seeds of these genetic changes. (That God did it is the
theory Nathan accepts for the first five episodes of Volume
3—until he discovers that he was given his power artificially.)
Maybe Adam was given a rapidly mutating genetic trait to
make him the progenitor of a new breed of humanity. These
design arguments are the only feasible explanation for the
rapid change that happens in the series.

NOTES

1. George K. Michalopoulos, and Marie C. DeFrances, "Liver Regeneration," *Science* 276, no. 60 (1997).

2. See the graphic novel, chapter 66, "The Ten Brides of Takezo Kensei."

3. Dr. Aubrey de Grey, *Ending Aging: The Rejuvenation Breakthroughs That Could Reverse Human Aging in Our Lifetime* (New York, NY: St. Martin's Press, 2007), p. 30.

4. Although this notion may seem logical, it is not self-evident. Many natural philosophers of Newton's day believed that the natural tendency of an object was to be at
rest, because every moving object they had observed, on Earth, eventually came to a rest.
Newton recognized that this happened because frictional force acting on the objects
slowed them down until they stopped—not because they were "naturally at rest."

5. Try "High Field Magnetic Laboratory," www.hfml.ru.nl/, or YouTube-ing "floating
grasshopper."

6. A rough estimate indicates a human body at about 1.5 million drops of water, by
taking an estimate of the human body's volume (2.5 cubic feet) and dividing by an estimate for the volume of a drop of water (0.05 milliliter), with proper unit conversions
taken into account.

7. When light passes through water, glass, or even air, it does slow down a bit, but for
the purposes of most discussions the difference can be ignored.

8. If the speed between the two frames is constant, the theory of special relativity
dictates the relationships between the two frames. In the case where two frames are
accelerating, the relationships are dictated by the theory of general relativity. Recall
from earlier that the force exerted by gravity results in an acceleration. Newton himself described the law of universal gravitation but provided no real explanation as to the

mechanism by which the force of gravity worked. Einstein's model of gravity through general relativity finally provided such a mechanism.

9. A very practical example of this concept exists within the global positioning system (GPS). Each satellite suffers an overall time lag, due to both movement and lower gravity, of about 38 microseconds per day. Even this small error would make the system fail, so a time differential had to be built into the clocks on the satellites before they were put into orbit. On Earth, the satellites are a bit off. In orbit, their timing is perfectly in sync and allows the system to function.

10. If you find this talk of quantum physics confusing, you're in good company. Einstein found the implications so contrary to reason that he spent the last third of his life trying to disprove it. Niels Bohr (1885–1962), one of the key figures in the development of quantum physics, is reputed to have said, "If anybody says he can think about quantum physics without getting giddy, that only shows he has not understood the first thing about them."

11. The entire transition of knowledge from Darwin and Mendel to Watson and Crick is itself an intriguing analysis of scientific progress. See Bill Bryson, *A Short History of Nearly Everything* (New York, NY: Broadway Books, 2003).

12. This would be like the X gene in *X-Men*. For more *Heroes* and *X-Men* similarities and possible accusations of plagiarism, see chapter 4, "With Great Creativity Comes Great Imitation: Problems of Plagiarism and Knowledge," by Jason Southworth.

TWELVE

PSEUDOSCIENCE, SCIENTIFIC REVOLUTIONS, AND DR. CHANDRA SURESH

David Kyle Johnson and
Andrew Zimmerman Jones

Poor Chandra. His book *Activating Evolution* was rejected by everyone in the scientific community, even his son, Mohinder. And yet, it turns out, he was right! Of course, in reality, we think his theory is false. But wait—has anyone gone out and tested it? Have we looked for people with powers? Isn't it at least possible that they are hiding out there somewhere? If we just laugh it off, how will we ever know? Shouldn't we check it out? The problem is, there are so many "fringe theories" that if we take time to examine them all, we will never get any real science done. So, how can we tell which theories are good science and which are laugh-off-able pseudoscience?

Science versus Pseudoscience

There is no shortage of fringe theories whose proponents hope to make their mark on science. Consider the theory of biologist Rupert Sheldrake (1942–), who has spent years and much career credibility supporting his own brand of scientific revolution. Sheldrake's "hypothesis of formative causation" states that "in self-organizing systems at all levels of complexity there is a wholeness that depends on a characteristic organizing field of that system, its morphic field."[1] Morphic fields supposedly explain everything from the formation of fungi and the operation of elaborate ant colonies to the relationships people have with one another and their pets. We supposedly even have a genetic morphic field that impacts the inheritable traits we develop.

Could Sheldrake's morphic fields lift Nathan Petrelli into the sky? Perhaps Ted Sprague is able to take his morphic field and transform it into pure energy. Maybe Bob Bishop takes the morphic field of stainless steel and changes it into the morphic field of gold, thus changing the material itself along with it, in much the same way that Medieval alchemists believed they could alter the true name, the essence, of an object. It's as realistic an explanation for these powers as any presented on the series *Heroes*.[2]

For another example of a fringe theory, consider "intelligent design," as championed in Michael Behe's book *Darwin's Black Box*. Behe, a biochemist, offered a logical argument that the biochemical systems involved in many complex organic systems could not have evolved in a stepwise manner. He thus concluded that the currently accepted theory of evolution cannot fully account for the development of life as we know it. Examples he offered include the operation of flagella, blood clotting, and the human eye. Biochemical step A plus step B provides no evolutionary benefit, so they can't remain in the genetic code long enough to wait around for step C, which is required to give them the survival benefit demanded by Darwinian evolution. Behe called this sort of complex system "irreducibly complex," indicating that removing any single component of it causes the entire system to fail. So, to develop such things as eyes and flagella, evolution must have been assisted by an outside source. According to Behe, that outside source is God. But, on Behe's own admission, the explanation could also be alien technology. Maybe, as in *2001: A Space Odyssey*, our evolutionary process has been pushed along by alien forces.

Nearly everyone laughs at Sheldrake's morphic fields, but because of religious devotion, not as many laugh at Behe's intelligent design theory. Still, most people scoff at the suggestion that aliens had anything to do with species development. And the intelligent design theorists are embarrassed by the fact that the "evidence" for their theory counts just as much for their theory as it does for the alien one. People laughing at a theory doesn't make it false, however. People laughed when it was said that the world was round; they laughed at Copernicus and Galileo when they said the Earth wasn't the center of the solar system (but the sun was); and they laughed at the Wright brothers when they said they could fly. People even laughed at Newton and his laws of motion and theory of gravity, Darwin and his theory of evolution, and Einstein and his theories of special and general relativity.

So, What Is the Difference?

Well, truth be told, there is no five-minute method for telling science from pseudoscience. You have to give it time. But if a theory *is* true, it will eventually be accepted. This is what a scientific revolution is: a laughable theory eventually being accepted in place of a traditional one. A simple but interesting example is alchemy. Although it is often associated with the notion of turning certain things into gold—as Bob, the now-deceased former head of the Company, could—alchemy can be more accurately understood as the notion that one element can be transformed into another. The theory was popular in the Middle Ages, but it has been rejected by the scientific community for a long time. It is still true that you can't turn anything into gold; however, the discovery of radioactivity, where an element spontaneously transforms, or decays, into another element through natural processes, confirmed the theory that elements can indeed transform. Such transformation can even be performed in the lab: for example, the transformation of nitrogen into oxygen through artificial disintegration.

The work of the philosopher of science Thomas Kuhn (1922–1996) focused heavily on the notion of scientific revolutions. Kuhn viewed science as long periods of relative consistency broken by scientific revolutions that fundamentally change the entire scientific landscape. During these periods of consistency, "science does not aim at novelties of fact or theory and, when successful, finds none."[3] Anomalies do arise during these periods of consistency—occurrences for which there is no explanation within the existing scientific paradigm—but it is not until the anomalies reach a critical mass and spawn a revolution, accompanied by sufficient numbers of scientists who are willing to accept it, that the consistency is broken. Like Mohinder Suresh, sometimes it takes scientists a while to accept revolutionary ideas, to abandon the existing scientific paradigm and begin forging a new one. But when confronted with enough evidence, scientists will eventually do so. Generally, they are led by a younger generation of scientists seeking to make their mark. The revolutions of Newton, Darwin, and Einstein followed this pattern.

So, if we don't know whether a theory is pseudoscience, we need to give it time. If the theory really is true, those who proposed it will keep promoting it, the evidence will pile up—evidence that the current scientific theories can't explain—and finally it will be accepted. If Chandra Suresh's "Activating Evolution" theory (or Mohinder's version of it) is true, eventually the presence of those with powers will not be denied, and the scientific community will have to accept it.

Sometimes the conflict between the old theory and the new theory comes to a head, and one single experiment can decide each theory's fate. This happened with Newtonian physics and Einstein's relativity. Newton predicted that gravity would not affect light, but Einstein said that it would. In 1919, when Arthur Stanley Eddington observed a star's light bending around the sun—he could see it, despite the fact that it was behind the sun—the British newspaper the *Times* announced that Newton had been overthrown. (Of course, things weren't so simple. The experiment was challenged, but the findings were eventually confirmed.) Perhaps Nathan's announcing to the public that he can fly and then flying off into the sunset would be just the evidence that Suresh needs to overthrow the current theories and establish his own.

Good Scientific Method

Most often, time will tell you that a theory is pseudoscience. Intelligent design is a perfect example. The motivation for intelligent design has been shown to be faulty—it merely took a little time. Recall that Behe suggested that if some beneficial trait required simple steps A, B, and C, the trait was too complex to be developed by evolution. The entire explanation is a bit complicated, but the response by mainstream scientists has been to point out that steps A and B can be present in the genetic code, even if they don't have a benefit. With no benefit or detriment, sometimes these genetic traits might spring up and sometimes they won't, in a seeming random distribution. But when beings with step A and step B in place also gain step C, they and their offspring get a

PSEUDOSCIENCE, SCIENTIFIC REVOLUTIONS

decided survival benefit that allows them to flourish in comparison to people who do not have these traits. For example, let's say that Claire Bennet's healing power is studied, and Mohinder discovers that it involves the operation of a dozen distinct biochemical actions, controlled by Claire's genome. Perhaps Nathan also has six of these encoded in his DNA. This doesn't mean that he heals at half the rate of Claire; it merely means that his DNA combined with that of Claire's mother results in a very resilient set of DNA.

Yet time can also show that a theory is a bad one in another way: by revealing bad scientific method. A good scientist operates by proposing a hypothesis and testing it. The way to test a hypothesis is to see what observable predictions it makes, and then go out and observe and see whether those predictions come true. If they do, the theory gains confirmation, and you continue to test it. If they don't, good scientists will reject the theory. But this is not how the scientific history of intelligent design goes. Intelligent design finds its scientific roots in creationism—the theory that the Earth was created about six thousand years ago, by God, with every species being pretty much as it is now. Creationists believe this because they believe that the Bible says this is true, and they refuse not to believe any piece of the Bible. When the evidence came in against their theory—such as million-year-old fossils and visible stars billions of light-years away and thus billions of years old—they did not give up their creationist theory, as good scientists should. Instead, they protected it. They did everything they could to discount the evidence against them. "God must have created those stars with their light already on the way," they said. When they had to reject that (it made God a liar, after all), they said, "The speed of light must be slowing down over time." When that was proved false, they tried again. The current story has something to do with the Earth being toward the center of the universe (which has no center, by the way) and relativity.

(You don't want us to explain it.) Maybe they will eventually find something that can't be disproved, but that won't make it true. Any theory that is developed to protect an idea—especially one that has already been disproved—deserves a lot of initial skepticism.

Intelligent design falls into this category; it is a theory that was developed to protect another. The age of fossils was first challenged by creationists on the grounds that the dating method (carbon dating) was inaccurate. That was dismissed—it would have to be off by millions of years, after all—and now creationists pretty much can't deny the age of the Earth. They also can't deny that the fossil record seems to indicate that species developed through a gradual change over the Earth's history, via evolutionary processes. To protect their theory that God created the universe (and that evolution can't explain it all), they looked for something that evolution had yet to explain and announced that it could never explain it. They started with "gaps" in the fossil record. But as those gaps became filled, they turned to complex traits such as eyes and announced that evolution can't explain them. As far as we know, creationists are still coming to terms with the fact that it can.[4]

Can Only Time Tell?

There are quicker ways to spot a pseudoscientific theory, and these could be used to call out Sheldrake's "morphic fields" and Chandra Suresh's "Activating Evolution" theories. For one thing, they have sketchy evidence: the kind that hasn't been or can't be duplicated and is rejected by the scientific community.[5] (Any time someone tries to debunk a current scientific theory by saying, "This one guy did this one thing—how can you explain that?" simply ask, "Has anyone else repeated his results? No? When they do, come talk to me again.") In addition, these theories interject into a process (evolution) an organizing principle that does not appear to be necessary. Good scientists attempt to devise theories that offer the least number of unnecessary rules (a practice known as Occam's razor). And Sheldrake's and Suresh's theories create more problems than they solve with their added rules. This not only makes them bad science, but also makes their adoption by the scientific community unlikely. In Kuhn's view, the scientific community is unlikely to accept a theory unless it resolves a critical flaw, a theoretical crisis, in the very foundations of the science. Such a crisis is not at hand, nor does it appear imminent, in the field of evolution.

Of course, things would be different if there was a widespread appearance of humans who flew, healed, controlled fire, turned invisible, and the like; this would indeed trigger a scientific crisis. Current evolutionary theory cannot account for such things, and a radical revision of the theory would absolutely be necessary. In the wake of such a crisis, the scientific community would perhaps come to accept Suresh's theories (or ones like them) as correct.

Still, even in our world, there are people such as Behe and Sheldrake who would cling to the belief that there are mysteries that have yet to be fully explained, who attempt to see the crisis that is looming on the horizon (real or imagined) well before it manifests. History shows us that at least occasionally, such unorthodox viewpoints are correct and, when they are, people who dismiss them look very foolish to posterity. So maybe we should tread lightly—just maybe.

NOTES

1. Rupert Sheldrake, *Dogs That Know When Their Owners Are Coming Home* (New York, NY: Three Rivers Press, 1999).

2. For more on the scientific viability of the *Heroes* story, see chapter 11 in this book, "The Science of *Heroes*: Flying Men, Immortal Samurai, and Destroying the Space-Time Continuum," by Andrew Zimmerman Jones.

3. Thomas S. Kuhn, *The Structure of Scientific Revolutions* (Chicago, IL: University of Chicago Press, 1970), p. 52.

4. This is one danger of believing in God because you think his existence explains something (such as lightning or earthquakes.) If that thing is eventually explained by something else (static electricity or plate tectonics), your reason for believing in God will be pulled out from under you. If you are going to believe in God, it's safer to simply have faith.

5. And sometimes the evidence is just not there at all.

PART FOUR

THE MINDS OF *HEROES*

THIRTEEN

PETER PETRELLI, THE HAITIAN, AND THE PHILOSOPHICAL IMPLICATIONS OF MEMORY LOSS

Peter Kirwan

We are all connected, joined together by an infinite thread, infinite in its potential and fragile in its design. Yet, while connected, we are also merely individuals—empty vessels to be filled with infinite possibilities, an assortment of thoughts, beliefs, a collection of disjointed memories and experiences. Can I be me without these? Can you be you?

—Mohinder, "An Invisible Thread"

It's the evening of April 23, 2007, and you are watching the *Heroes* episode ".07%" as it first airs. Daniel Linderman just asked Niki Sanders whether he could "borrow" Micah to rig

Nathan Petrelli's election, but she refused. But now Niki, apparently, stands in front of Micah, trying to convince him to help Linderman. How could this be? Didn't she just say no? But then you remember Candice Wilmer the shape-shifter, who can look like anyone. And she works for Linderman. So you wonder, Is that person talking to Micah the *same person* who I just saw saying she wanted to keep Micah out of this affair at all costs? Is the person talking to Micah, Niki? Here we're concerned with what philosophers call "numerical" identity. You want to know whether the object in question is the same "thing" as the one before.

When Matt Parkman and Janice first got married, Janice was loving and attentive. In Volume 1, she is distant and having an affair. "She is just not the *same person* I married," Matt might have said. Here, we're *not* concerned with numerical identity. Matt does not think that Janice died and some new person has taken her place. He merely thinks she doesn't act the *same* as she used to.

Questions of numerical identity abound in superhero literature. Lois Lane wonders, Is Clark Kent the same person as Superman? Of course, we know the answer to that. But we might also wonder, Is Bruce Banner the same person as the Hulk?[1] And this is not so easy to answer. Not only do Bruce and the Hulk act very differently, but the Hulk doesn't remember anything that Bruce does, and Bruce doesn't remember anything the Hulk does. Couldn't they thus be considered two different people?

The same questions come up in *Heroes*. Niki doesn't remember what Jessica does. So are Niki and Jessica the same person? The Haitian has wiped out the memories of so many people, so many times, I have lost count. When he wipes Peter Petrelli's memories between Volumes 1 and 2, Peter awakens with total amnesia. So Volume-2-Peter knows nothing about Volume-1-Peter, and vice versa. This makes us wonder, Is Peter, numerically, the same person when he wakes up in the crate at the beginning of Volume 2? Or did the old Peter "cease to be" and a new person "take his place"? And then there is what Matt does to Sylar at the end of Volume 4, making him awaken with Nathan's memories but none of Sylar's. Is he still Sylar? Is he now Nathan? Is he neither?

Are You Really *You*? Is Mohinder Really *Mohinder*?

Questions of numerical identity aren't new to philosophy. Consider this classic scenario. What if a ship, made of wood and containing a large number of barrels, sets out across the sea. As it sails, its crew starts to replace each board of the ship with boards from the barrels, throwing the old boards over the side. By the time the ship finally arrives at port, each of the original boards that made up the ship is gone—replaced by boards from the barrels—and all of the barrels are gone. Question: is the ship that set sail (numerically) the same ship that arrives at port? Yes? What if I told you that someone was following it, collecting all of the wood the crew threw over the side, and built a ship in the same design out of it. Would that change your answer? Philosophers call this the "Ship of Theseus Paradox."

It may seem like a silly thought experiment, but it actually hits closer to home than you might think. When you scratch your arm, skin cells flake off, but those cells are replaced. Your body uses material and energy from the food you ingest to replace them. Yet over time, this happens to every cell of your body, inside and out; it is damaged and replaced, using material that you have ingested from outside your body. Even the atoms that make up the cells of your brain go through this process. Gradually, over roughly seven years, all of the material that currently makes up your body will be discarded and replaced by material that is currently not a part of your body.[2] In other words, in seven years, you will have a totally new body: one made of material that is not a part of you now. What's more, if someone was really careful and smart, he or she could follow you around, collecting all of the bodily material that you slough off, and—after seven years—put it back together in the way it was seven years ago. If this person did that, where would *you* be?

At age sixteen, Mohinder was a teenager, intelligent but immature and not yet fully educated, living with his father but ignorant of his father's theories. At age thirty, Mohinder is on his own, superintelligent, mature, fully educated, and seeking to prove his father's theories. What's more, sixteen-year-old Mohinder's body is not even made of the same material that thirty-year-old Mohinder's body is made of. It has actually been replaced, two times over. Question: are sixteen-year-old Mohinder and thirty-year-old Mohinder (numerically) the same person? You probably think they are, but how can you defend your answer? You certainly can't say, "It's because they have the same body," because they don't.

Quite often, when we are trying to answer questions of numerical identity, we look at properties. Suppose someone steals my car; maybe I am not too bright and I left it unlocked with the keys inside, as Claire did with her shamelessly plugged Nissan Rogue. If the police then find a stolen car of the same make and model, I check to see whether it has the same properties as my original car: Is it the same color? Does it have that same scratch down the side? Is the serial number the same? If it does, then I conclude that it is the same car: my car. The problem is, appealing to "sameness of properties" will not help us in the case of Mohinder. When Mohinder was sixteen, he was immature and uneducated; at thirty, he is not. So if we think he is the same person over time, we can't think it is because of sameness of properties.

Do You Remember? Mohinder's Past, Present, and Future

John Locke (1632–1704) developed a theory that tried to answer this question; he suggested that we could find a suitable criterion for "personal identity over time" in "memory access."

It's pretty obvious that personal identity depends on memory, Locke argued, when you just think about what we mean by the word *person*. Persons are, for Locke, conscious beings and so are distinguished from one another by the different experiences of which they are conscious. When Nathan catches Peter ("Genesis"), they are different persons, because they are conscious of different things. Peter is conscious of the experience of falling from the building, whereas Nathan is conscious of the experience of catching his brother.

Given that we use this way of distinguishing persons from one another, Locke argued, it follows that two persons will be identical with each other if one is conscious of the other's experiences. Now, bearing in mind that memory gives us a sort of consciousness of past events, it also follows that memory will be the correct criterion for personal identity over time. According to Locke, thirty-year-old Mohinder is numerically identical with sixteen-year-old Mohinder because thirty-year-old Mohinder is capable of remembering an experience of sixteen-year-old Mohinder's.[3] We can call this "the simple memory criterion."

The most famous objection to the simple memory criterion comes from Thomas Reid (1710–1796), who argued that Locke's memory capacity is not a transitive relation and so cannot be a criterion of identity, which is transitive. What does Reid mean by "transitive"? Well, think about identity (or "equals") in math. Because $1 + 3 = 4$, and $2 + 2 = 4$, then $1 + 3 = 2 + 2$. Or, we might say, in general, "If $A = B$, and $B = C$, then $A = C$." Simple enough. Reid is suggesting that personal identity works the same way—and he seems to be right. Reid argued that with Locke's theory, however, personal identity isn't transitive as it should be. Thus, Locke's theory must be wrong.

Why is Locke's theory of personal identity not transitive? Recall the dark future of "Five Years Gone," where Mohinder stands in the Oval Office as chief medical adviser on the day before the fifth anniversary of the explosion. Then imagine him, five years previously, as the young professor who holds Sylar captive and tries to shoot him in the head in "Parasite." Finally, imagine him as the two-year-old at the time of Shanti's[4] death.[5] Now suppose, counter to fact, of course, that the chief medical adviser can remember shooting Sylar but not Shanti's death and that Sylar's captor actually does remember Shanti's death. According to Locke's criterion, the chief medical adviser is identical with the young professor and the young professor is identical with the child ("chief = captor" and "captor = child"). So far, so good. But given that identity is transitive, the chief must be identical with the child (chief = child). Yet the fact that the chief is identical with the child is precisely what Locke's criterion would have us deny! Why? Because the chief cannot remember Shanti's death, but, according to Locke, this is what he must do to be identical with the child. So Locke's theory must be flawed.

Chains of Memory: Heroic Ancestors

Paul Grice (1913–1988), responding to this objection, suggested weakening Locke's criterion to an ancestral relation.[6] What is an ancestral relation? Micah has the relation *child of* to Niki; Niki has the relation *child of* to Hal Sanders, right?[7] We all know that this means that Micah is the *grandchild of* Hal. Well, "*grandchild of*" is an ancestral relation of "*child of*." It's what you get when you chain two "child of " relations together; Micah is the child of the child of Hal. But it doesn't stop there. *Great-grandchild of* is also an ancestral relation of the *child of* relation; you are the child of your great-grandmother's child's child. And so on. Any relation had in virtue of a "chain" of *child of* relations will be an ancestral relation of the *child of* relation. We could simply say that all of your predecessors, besides your parents, are your ancestors.

Do you remember starting to read this chapter? Yes? Good. Well, think about Locke's simple memory access relation. Now, do you remember reading the first sentence of this paragraph? (I hope so.) Locke's memory relation holds between "you right now" and "you reading the first sentence of this paragraph." But because you answered yes at the beginning of the paragraph, Locke's memory relation also holds between "you reading the first sentence of this paragraph" and "you starting this chapter." So, an ancestral relation of *Locke's memory relation* holds between "you right now" and "you starting this chapter." We could say that "you starting this chapter" is a *memory ancestor* of "you right now."

But it doesn't stop there. If you remembered picking up the book when you started this chapter, then "you picking up the book" is a memory ancestor of you right now. And this is true, even if right now you can't remember the moment you picked up the book. The memory ancestor relation is simply what you get when you "chain" two or more of Locke's memory relations together—you may not currently remember all of your memory ancestors (just as you have genetic ancestors about whom you know nothing).

Grice considered using the "memory ancestor" relation, instead of Locke's simple memory access relation, as a criterion for personal identity. It solves the "forgetful Mohinder problem" quite well. Even if Chief Mohinder doesn't remember being child Mohinder, he does remember being captor Mohinder—and the captor remembers being the child. So the child is the memory ancestor of the chief. Thus, the chief is identical to the child, despite the memory loss. The memory ancestor criterion seems to get us the transitivity we need.

We could reformulate Locke's criterion by adding the memory ancestor relation to avoid Reid's objection. It could go like this: two persons are numerically identical with each other if one of them can remember the experiences of the other *or* if one is the memory ancestor of the other. We appear to have the criterion we need.

The Problem of Hiro's Memory Loss

As Candice demonstrates to Sylar in "Kindred," initial appearances can be deceptive. So it is with this criterion. On closer inspection, we will see that it is not transitive after all. That this is so was demonstrated by Grice himself, whose argument the contemporary philosopher John Perry helpfully illustrated with a thought experiment very much like what happened to Hiro in Volume 3; we will call it "the Senile Hiro problem."[8]

Recall, at the end of "Villains," Arthur Petrelli surprises Hiro after his "spirit walk" and wipes Hiro's memory—all the way back to when he was ten years old. Let's call Hiro in this state "Forgetful Hiro." Forgetful Hiro can remember everything up to being ten, but nothing since then, including stabbing Sylar at the end of Volume 1. But, of course, "Stabby Hiro" can remember being ten as well. So Forgetful Hiro can remember Ten-Year-Old Hiro, and so can Stabby Hiro, but Forgetful Hiro can't remember Stabby Hiro. Hiro's situation here is not unlike the forgetfulness that can onset with Alzheimer's: memories of days long gone by are vivid, but memories of the events of yesterday disappear as soon as the events are over.

Because Forgetful Hiro remembers being ten, on the ancestor criterion, Forgetful Hiro and Ten-Year-Old Hiro are identical. And Stabby Hiro remembers being Ten-Year-Old Hiro—so they are identical, too. From this, it logically follows that Forgetful Hiro and Stabby Hiro should be identical, right? But because Forgetful Hiro doesn't remember being Stabby Hiro, nor is Stabby Hiro a memory ancestor of Forgetful Hiro—Arthur's memory wipe broke the memory access chain—Forgetful Hiro and Stabby Hiro, on the ancestor criterion, are not identical. Thus, the ancestor criterion fails.

All is not lost, however. To deal with the Senile Hiro problem, we can create a Gricean memory criterion that *is* transitive.[9] How? If someone is your ancestor, then you are that person's descendant, right? So, we could say that you are a memory descendant of your memory ancestors. And it would seem that people are identical with their memory descendants, just as they are with their memory ancestors. In other words, not only does personal identity "flow back" on the ancestry memory chain, it "flows up" the descendant memory chain. Therefore, it would make sense to have a personal identity criterion that allows personal identity to "flow both ways." And according to this criterion, you would also be identical to your ancestor's descendants and to your descendant's ancestors. We could call this "the final criterion": Two persons are identical if one can remember an experience had by the other or one is a memory ancestor of the other, one is a memory descendant of the other, one is a memory ancestor of a memory descendant of the other, or one is a memory descendant of a memory ancestor of the other.

That may seem a bit complicated, but showing how it solves the Senile Hiro problem should make it clear. Ten-Year-Old Hiro is a memory ancestor of Forgetful Hiro and Stabby Hiro, but Stabby Hiro is not a memory ancestor of Forgetful Hiro. Yet because Stabby Hiro is a memory descendant of Ten-Year-Old Hiro, who is a memory ancestor of Forgetful Hiro, we can trace personal identity from Forgetful Hiro down the ancestor chain to Ten-Year-Old Hiro and then up the descendant chain to Stabby Hiro. Thus, Forgetful Hiro and Stabby Hiro are identical according to the new criterion, as transitivity demands.

Unlike the previous criteria, the final criterion allows us to give a clear and unequivocal answer in the case of Jessica and Niki because we can establish chains of memory between Niki at any particular time and Jessica at any particular time. For example, Niki might not remember Jessica's murder of

Linderman's thugs at the house, but Niki remembers Jessica's attempted assault on D.L. at the cabin, and Jessica at the cabin can remember killing Linderman's thugs at the house. In short, according to this criterion, we would have to say that Jessica and Niki are the same person.

But What about Total Amnesia?
The Case of Peter Petrelli

The final criterion seems to run into problems, however, when applied to cases where someone has total amnesia regarding *all* past experiences. In this case, it seems that the final criterion will force us to say that the Peter who wakes up in Ireland at the beginning of Volume 2 with total amnesia is not numerically identical with the Peter of Volume 1. If you like the final criterion, you might just be willing to accept this result, but not many philosophers are going to follow your lead. Bernard Williams (1929–2003) used a famous thought experiment to show that accepting this result is contrary to our intuitions about personal identity.

Suppose that you and the Haitian are about to be captured and tortured by Sylar before he takes your powers. (What power do you have? Any power you want. We're just making this up.) The Haitian says that to protect *you*, before you are captured he will knock you out and wipe your memory clean; as far as the person being tortured is concerned, his or her first memory will be of waking up right before the torture.[10] Would you take consolation in the Haitian's idea? Would you think that *you* are going to be spared the torture? If you accept the final criterion, you should. The person being tortured will not be your memory descendent, ancestor, or any combination thereof—the memory chain will have been broken by the Haitian's memory wipe. Williams argued, however, that anyone who imagines himself in this thought experiment is inevitably terrified of the impending torture and thinks the

Haitian's guarantee that the person being tortured will not have access to your memories is scant consolation.

Now, because this sort of fear is a self-regarding emotion—an emotion about oneself—it follows that one intuitively thinks that the person who is going to be tortured tomorrow *is* identical with oneself. In short, the final criterion is totally out of sync with our intuitions about personal identity. If we intuitively identify ourselves with someone who does not satisfy the final criterion, then it is insincere to claim that it succeeds as a criterion for personal identity.

As if that weren't enough, the final criterion can also be challenged by a variant on Derek Parfit's "psychological spectrum" argument.[11] In this thought experiment, I am again kidnapped by Sylar. This time, he connects my brain to a machine with a great many switches all in a row. If Sylar flicks the first switch, I will lose one experiential memory and gain one of the memories of Chandra Suresh. If he flicks another, I will lose a few more such memories, while gaining a few more of Chandra's memories. Another, and I lose yet more of my own memories and gain more of Chandra's. This pattern of small memory loss and gain continues until all of the switches are flicked and I have lost all of my memories and gained all of Chandra Suresh's.

The problem is deciding how many switches it takes before I become a numerically different person. This is a problem, because the difference between any two adjacent cases (such as the difference between flicking two switches and flicking three) is very slight. Wherever one draws the line (our final criterion would draw the line at the very last switch), it seems that one is making the survival of one's personal identity depend on a tiny number of memories, and that sounds implausible.

One might respond by observing that the problem regarding *where to draw the line* (which philosophers call "the problem of vagueness") is found in many of our everyday concepts where we do not consider it to be a serious problem. It is not clear exactly how many people Sylar needs to kill before he can be called a serial killer, but we are content to solve the problem with an arbitrary stipulation. "Three seems about right," we might say. If it turns out that we thought he murdered three, but he really murdered only two—the death of his adoptive mother was an accidental homicide, not a murder—Sylar's perceived status will go from *serial killer* back to *murderer* because of one simple change. Yet this fact does not keep us awake at night. It's really just a matter of semantics: how do you define "serial killer"?

Anticipating this objection, Parfit and Williams responded that although there are many concepts where we happily draw arbitrary borderlines, personal identity is not one of these concepts—whether a person survives is not merely a matter of semantics. We are inclined to think that questions about personal identity have a determinate answer; even in borderline switch cases, the question "Have I ceased to exist?" has an answer that is either yes or no.[12] It is not a matter of how you define "person." Because no memory criterion for personal identity can give us such a definite answer—there will always be borderline cases—it follows that no memory criterion can provide a convincing definition of personal identity.

The Evan-the-Human-Xerox Problem

A necessary condition is something that must be true in order for another thing to be true. For example, it is a necessary condition for Sylar to acquire another hero's power that he be in close proximity to that hero. Sylar has to be close to examine the person's brain and see how it works. Necessary conditions aren't a guarantee, however. Being in close proximity to someone does not, in and of itself, guarantee Sylar's acquisition of the person's power. He or she may escape Sylar's grasp, as Claire did in "Homecoming."

By contrast, a sufficient condition is something that, if true, guarantees the truth of some other thing. For example, in Volumes 1 and 2, Peter's being in close proximity to another hero was a sufficient condition for him to obtain that hero's power, because such proximity guaranteed that he obtained the power in question. If something is a sufficient condition for an event, however, it is not necessarily the only way to make that event occur. Although being near Claire was sufficient to bring about the spontaneous-tissue-regeneration power in Peter, he could have also obtained it by being near Adam Monroe.

Why mention all of this? Well, if taken alone, the preceding arguments show that the final criterion fails to provide a necessary condition for personal identity. Two things can be identical, even though they don't fit the criterion. But to demonstrate its failure as a sufficient condition, we must turn to a second thought experiment.[13]

In the *Heroes* graphic novel chapter titled "Revolutionary War," Adam is fighting in the American Revolution, looking for a "worthy adversary."[14] He comes across Evan, a man with the power to copy himself. He doesn't merely clone himself— a clone is only a genetic copy. Evan's copies are genetic clones, but they are also created, right before Adam's eyes, with all of the memories that Evan had at the time of their creation. (This is evidenced by the fact that when they are created, they all know exactly who they are, where they are, what they are doing, and so on—just as Evan does.)[15]

Now, because the genetic copies all come from Evan and have his memories, there is a giant complex ancestor-descendant memory chain running through the whole bunch. So, according to the final criterion, they would all be, numerically, the same person. But that is ridiculous. Adam doesn't kill the *same person* over and over again—he kills versions of the same person. One and the same person cannot be both living and dead. Adam even realizes this; he calls them brothers. They are separate entities. The final criterion as a sufficient condition for personal identity would force us to call these separate entities identical. But the quintessential aspect of numerical identity is that it picks out one and only one thing.

One way to deal with this problem is to add on to the final criterion by saying, "No branching allowed." In other words, for Evan to be identical with some person, not only must Evan satisfy the final criterion, but he must be the only person who does.[16] At best, this is an awkward fix. Not only does it seem highly arbitrary, but it openly flouts our intuitions. The fix would make Evan's personal identity depend on things that are completely external to him—for example, whether he has copied himself—and that just seems wrong. Evan is still Evan, regardless of whether he has copied himself.

Another traditional response to the Evan problem is to add to the criterion the stipulation that the memories must be caused in "the right way" to qualify as bona fide memories. Normally, the choice for "the right way" is between any reliable cause and the normal cause.[17] Evan copying himself, however, seems like a pretty *reliable* memory cause—he gets it right every time. And it is unclear why only *normal* causation should count. When the late great Bob Bishop turns a spoon into gold ("Four Months Later"), it's still a gold artifact, regardless of its abnormal causation.

Why Claire Should Keep Her Promises

Perhaps the best argument for the fact that no memory criterion will be serviceable as a tool for determining personal identity can be found at the end of Volume 4. Matt uses his power to convince Sylar that he is Nathan, thus erasing all the memories of Sylar's life, leaving only memories of Nathan's life in Sylar's head. Presumably, after Sylar's "Clairsentience" has "filled in the gaps," Sylar has all and only Nathan's memories. On any of our memory criteria, that would mean Sylar was Nathan (or, more accurately, it would mean that Sylar no longer exists and that Nathan still does, inside what used to be Sylar's body). But I think that most agree this isn't true. Even if the change Matt made were permanent, it would still just mean that Sylar had Nathan's memories and thus thought he was Nathan. As Matt says, "He would never really be Nathan; he would always be Sylar." ("An Invisible Thread")

That said, although no memory criterion will be serviceable as a tool for determining personal identity, so we should look elsewhere for a criterion. That said, although memory does not determine or prove personal identity, it still has an important role to play regarding our identity over time. Regardless of what the truth is about our identity over time, one thing is certain: most of the time we must be able to act *as if* we are the same person across time. If we don't, basic elements of our relationships and lives will not function.

Recall the homework assignment on the manatee that Claire is "assigned" in "The Fix."[18] If Claire Bennet does not act *as if* she is the same person across time, then she will have little or no reason to finish the assignment. Why bother, right? If the Claire who gets the grade for the assignment is a person different from the Claire of "The Fix," then why do all of the work? It is someone else who will be reaping the benefits. In "Genesis," Claire promises Zach that she will talk to him in front of people at school the next day. The Claire whom Zach sees at school the next day, however, will have no reason to fulfill the promise if Genesis Claire and Next Day Claire are different people. After all, you don't feel obligated to keep promises your neighbor makes, do you? In fact, Claire won't even care who her real parents are. Whoever they are, they haven't given birth to *her*—but simply to some baby they named Claire.

By allowing Today Claire access to the experiences of Yesterday Claire and letting her know that Tomorrow Claire will probably have access to her experiences, memory gives Today Claire the feeling of an incredibly close tie with these future and past selves. This feeling of closeness will normally be enough to make Today Claire feel, at the very least, that their interests *are* her interests and so cause her to act *as if* they are identical with her. As a result, she will be motivated to engage in projects and relationships over time. So, too, with us. Even though memory doesn't constitute personal identity over time, it plays an important role regarding identity. We wouldn't be who we are without it.

NOTE

1. Someone has already written on this question! See Kevin Kinghorn's chapter "Questions of Identity: Is the Hulk the Same Person as Bruce Banner?" in Tom and Matt Morris, eds., *Superheroes and Philosophy: Truth, Justice, and the Socratic Way.* (Chicago: Open Court, 2005).

2. The seven-year number is an estimate. Various cells replace themselves at different rates.

3. John Locke, *An Essay Concerning Human Understanding* (Oxford: Clarendon Press, 1979), section 9, p. 335. Locke also repeats this claim in section 16, p. 340.

4. There is, of course, a minor continuity error regarding Mohinder's age at the time of Shanti's death. In "The Hard Part," Mohinder says that he hadn't been born at the time of Shanti's death, while in "Seven Minutes to Midnight" Mohinder's mother tells him he was two years old when his sister died.

5. My language here obviously implicitly assumes in advance that these persons are numerically identical. This is, unfortunately, often an unavoidable linguistic inevitability when talking about personal identity.

6. Paul Grice quoted in John Perry, ed., *The Problem of Personal Identity* (Los Angeles: University of California Press, 1975), p. 18.

7. If you don't remember, Hal is the mean guy who gave Micah a laptop that Micah tore apart in "Six Months Ago."

8. Perry, *The Problem of Personal Identity*, p. 19.

9. In the description of the new memory capacity criterion, I borrow heavily from Perry (who himself is paraphrasing Grice), although, for stylistic reasons, I have made minor changes in the exact phrasing.

10. Derek Parfit, *Reasons and Persons* (New York: Oxford University Press, 1987), p. 230.

11. Ibid., pp. 231–233.

12. Ibid., pp. 232–233.

13. Ibid., pp. 287–289.

14. Chaps. 60 and 61.

15. Evan's power is very similar to Julien Dumont's. See the graphic novel chapters 88–90.

16. Perry, *The Problem of Personal Identity*, p. 19.

17. Parfit, *Reasons and Persons*, pp. 206–207.

18. Actually, she made up that assignment as an excuse to visit her biological mom, Meredith Gordon.

FOURTEEN

UNDERSTANDING OTHER MINDS: PHILOSOPHICAL FOUNDATIONS OF *HEROES'* MIND-READING POWERS

Fabio Paglieri

Mind reading, or telepathy, is ordinarily understood as the capacity to directly perceive the thoughts of other human beings. It figures prominently among the vast array of mind-related superhuman powers portrayed by the characters of *Heroes*, together with clairvoyance, memory modification, empathy with technological devices, mind shielding, lie detection, and many more. Matt Parkman and his shady father, Maury, are capable of literally hearing the thoughts of other people. Over time, both men also become adept at manipulating the minds of others; they inserted thoughts into others' minds, trapped people in their worst nightmares, altered their perceptions, and even compelled them to obey specific orders. The arch-villain Arthur Petrelli also shows similar abilities but with a slightly different twist.

Although we normally think such mind-reading powers are purely fictional, the issue of mind reading is just as
prominent in philosophy, psychology, and neuroscience
as it is in *Heroes*. Mind reading is thought of differently in
these disciplines, however. In *Heroes*, mind reading is (basically) the ability to "hear" the thoughts of others as if they
were communicating these to you verbally. In philosophy,
psychology, and neuroscience, mind reading is the ability to
use insight and observation to infer the thoughts of others.
Although the methods differ, the result of both activities is
the same: acquiring precious information about the minds of
others. One might object that calling both of them "mind
reading" is confusing and even silly, but, as we'll see, they
have more in common than meets the eye.

Supernatural and Mundane
Mind Reading

In "One Giant Leap," Matt visits a bar immediately before
being abducted by the Haitian. While picking up random
thoughts of the other customers, Matt notices a middle-
aged woman sipping a glass of red wine and realizes that
she's feeling really depressed and contemplating suicide.
Matt hears her thinking, "What if I'd just disappear? Would
they care? Would anybody care? Would anybody notice that
I'm gone?"

Now imagine yourself in that bar, seeing the same woman
sadly sipping her drink, eyes downcast and an expression of
deep concern on her face, exactly as she appears to Matt.
Without much reflection, you'd probably conclude that she
must be feeling awful; you might also speculate that she's
badly depressed and possibly entertaining suicidal thoughts.

In the blink of an eye, you have harnessed a remarkable
amount of information about her mind, concerning both her
thoughts (contemplating suicide) and her emotional state

(sadness and despair). This is not so far from what Matt did, even if you don't have, I presume, any supernatural mind-reading talent. The similarity is in the final result: both Matt and you end up gaining some insight concerning the mental states of the subject under observation. The only major difference is in how this insight is achieved: Matt can directly perceive the thoughts of others, usually by hearing them as sentences, whereas you and I have to resort to inference to "read" the minds of the others, making guesses on the grounds of people's behavior and demeanor.

Let's call the kind of telepathic ability possessed by Matt "supernatural mind reading" and the inferential talent that we all share to some degree "mundane mind reading." The first phenomenon has received little consideration in philosophy.[1] The latter, however, is a major topic in the philosophy of mind, which is the branch of philosophy that studies the nature of mental phenomena and their connection with behavior and the physical body, particularly the brain. Even though philosophers have been mainly concerned with mundane mind reading and have been rather skeptical of the existence of its supernatural cousin, close observation of the heroes' mind-reading powers is very instructive on a variety of classical philosophical problems. This should not come as a surprise. Superheroes were always intended to be an allegory of real human beings, merely with exaggerated powers and problems. Mind reading is no exception to this rule.

Is Anyone in There? Telepathy and the Problem of Other Minds

The *problem of other minds* is a classic philosophical issue. How can our assumption that our fellow humans are governed by minds like our own be justified? Philosophers often put this problem in terms of zombies. Philosophical zombies have little in common with Haitian undead creatures or with the mindless villagers who were struck by the Haitian's unleashed power when he was young (see the graphic novel chapters 36–38), but they're pretty scary all the same. According to David Chalmers, "[A philosophical] zombie is just something physically identical to me, but which has no conscious experience—all is dark inside."[2] Philosophical zombies are perfect physical replicas of their human counterparts; their behavior, body, brain, guts, expressions, and reactions are the same as ours. They don't experience anything *inside*, however; they have no inner mental life. They are perfectly functioning input-output machines that behave precisely like us but have no minds.

So, the problem of other minds is this: we cannot know— *for sure*—that all other people are not actually philosophical zombies. There is a striking difference in the kind of access we each have, respectively, to our own mind and to the minds of others. We're usually immediately in touch with our own inner states: we experience the contents of our sensations, we feel our emotions, introspect our thoughts, and monitor most of our reasoning. But when it comes to assessing the mental states of others, we don't have such privileged access. All that we have is observation of other people's external behavior and the context where this behavior occurs. From this, we make an informed guess regarding what they're thinking, but we have no way of knowing whether that guess is correct. The point, of course, is not to argue that people are in fact zombies but simply to show that they *could* be, and that we have no way of knowing *for sure* that they aren't.

In philosophy, this kind of skepticism is rooted in the work of René Descartes (1596–1650). This is somewhat ironic because Descartes' ultimate aim was to provide a stable foundation for human knowledge by finding some belief that was indubitable. To achieve this, Descartes submitted all beliefs—including his belief in other minds and in the existence of the world itself—to the severest methods of doubt,

and he considered what could be salvaged after such a mer-
ciless cross-examination. If Descartes had been able to watch
Heroes, he could have used many examples from the show:
we know it *seems* like the world exists, and in it there are
other minded creatures, but what if the world we experience
is merely a dream created in our minds by Maury Parkman's
devious telepathy or an illusion generated by Candice
Walker's power to make us see whatever she wants?

Even in such extreme cases, Descartes pointed out, there
is one certainty that I cannot be stripped of: the fact that
I think and therefore exist. As he famously phrased it, *cogito
ergo sum.*[3]

> If I convinced myself of something, then I certainly
> existed. But [what if] there is a deceiver of supreme
> power and cunning who is deliberately and constantly
> deceiving me. In that case I too undoubtedly exist, if
> he is deceiving me; and let him deceive me as much
> as he can, he will never bring it about that I am noth-
> ing so long as I think that I am something. So, after
> considering everything very thoroughly, I must finally
> conclude that the proposition "I am, I exist" is neces-
> sarily true whenever it is put forward by me or con-
> ceived in my mind.[4]

The problem is that this strategy works only in the first-
person case. *You* can be sure that *you're* thinking and therefore
exist—you know that you exist and are not a philosophical
zombie—but you do not know this of others. What started
as a problem about knowledge has become a problem about
reality: we moved from epistemology to metaphysics. Lacking
the safety of the *cogito* in the case of other minds, their very
existence is put in jeopardy by Descartes' skeptical inquiry.

Now, one might think that supernatural mind reading
could put an end to this problem. If Matt existed in reality,
his ability to hear the thoughts of others could quench any

doubt of the existence of other minds—at least, for Matt. But such hopes are misguided.

For the skeptic, Matt's powers have the same limitation that all other senses have: they can be fooled. When I access my own thoughts, I do not actually "hear" them. The same is true of everyone. Instead, we all experience our own thoughts directly, as part and parcel of the very act of thinking. (This is why we can't doubt that we think and exist.) But when Matt hears the thoughts of others, it is as if someone's talking to him ("One Giant Leap"); he's able to listen to someone else's inner language in the absence of overt communication. He's fully aware that the thoughts he hears are not his own, because he experiences them as a special kind of external communication. So, as far as Matt knows, his mind-reading experience may be part of a grand illusion he's living in. Indeed, on first discovering his powers, Matt for a time fears being delusional.

Even if we grant that the world and other people exist, Matt's mind-reading powers still won't solve the problem of other minds—that is, they won't allow Matt to prove that other people aren't philosophical zombies.[5] Matt's powers work by directly interfacing his brain with the brains of other people. When Matt succeeds in sending a thought into Molly Walker's head during her coma, it produces a spike in her electroencephalogram ("Out of Time"). In the same episode, Bob Bishop says to Matt, "Everything the brain controls, you control: senses, actions, thoughts." But even if Matt's brain happens to be perfectly "tuned in" to the brain of another person, and the resulting brain activity is then "translated" into thoughts by Matt's own brain and experienced as part of his own mental life, Matt cannot be sure that the exact same thing is occurring in the head of the other person. Perhaps the brain of that person is simply a well-functioning biological machine, one that doesn't give rise to any mental experience. It would be like tuning your radio to a station that no one—not even those at the broadcast location—is listening to. Sure, this sounds unlikely and maybe a little crazy, but it cannot be excluded for certain. So even Matt's "mind reading" can't guarantee that others aren't just mindless biological machines, rather than minded creatures like you (I guess) and me (I know!).

So, are we stuck in a blind alley on the problem of other minds? Not completely, for at least two reasons. The first is that our own puzzlement teaches us an important lesson: *skepticism is pandemic,* like a philosophical version of the Shanti virus. If you allow radical doubt to infect something as commonsensical as the idea that other people have minds, then you'll have to be skeptical about nearly everything. And if not even Matt's supernatural mind reading could solve the problem, it's unlikely that anything could. When this kind of stalemate happens in philosophy, you have either encountered one of the great mysteries of life or started from the wrong assumptions and ended up with a false dilemma. Regarding the problem of other minds, the latter may be the case.

A second reason for optimism is that in real life, we cope with the problem of other minds all the time, and we do so quite successfully. Our reasoning in attributing minds to others is usually based on *analogy.*[6] Because you behave more or less like me, I assume that you have a mind like my own. We use knowledge of our own mental lives to infer the existence of other minds. When we consider our own behavior, we can experience the antecedent conditions that prompt us to act (a sudden downpour that catches us in the street without an umbrella), the inner states that guide our actions (the desire to find cover), and the resulting conduct (running toward a nearby café). When we see others facing the same predicament, we're able to observe only the beginning and the end of this sequence, while their inner states remain hidden to us. Because they consistently react similarly to analogous conditions, however, it seems warranted to conclude, by analogy, that they experience mental states like our own—in the example, a sudden desire to find cover from the rain.

This analogical reasoning is very pervasive and quite effective. FBI agent Audrey Hanson, while interviewing Claire Bennet after Sylar's aggression at Union Wells High School, recognizes the telltale signals of Claire's insincerity and, by analogy, concludes that the girl is harboring some secret. As Audrey correctly points out to Matt, "You don't have to be a mind reader to know she's hiding something!" ("Fallout").

Although quite satisfactory for most people, the argument from analogy still fails to convince radical skeptics, because their doubts will infect the very reasons for drawing the analogy in the first place. How can I be sure that other people are "like me" in all of the relevant respects? But this will worry only hard-core metaphysicians (that is, people looking for incontrovertible proof of the existence of things), not ordinary people. In our dealings with others, we're fully justified in attributing to them minds similar to our own, even if we cannot prove beyond doubt that they have these minds. When we assume that their actions are guided by certain beliefs, intentions, values, and emotions, we are often successful in predicting and understanding their actions—mundane mind reading works—and this *pragmatic success* is justification enough, insofar as our everyday lives are concerned.[7] As Sylar might put it, we just know how things work, and this is no trivial trick. Besides, this is also the most likely reason that our ability to interpret one another's minds has evolved in the first place.

Changing Minds: The Evolutionary Value of Mind Reading

Evolution is a recurrent theme in *Heroes*. The heroes of the series, "ordinary people with extraordinary abilities," are presented as the next stage of human evolution: an adaptation of the species to the ever-changing environment. Both Chandra

Suresh and his son, Mohinder, are geneticists, and Chandra's book is titled *Activating Evolution*. A fictional introduction is available online, stating that "the human species is at the very dawn of an evolutionary renaissance."[8] As Dr. Suresh describes it, "Evolution is a matter of choice. When a mutation is introduced, a decision is made. Nature asks: Does this new characteristic have value? Does it represent progress? Will it benefit the species?"[9]

Apart from the "romantic take on evolution" that is characteristic of Chandra's work ("Collision"), the concern with the *evolutionary value* of a given trait or ability is also paramount in the contemporary philosophy of mind. It's no longer enough to describe how our minds work, we also need to have a plausible story about how they evolved—and this story requires highlighting its specific adaptive value.[10] This also applies to mundane mind reading. Because a consistent part of our actions and thoughts about others hinges on the assumption that they are minded creatures, we need to understand why and how this particular attitude has naturally evolved in our species.

So, it's not surprising that the adaptive relevance of mundane mind reading has been the object of speculation, both in philosophy and in cognitive science. Why are we inclined to interpret the behavior of others as being determined by inner states that we cannot directly observe? What is the advantage of speculating about the minds of our fellow humans? Provided that mundane mind reading is specific to the human species, does it grant us an edge over other animals? If it does, how is this possible?

The mere presence of a capability or a trait isn't enough to conclude that it must have some adaptive value or that it evolved because of that value. Mind reading, as with any other human skill, could either be an *adaptation*, an *exaptation*, or a *vestigial residue of an extinct functionality*. Adaptations are traits that increase the overall fitness of the individual, thus improving the chances of survival and reproduction. Bipedal locomotion (aka walking on two feet) is an adaptation for our species, because it ensures good mobility and at the same time frees our hands. This increased our capacities for physical manipulation and opened the way to tool use. Exaptations are traits that, although still beneficial for the individual's fitness, have changed their function over time. A well-known example is the evolution of feathered wings in birds. Feathers started as a mechanism for regulating body temperature but then became large enough to allow gliding, producing a functional shift from thermic regulation to airborne locomotion. Finally, some traits or capacities can be mere residues of previous functions that are no longer in use. A standard case is the human coccyx, or tailbone. It is the vestigial remnant of a tail and no longer serves the original function of improving balance and mobility.[11]

So, the first question is whether mundane mind reading has any function at all. In the contemporary philosophy of mind, the unanimous answer to this is affirmative. The disagreement comes in determining exactly what the function is. Here the debate is dominated by several hypotheses, some of which might be combinable. The general idea is that mind reading is a *social skill*: one that improves our ability to interact with other intelligent beings to our advantage. But four different functions have been proposed in the philosophical and psychological literature:[12]

1. Mind reading for *interpretation*: By attributing motives and reasons to the actions of others, we make sense of their behavior and gain insight into why they did what they did.
2. Mind reading for *prediction*: By divining the goals and beliefs of others, we can predict what they will do in the future and thus ready ourselves to cope with the consequences.
3. Mind reading for *coordination*: Understanding the intentions of others is often needed for coordination—someone

will need to adjust his or her behavior to suit the goals of
the others.

4. Mind reading for *influence*: If I understand what you're
   thinking, I can try to change your mind by giving you reasons to reconsider your past decisions or current actions.

If we now turn to consider how mental powers are portrayed in *Heroes*, we'll find excellent examples for all of these
different functions. This proves once again that supernatural
mind reading in *Heroes* is meant as a fictional exaggeration
of our own mundane mind-reading skills. In particular, the
development of Matt's skills is a recurrent topic in the series.
As Matt's father puts it, "It only begins with reading minds,
then it becomes so much more!" ("Fight or Flight").

Matt's ability is initially limited to hearing thoughts. It
first helps him locate people whom he cannot see. This is how
Matt finds Molly's hiding place ("Don't Look Back") and how
he tracks the movements of Niki-Jessica when she's trying to
kill him and Aron Malsky ("Run!"). Matt confesses that he
has little control over his talent and is easily overcome by the
white noise of people's thoughts: "I really can't control this"
("One Giant Leap"). "Lately it's been hard for me to filter the
voices, and hearing what they're really thinking. . . . It can be
ugly!" ("Nothing to Hide"). Others' thoughts were perceived
verbally: "It was like someone was talking to me, except it was
in my head" ("One Giant Leap"); "Honey, I can't see your
thoughts, I can only hear them" ("The Fix"). This is confirmed
by the fact that Noah Bennet successfully counteracts Matt's
ability by thinking in Japanese, so that Matt cannot understand
the thoughts he hears ("Company Man"). It's only when Matt
masters the ability to manipulate nightmares, as his father can,
that he begins to perceive people's thoughts as sequences of
images ("Fight or Flight" and "Out of Time").

Initially, Matt's telepathy is monodirectional: he can perceive what others are thinking, but he cannot project his own
thoughts into their minds. Matt's ability to hear thoughts

is often exploited by those who know of it, as they communicate with him covertly by thinking what they want to say to him. His wife, Janice, chooses this way to let him know that she's pregnant with their first child ("The Fix"); Bennet uses his own thoughts to tell Matt how to calm down Ted Sprague before Ted goes nuclear ("Company Man") and later on employs the same trick to guide Matt during their escape from the Company: "You might wanna argue, but luckily this is a one-way conversation" (".07%"). Similarly, Angela Petrelli mentally asks Matt to accept her fake confession to Kaito Nakamura's murder ("The Kindness of Strangers") and then instructs him on how to kill Peter if he should lose control of his powers, without making Nathan aware of her intentions ("Powerless").

But later on, Matt develops the ability to insert his own thoughts into the minds of other people, as his father before him did ("Out of Time"). This includes projecting visual scenes into other minds, making people see, hear, smell, and even feel as if they're touching something that is not there. Maury uses this ability to have Nathan converse with the spirit of Daniel Linderman ("The Second Coming," "The Butterfly Effect," "I Am Become Death," "Angels and Monsters") and to have Linderman deal orders to members of the Pinehearst crew of superhumans, such as Daphne Millbrook ("Dying of the Light," "Angels and Monsters"). Similarly, Matt uses the same trick to make Knox believe that he killed both Matt and Daphne ("Eris Quod Sum").

Thought insertion quickly evolves into a talent for compulsion, akin to Eden McCain's power, but with no need for speaking orders aloud. In "Cautionary Tales," Matt discovers that he can also give mental orders to other subjects, obtaining instant obedience—and it works quite well. Matt successfully manipulates not only Molly and his boss at the NYPD, but also Angela ("Cautionary Tales"), who on previous occasions was able to resist his mind-reading skills ("Lizards"). Moreover, it's hinted that mental compulsion might also work on large groups of people.

In "Powerless," Nathan enlists Matt's help to "make sure every-body listens" at his press conference. Obviously, it would have worked; that is why Peter comes back from the future to shoot him and stop him from making his announcement. By Volume 4, Matt's skills of compulsion include the ability to make others see (or not see) what he wishes ("I am Sylar") and the ability even to make Sylar think he is Nathan ("An Invisible Thread").

Looking at the evolution of Matt's mind-reading talents, it's remarkable how much they mirror the adaptive functions usually assigned to mundane mind reading in philosophy: interpretation, prediction, coordination, and influence. Under the metaphorical cover of Matt's supernatural powers, *Heroes* is telling us something about the reasons we all engage in mundane mind reading during daily interactions with others. We are so obsessed with understanding other minds precisely because we want to make sense of past deeds and predict future moves, in order to know how to coordinate with other people and how to change their plans, if needed. What makes our everyday mind-reading skills so useful is also what makes Matt's telepathy so powerful: even if the former capacity is real, while the latter is fictional, their adaptive function is the same.

This similarity extends to some thorny moral issues involved in mind reading, both supernatural and mundane. In *Heroes*, Matt frequently indulges using his powers for per-sonal gain. For example, he uses them to salvage his mar-riage with Janice (Volume 1), to find and keep for himself some stolen diamonds ("Run!"), to improve his career pros-pects ("Four Months Later . . . "), to exact revenge on Emile Danko ("Turn and Face the Stranger"), and in general to have his way with other people ("Cautionary Tales"). This seems to be the same slippery slope that Matt's father encountered in his youth, ultimately becoming a thoroughly evil charac-ter: "When I found I could read minds, it was a temptation, I was weak. I used people, I was a real scumbag" ("Fight or Flight"). Indeed, it's been explicitly hinted that Matt is at risk of following in his father's footsteps. Angela voices this danger when Matt forces her to reveal Victoria Pratt's secret location: "I made her a promise! If you make me tell you her secret, you're not just like your father—you *are* him!" ("Cautionary Tales"). Angela herself is all too familiar with this kind of violation of one's own basic freedom, having been subjected to repeated mental manipulation by her husband, Arthur ("Villains").

Again, the ethical hazards associated with mundane mind reading are reminiscent of those faced by *Heroes* telepaths. In the same way that Matt risks ending up treating people like puppets, as his father did (but not quite like Eric Doyle, the puppet man ["The Butterfly Effect"], so we're in danger of making inappropriate use of our own skills—for instance, by *manipulating* our friends thanks to a subtle understanding of their deepest passions. It's with good reason that highly manipulative characters are regarded with suspicion and condemnation in our society, and it is no coincidence that one of the worst villains in the show, Arthur, specializes in manipulation. We intuitively perceive that certain uses of one another's inner motives are immoral, and we fear people who might be able and willing to take advantage of others this way. The dangers of clever manipulation are frequently portrayed in *Heroes*, where the most accomplished manipulators are not necessarily endowed with telepathic skills. Consider, for instance, Sylar, Noah Bennet, Daniel Linderman, Angela Petrelli, Bob Bishop, Adam Monroe (aka Takezo Kensei), and Emile Danko. Their success at manipulating other people proves that humans don't need supernatural mind reading to masterfully influence one another—the mundane mind reading we are so good at is already more than enough.

Mind Reading and Technology: Myth or Reality?

Heroes presumes that the nature of the mind is essentially materialist. Our thoughts and our cognitive abilities are the emergent result of the workings of our brains, with no room left for any "additional ingredient" outside of scientific explanation. As Dr. Chandra Suresh says, "The brain controls every human action, voluntary or involuntary. If the soul exists, scientifically speaking, it exists in the brain" ("Six Months Ago"). The untapped potential of the human brain is a recurrent topic in the series from the very first episode. In "Genesis," Mohinder explains to his students that "man uses only a tenth of his brain power. Another percent and we might actually be worthy of God's image. Unless, of course, that day has already arrived."[13] Supernatural powers, either naturally developed or artificially induced, are depicted as dependent on mutations in the subject's brain, and pseudoscientific explanations are offered for them. Here is an excerpt from the fictional introduction of Chandra Suresh's *Activating Evolution*:

> Though the human brain is the most remarkable mechanism we know of on earth, it is still highly inefficient and can only interpret the most obvious and base of senses: sight, smell, sound, passion, fear. But add a mere two additional neural pathways and the brain could interpret wavelengths at a frequency a thousand times greater than our current capacity, giving us the ability to hear each others' thoughts.

Since the second half of the twentieth century, incredible progress has been made in the scientific study of the brain and the central nervous system, and today neuroscience is a leading discipline around the globe.[14] Much of its success depends on technological breakthroughs in *neuroimaging* systems—the methods and the devices by which the workings of the brain can be objectively recorded and studied. Neuroimaging techniques currently in use include, among others, *electroencephalography* (EEG), which records the electric activity in different areas of the brain by placing electrodes on the scalp; *positron emission tomography* (PET) and *functional magnetic resonance imaging* (fMRI), which use different methods to measure the quantity and quality of the blood flow in different brain areas; and *single unit recording*, which uses an electrode to record the electric activity of either a single neuron or a small cluster of neurons.

These technologies have captured the attention of the media and are frequently portrayed by popular culture. In fact, references to neuroimaging techniques are numerous both in the *Heroes* TV series and in the graphic novel. The most common technology in the *Heroes* universe is electroencephalography (for instance, in "Collision," "Six Months Ago," "Company Man," and "Fight or Flight"), whereas various forms of magnetic resonance are rarer (in the graphic novel's chapter 14 and possibly in the episode "Company Man"). At other times, the kind of neuroimaging techniques being displayed are either hard to assess (for instance, in the trilogy dedicated to Matt Neuenberg, graphic novel chapters 68–70) or openly fictional. An example of the latter is in the file on Sanjog Iyer briefly shown in "Seven Minutes to Midnight," which includes a neuroscientific article on sleep research, allegedly conducted with a mysterious "DCX imaging" technique.

The availability of increasingly sophisticated tools to monitor and measure brain activity is also responsible for the growing relevance of neuroscience in the philosophy of mind. As we obtain a wealth of information on what the brain is doing, our theories of how the mind works are tested against it. In the general public, this has engendered the expectation that we're close to achieving a form of *technological mind reading*. Using cutting-edge neuroimaging technologies (that is, brain-scanning techniques), so the story goes, we're about to acquire a window into the human mind. In the near future, we'll be able to read other people's thoughts on a monitor. Eventually, we could have the scanning hardware and interpretation software installed directly into our brains and could even read minds just as Matt Parkman does.

Unfortunately, this is a pipe dream—at least, for the time being. Disappointing, I know. And we will remain disappointed for several decades, perhaps longer. Three formidable obstacles bar the way to this project: the *nature of the phenomenon* under consideration, current *limitations of neuroimaging technologies*, and *conceptual difficulties* in the interpretation of the resulting data.

Let's start with the first factor. The sheer complexity of the human brain is flabbergasting: the number of neurons is estimated to be around 100 billion (10^{11}), with each neuron having on average 7,000 synaptic connections to other neurons, with a resulting estimate of about 100 trillion (10^{14}) connections in the brain of an adult human. These figures truly defy the imagination, and yet they refer only to neurons, which constitute just a rough 10 percent of the brain: the rest is made up of glial cells, that is, nonneuronal cells that serve many vital functions, including participating in signal transmission in the nervous system. In addition, the brain uses two main mechanisms for propagating information across neurons, and they constantly interact with each other. First, *neurotransmission* is the process by which a single neuron transfers an electric impulse to another single neuron. Second, *neuromodulation* is the process by which chemical substances secreted by small groups of neurons spread across large areas of the brain, thus modulating the activity of multiple neurons.

As a result of the brain's complex structure, it works as a highly *distributed* and *parallel* machine, in which there is no fine distinction of local functions. Indeed, the current functional map of the brain used for clinical exams and treatment is just a rough sketch of mental capabilities on a very large and coarse scale. As such, it cannot provide the kind of fine-grained insight that would be needed to "read" specific thoughts via neuroimaging. What *Heroes* telepaths do as a matter of course requires in fact an astonishing computational power, given the complexity of the human brain. In other words, although the chances of someone naturally evolving Matt's abilities are abysmal, our current chance of building a machine with those capacities is even smaller.

The second problem with technological mind reading concerns what can actually be recorded by current neuro-imaging techniques. So far, what we can *read* is the level of activity in localized areas of the brain. But this is only *quantitative* data, not qualitative; we know that a certain area of the brain is doing something, but not *what* that something is. Moreover, the brain never sleeps—that is, it's constantly active, even when we're unconscious. Recent research has focused on the so-called *default mode of brain function*, or baseline activity.[15] Observation has revealed that the performance of specific tasks involves not only increases of activity in certain brain regions, but also corresponding *decreases of activity* in other regions. This suggests that there is an intrinsic activity being performed by the brain in the absence of any specific task. So, the traditional view of the brain as a machine waiting to get started on a given activity is deeply mistaken.

To understand human intelligence, task-related inhibition of brain functions is as important as the corresponding activation, but studying their interaction further complicates the task of neuroscientists. This difficulty is aggravated because the most precise neuroimaging technologies, like single unit recording, are still *unusable on humans*. They are highly invasive and compromise the brain of the subject under study—so much so that even their current application on nonhuman animals is considered ethically controversial. Current neuroscience still lacks the luxury of Matt's noninvasive, precise, and qualitative methods for probing the thoughts of other human beings.

Finally, technological mind reading faces a severe conceptual problem: the "language of the brain" is, in and by itself, a *language without meaning*—a syntax without semantics. To give meaning to a certain brain activity that we register with our instruments, we need to associate it with either a bodily action or a mental process. This raises at least two difficulties: how to separate the task under consideration from other processes the brain might be performing at the same time, and how to make sure that the experimental subject is executing exactly the required task.

The first problem depends on the highly parallel nature of human cognition: even when we're focused on a given task, the central nervous system is taking care of a variety of other functions (monitoring basic bodily functions, perceiving the surrounding environment, rehearsing current plans, plus indulging in any daydream we might concoct), which results in complex patterns of brain activity, extremely difficult to disambiguate.

The second problem is a plague for any neuroscientific experiment, especially those that attempt to study mental processes. The main access we have to what's going on in the subject's mind while his or her brain shows a certain activity is *subjective introspective reports*. Basically, we have to ask the subject to perform a certain cognitive process, such as remembering, planning, or deciding, and trust the person to do it and nothing else. But introspection is a highly dubious source of scientific evidence, and this undermines the reliability of the resulting neuroimaging data. Thus, while the recordings of brain activity are highly uncontroversial, their interpretation is often subjected to vigorous debate. The difference with *Heroes* telepathy is striking: where Matt perceives the thoughts of others as already decoded in a comprehensible format, either sentences or images, we are stuck with quantitative figures that, more often than not, lack any obvious translation.

In view of all of these difficulties, extreme prudence on technological mind reading is widespread among philosophers—including those who are adamantly convinced that it's possible to achieve a fully scientific explanation of the mind.

But to state this possibility in principle is very different from claiming that we're anywhere near obtaining such an explanation in practice. On the contrary, for the time being mind reading will have to be confined to our mundane skills at interpreting one another's plans and to the kind of fictional telepathy that *Heroes* so beautifully portrays. All things considered, I'd say this is a comforting thought—one that you can still hold safe in the privacy of your mind, free from any danger of supernatural or technological mind readers.[16]

NOTES

1. For a sympathetic outlook on parapsychology from a philosophical standpoint, see David Ray Griffin, *Parapsychology, Philosophy, and Spirituality: A Postmodern Exploration* (Albany: SUNY Press, 1997). For a more skeptical and sobering view, see James Alcock, *Science and Supernature: A Critical Appraisal of Parapsychology* (Buffalo, NY: Prometheus Books, 1990).

2. The quote is from page 96 of David Chalmers, *The Conscious Mind* (Oxford: Oxford University Press, 1996). Although Chalmers is a major proponent of the relevance of zombies for philosophical debate, other philosophers are skeptical of their significance. For a highly enjoyable critique of the "zombie affaire," see Daniel Dennett, *Sweet Dreams: Philosophical Obstacles to a Science of Consciousness* (Cambridge: MIT Press, 2005).

3. For the record, even if Descartes made this motto famous for eternity, he was in fact borrowing ideas already introduced by earlier scholars. Among them, most noticeably, was St. Augustine (354–430), who coined a similar principle in *De Civitate Dei*: *Si fallor sum* ("If I am mistaken, I am," Book XI, 26).

4. Descartes, *Meditations on First Philosophy*, originally published in Latin in 1641. The quoted passage is from the Second Meditation in the English translation by John Cottingham, Robert Stoothoff, and Dugald Murdoch, in *The Philosophical Writings of Descartes*, vol. 2 (Cambridge, UK: Cambridge University Press, 1984).

5. Interested readers will find additional discussion on how telepathy cannot solve the problem of other minds in John Wisdom, *Other Minds* (New York: Philosophical Library, 1952); and Irving Thalberg, "Telepathy," *Analysis* 21 (1961): 49–53.

6. This view was defended by, among others, John Stuart Mill (1806–1873) and A. J. Ayer (1910–1989). See John Stuart Mill, *An Examination of Sir William Hamilton's Philosophy* (London: Longmans, 1865); and A. J. Ayer, *The Concept of a Person* (London: Macmillan, 1963).

7. More extended discussion of this line of thought on the problem of other minds can be found in Daniel Dennett, *Brainstorms: Philosophical Essays on Mind and Psychology* (Cambridge: MIT Press, 1978); and Anita Avramides, *Other Minds* (London: Routledge, 2001).

8. Chandra Suresh, "Activating Evolution," http://activatingevolution.org/book.shtml.

9. This quote comes from chapter 5 of the book that is mentioned in the graphic novel's chapter 51, "Maya y Alejandro," www.nbc.com/Heroes/novels/downloads/Heroes_novel_051.pdf.

10. For more on whether the *Heroes* story makes scientific evolutionary sense, see chapter 11 of this book, "The Science of *Heroes*: Flying Men, Immortal Samurai, and Destroying the Space-Time Continuum," by Andrew Zimmerman Jones.

11. This distinction was already clear to Charles Darwin (1809–1882), although he used partially different terms to label these concepts. See Charles Darwin, *The Origin of Species*, 6th Edition (London: John Murray, 1872).

12. Interested readers will find excellent introductions to this topic in the following: Daniel Dennett, *The Intentional Stance* (Cambridge: MIT Press, 1987); Simon Baron-Cohen, *Mindblindness: An Essay on Autism and Theory of Mind* (Cambridge, MA: MIT Press, 1995); Michael Tomasello, *The Cultural Origins of Human Cognition* (Cambridge, MA: Harvard University Press, 1999); Shaun Nichols and Stephen Stich, *Mindreading: An Integrated Account of Pretence, Self-Awareness, and Understanding Other Minds* (Oxford: Oxford University Press, 2003); and Kim Sterelny, *Thought in a Hostile World: The Evolution of Human Cognition* (Oxford: Blackwell, 2003).

13. Incidentally, this indication of how much of our brains we use is dangerously ambiguous and may lead to severe misconceptions. It does *not* mean that there is a large area of the brain that we never use. This would make no sense in evolutionary terms; how could we evolve such a highly inefficient brain and still survive? Besides it's just factually false: virtually all areas of our brains have a known use and often more than one. Instead, it is somehow correct, although very imprecise, to say that there's a stronger brain activity in only a (different) small portion of the human brain at any given time. This, however, doesn't mean that the rest of the brain is "sleeping" or that its background activity is less important than what's happening in the foreground. On the contrary, we'll soon see that the default mode of brain functioning is crucial to our understanding of human intelligence. Finally, when Mohinder hints that using more of our brains would certainly be an excellent thing, making us "worthy of God's image," he is actually overlooking the most basic law of physics: activity requires energy, and energy is limited. Our brains are no exception: to use "more of our brains" would require, among other things, a stronger blood flow to be pumped in our brain cells, which could easily cause a hemorrhage and thus provoke either death or permanent cognitive impairment—something similar to what Peter risks when he absorbs too many powers too quickly ("Fallout" and "Godsend"), before Claude teaches him how to control them ("The Fix," "Distractions," and "Unexpected").

14. There are several excellent books that provide exciting and updated introductions to contemporary neuroscience and also discuss its implications for philosophy. In particular, I suggest the following: Antonio Damasio, *Descartes' Error: Emotion, Reason, and the Human Brain* (New York: Avon Books, 1994); Vilayanur Ramachandran and Sandra Blakeslee, *Phantoms in the Brain: Human Nature and the Architecture of the Mind* (New York: William Morrow, 1998); and Chris Frith, *Making Up the Mind: How the Brain Creates Our Mental World* (London: Blackwell, 2007). For a more technical overview, there is the excellent textbook by Nobel laureate Eric Kandel and colleagues: Eric Kandel, James Schwartz, and Thomas Jessell, *Principles of Neural Science*, 4th Edition (New York: McGraw-Hill, 2000).

15. This field was pioneered by Marcus Raichle and colleagues at the beginning of this century. For a survey of their results and the implications for behavioral studies, see Marcus Raichle, "The Brain's Dark Energy," *Science* 314 (2006): 1249–1250; and Marcus Raichle and Abraham Snyder, "A Default Mode of Brain Function: A Brief History of an Evolving Idea," *NeuroImage* 37 (2007): 1083–1090.

16. I am grateful to the editor, David Kyle Johnson, for his helpful comments and suggestions on previous versions of this essay.

PETER PETRELLI: THE POWER OF EMPATHY

Andrew Terjesen

When *Heroes* first began, fans speculated endlessly about what (if any) power Peter Petrelli had. We were faked out by his walking on air and prophetic dreams ("Don't Look Back"), until it became clear that Peter's power included the ability to duplicate the powers of others ("Collision"). Most fans of the show then described his power as "power mimicry." In addition, most thought his power to be different from Sylar's in method only—Sylar has to examine the brains of those he gains his powers from, but Peter only needs to be near them. Sylar steals powers; Peter copies them.

But this view of Peter's power is incomplete. On the fan Web site HeroesWiki, Peter's power is called "empathic mimicry" (not "power mimicry"), and Claude Rains refers to Peter as an "empath" ("The Fix"). Later, Peter's father suggests that Sylar could acquire powers through empathy (as Peter does), instead of by examining the brains of his victims ("It's Coming"). Series creator Tim Kring, when comparing Peter's and Sylar's powers, even stated that Peter's power "is based on his empathy and his ability to connect with people."[1] The suggestion is that Peter's power is actually the ability to empathize—in a deep and significant way—with others, and it is only by virtue of having this ability that he is able to copy the powers of others.[2] But how could empathy be a real power, much less the most powerful one? What would such a power really amount to, and how could it let Peter "copy" powers? And how might Peter's power teach us all to be better people?

What Is Empathy?

Look up the words *empathy* and *sympathy* today and you will probably conclude that they mean the same thing. *Sympathy* comes from the Greek *sympatheia*, which, when translated from its Greek roots, means "experiencing or suffering with (in the sense of *together* or *at the same time*)." Sympathy usually describes all forms of *feeling and understanding the pain of others*. The modern dictionary definitions of *empathy* are practically interchangeable with such descriptions.

But the complicated history of the word *empathy* reveals that in a certain way, empathy doesn't really mean what we think it does. Empathy was actually introduced into the English language in the twentieth century by E. B. Titchener (1867–1927) as a translation of the German word *Einfühlung*. In German aesthetics and psychology, *Einfühlung* describes how people project their feelings into an *inanimate object* (in the process giving it a certain life and dignity). So, that is what empathy should mean. But because *empathy* kind of sounds like *sympathy* and both words involved the projection of emotion, the two words began to be used as synonyms. (At least, that is how one imagines the process; such things are hard to track.) And since common usage—not academic decisions—actually determines the meanings of words, the two words are now synonyms.

Empathy involves "harmony" or "conformity of feelings." We have empathy when we share another's feelings or condition, and many people would argue this happens only when we imagine or replicate the feelings or condition of another.[3] For most people, the classic example of empathy is when we imagine ourselves in someone else's shoes, something Peter can do with ease.

Think of the time when Peter simply becomes *aware* that his brother, Nathan, has been hurt in an accident and Nathan tells him, "You're good with people" ("Genesis"). Also consider Angela Petrelli's comment to Peter: "You were always so sensitive" ("Don't Look Back"). And, of course, the fact that Peter was a hospice nurse leads Claude to comment, "A nurse who's an empath, very cute" ("The Fix"). Peter seems to respond to the presence of others' powers, experiencing them with the other person, in an unmediated fashion, without any direct contact or obvious exchange of energy. So, clearly, his power derives from his empathy. But we still wonder, how does "super-empathy" entail the ability to copy superpowers? Perhaps looking at specific kinds of empathy will help answer this question.

Empathy as Resonance

The idea of empathy as resonance (or contagion—as in "contagious") is found in the philosopher David Hume's (1711–1776) account of our interactions with other people. As Hume described it, empathy can be an unconscious transfer of emotion from one person to another.

> The minds of all men are similar in their feelings and operations, nor can anyone be actuated by any affection, of which all others are not, in some degree, susceptible. As in strings equally wound up, the motion of one communicates itself to the rest; so all the affections readily pass from one person to another, and beget corresponding movements in every human creature.[4]

For Hume, empathy seems to be a process by which I become infected with the emotions of others. But it's not spread as a germ is. More likely, when I see someone really agitated, I unwittingly begin to copy some of this person's behaviors, such as fidgeting, and that makes me feel agitated—just as making yourself smile starts to make you feel better. Perhaps seeing the person's agitation reminds me of stressful experiences, and I become stressed. Either way, someone else's emotional state sets off a similar emotional state in me because we are similarly constructed (like strings on a violin).

Maybe Peter's power works the same way. At least initially, Peter's power seems to work only as a form of resonance. The power requires the presence of another "hero." Peter seems to have little control over it, and he has the power only while the other person is around. As Claude describes it, Peter's power is "autonomic, like swallowing" ("Distractions"). But if Peter acquires his powers in this way, resonating with other heroes, then he should lose his abilities when they are no longer around—or, at least, the abilities should fade away over time. Yet we know this doesn't happen. Peter retains the powers (unless they are stolen from him), even far into the future (every Future Peter we have seen still has them). So, it looks like our answer isn't in empathy as resonance.

Empathy as Absorption

Mohinder Suresh describes Peter as a sponge, suggesting that he absorbs other people's powers. This would certainly explain how Peter retains these abilities after he is no longer in the presence of the hero in question. So, another kind of empathy may work to describe Peter's power: emotional identification.

Feeling the same things as another person is not enough to attain emotional identification. If both D.L. Hawkins and Niki Sanders are worried about Micah, they feel the same thing, but neither is empathizing with the other. According to the philosopher Max Scheler (1874–1928), emotional identification is identifying with another person to the extent that one becomes unaware of one's own individual identity— when one begins to see oneself as part of some other person or entity who is sharing the same feelings.[5] This is why, if Peter is experiencing emotional identification, he would actually be absorbing the other person.

Calling Peter's powers "empathy" in this sense seems consistent with what happens to Peter in Volume 2. When Peter uses Sylar's telekinesis, he almost kills Will and seems to delight in doing so ("Kindred"). It seems, then, that Peter has absorbed not only Sylar's powers but also his anger—his empathy is emotional absorption.[6]

But how does one absorb someone else's feelings? By definition, what I am feeling are my feelings—how in the world could I feel someone else's? Edith Stein (1891–1942) described empathy as "the experience of foreign consciousness in general."[7] Her point was that when empathizing, we never lose sight of the fact that what we feel are someone else's feelings. Consequently, it is not possible to become absorbed into someone else when we empathize. Thus, it seems that Peter's power cannot be described in this way.

Empathy as Duplication

Perhaps Peter's ability is really a process by which he duplicates the powers of other heroes. It's hard to say for sure how this process might work—especially since we're not sure how the powers themselves work. But Hume might be able to help us out:

> When any affection is infused by sympathy, it is at first known only by its effects, and by those external signs in countenance and conversation, which convey an idea of it. This idea is presently converted into

an impression, and acquires such a degree of force and vivacity, as to become the very passion itself, and produce an equal emotion, as any original affection.[8]

Later, Hume said that sympathy is "nothing but the conversion of an idea into an impression by the force of imagination."[9] Today we might say that for Hume, empathy is accomplished when seeing someone feeling a certain thing reminds us of what it is like to feel that way, and that memory produces in us a vivid sensation of feeling that way. The memory (an idea) is converted into a current vivid experience (an impression) by the imagination.

Peter, however, doesn't have to see someone use his or her power to get it; he got Ted Sprague's powers before seeing him become radioactive. But Hume can still help us describe Peter's empathic power. When Peter is in close proximity to Hiro Nakamura (for example), this gives rise to an idea in Peter's mind of how to stop time; then, by the power of imagination, that idea becomes an impression in Peter's mind of how to stop time, and thus Peter has that ability. But the question still remains: how could Hiro's proximity give rise to such an idea in Peter?

Sylar's method of power acquisition suggests that all powers have something to do with the brain. So, like Sylar, when Peter acquires the powers of heroes, his brain must duplicate their brain structures. Sylar replicates powers by looking at brains directly and seeing how they work. Peter's power must also be a power of brain duplication, but how does it work?

Modern neuroscience can shed some light on this question. For one thing, neuroscience has taught us that all mental functions, even emotions, are the result of the activity of the brain. When the neurons of your brain are wired and fire in certain ways, you feel certain emotions. In addition, neuroscience has taught us that neural activity and brain structure can be mimicked from person to person very easily.

One important experiment demonstrated that when monkeys rip a piece of paper, the same areas of their brains are active as when they see or hear someone ripping paper.[10] These so-called mirror neurons are thought to bridge the gap between knowing what something is like for me and knowing what something is like for someone else.[11] In addition, many of the same neurons that are active when you imagine an experience are the same ones that are active when you actually are having that experience.[12] Thus, empathy, even as Hume described it, would literally consist of replicating the brain structure and activity of the person you are empathizing with.

So, Peter's empathic mimicry is most likely the ability to copy the brain structures and activities of those around him; that is how he copies emotions. But because powers are also the result of brain structure, his empathic power makes him copy powers as well. Of course, he would do this unconsciously, and how his brain manages to do this is a mystery—but so are most other powers.[13]

And, given the TV series, this makes so much sense. Recall that when Peter is first learning to use the powers on his own, he realizes that to do so, he must remember the person from whom he acquired the power and how this person made him feel ("Distractions"). This includes remembering how the person felt when he or she was near him. As he replicates the person's past brain structure to bring about that emotion, he also replicates the part of his or her brain structure that is necessary for the person's power and—bingo!—he has acquired his or her power.

So, unlike Sylar, Peter gets the emotions of others. But what seems to separate Peter from Sylar even further is that Peter doesn't get only the power or even the emotions; he takes in a part of the person whose power it is. As part of that package, Peter can appropriate someone else's skills. His initial drawings of the future are pretty rudimentary, but later on, he seems to copy not only Isaac Mendez's ability but also his skill at painting ("Hiros").[14] Moreover, it seems that Peter might have tapped into Charles Deveaux's business skills when (in "Nothing to Hide") he discusses whether a stock would be a good buy.[15] That is also probably why Peter almost enjoyed killing Will with the telekinesis power he acquired from Sylar ("Kindred"). Peter even has trouble controlling his ability to travel through time, just as Hiro does, when Peter acquires that power from him.

In Volume 3, Sylar begins to develop the ability to acquire powers by empathy. Recall when Sylar is locked in the room at Pinehearst with Elle Bishop ("It's Coming"). She electrocutes him over and over, but Sylar refuses to take her powers by force. When she finally asks for death, he releases her instead and acquires her power. It seems that when he finally empathizes with her, he acquires her power. But his empathy is not as developed as Peter's; he does not acquire Elle's skill of using her power. She has to teach him. Of course, he later rejects this ability and goes back to getting his powers the old-fashioned way: by examining a person's brain. Some things never change.[16]

So Peter's power is not mere power mimicry. He acquires the powers of others *in virtue* of having the power of empathy: being able to empathize with those around him to the greatest degree by literally replicating their brain structures— emotions, powers, and all. By contrast, although Sylar has the skill of empathy for a while, he acquires the power of others at the cost of having true empathy; he is driven by a hunger that makes him disregard the emotions of others, while he takes people apart as if they were clocks in his shop, in order to learn how their powers work ("I Am Become Death").[17] Peter's power is emotional, whereas Sylar's is rational, but it is their differing attitudes that explains why Sylar is so much more fearsome than Peter, even though they both wield tremendous power.

Does Empathy Make You Moral?

The idea recurs throughout the series that Peter, because of his empathy, is uniquely suited to saving the world. Consider Charles Deveaux's observation that Daniel Linderman may have chosen the wrong brother. Charles tells Angela, "I look in Peter's eyes, I see compassion, empathy, but, most of all, I see hope" ("How to Stop an Exploding Man"). Only minutes later, Charles tells Peter that he will be able to save everyone because Peter's heart "has the ability to love, unconditionally." Angela sees her son's sensitivity as weakness compared to Nathan's self-centered determination, but Charles sees it as a source of moral strength. Peter's personality also makes him the kind of person who really seems to act for the good of all. While Nathan seems persuaded by the logic of Linderman's .07 percent argument, Peter cannot discount the loss of life and the suffering that such an act would create. Peter would rather have Claire Bennet shoot him than cause all of that damage to New York City.

But can having empathy, as Peter does, make us better people, too? No. Simple knowledge of how other people feel is not enough. After all, Elle presumably knows how Peter feels when she electrocutes him while the Company has him imprisoned ("Four Months Ago . . ."). In fact, she enjoys knowing that he is hurting and feeling trapped, and she would be unsatisfied if he wasn't. Likewise, Sylar acknowledges that he knows he is hurting Elle, just before he kills her ("The Eclipse, Part II"). The ability to make connections with others and even feel what they are feeling would appear to make Peter a great hero. But simply sharing someone else's feelings is not enough for moral goodness. Someone might, of course, feel your pain but not want to do anything about it. Mohinder Suresh could feel the terror of his subjects—even he was terrified by what he was doing—but it didn't stop him from experimenting.

Simply resonating the emotions of a few other people won't be enough, either. Noah Bennet could not help but fall in love with his adopted baby daughter, partly because he resonates her emotions, but Bennet's love of Claire causes him to do some pretty morally questionable things, such as repeatedly erase his family's memories. For empathy to make me a better person, it needs to do more than occasionally connect me with someone (like Claire and her dad); it needs to connect me with everyone.

Fortunately, Peter's power allows him to pick up a part of everyone he encounters. But morality requires more than this. If Peter is going to be a hero, it's not simply because he knows when people are scared or happy. It's because he knows what is scaring them and what will make them happy. So, his empathy also makes him mirror the worldviews of others. And this may even teach Peter about himself. As Edith Stein suggested, "It is possible for another to 'judge me more accurately' than I judge myself and give me clarity about myself."[18] Empathy makes Peter more moral, both by expanding his horizons and by chipping away at his self-centered bias.

So, Peter is being made better (in a moral sense) by all of the people he empathizes with. But can Peter teach us to be good? I think so. What we have learned is that the kind of empathy that helps make us better people is the kind that is directed at everyone and not only at those we care about. What really needs to happen when we empathize is that we not only replicate feelings, but that we also recognize that the feelings belong to someone who deserves our respect.

We need to consider the objects of our empathy. Empathizing too much with a particular person (especially when other people are involved) or not empathizing with everyone will lead us away from the right thing to do. Peter's difficulty in controlling his powers demonstrates this pretty well.

Ted Sprague (the original "exploding man") was always upset by his powers—after all, they had caused the death of his wife. If Peter's powers involve a form of mental duplication, then Peter probably duplicates Ted's fears about his ability to control that power. At inopportune moments, those feelings could surface and make Peter a walking bomb (which is precisely what happens at the end of Volume 1). So, if we're going to use empathy to become better individuals, we need to make sure that particular acts of empathy do not create emotions that overwhelm the feelings of all of the other people we've empathized with.

There is another lesson to learn from Peter. According to Claude, Peter's problem is that he has too many attachments. Claude's solution is that "We've got to get those people out of your head" ("Distractions"). Although Peter later claims, when using Claire's power, "I don't have to cut her out. I have to remember her. How she made me feel," Claude might still have a point. Peter gains some command over his powers by learning to focus on certain emotional attachments. The problem is that most likely he is being pulled in different directions by his powers and presumably by the personalities that come with them. Only by focusing on the right person at the right time is Peter able to access the power that is appropriate to the situation and keep his other powers in check.

Likewise, the empathy that will help me become a better person must not be too attached to particular people; it needs to reach out to everyone. In addition, it cannot treat everyone exactly the same; otherwise, we are likely to have a stalemate between competing people's desires. So, we need to figure out how to identify the most relevant perspectives in a given situation (we do not want to treat Linderman's, Adam Monroe's, or Arthur's perspective as special). If we're going to develop morally, we need to learn how to rein in our empathy. But how will we know when to limit our empathy?[19]

Limiting Our Empathy in Order to Be Moral

Although empathy is helpful to us, we have to worry about feeling *too much* attachment and about not feeling enough to overcome competing interests or sadistic passions.[20] Hume recognized this, insisting that one's sympathy be filtered through what he called a *general point of view.*

The problem, as Hume saw it, is that we do not properly weigh pleasures and pains—we often give undue emphasis to our own present condition. A general point of view keeps us from doing that. In order to discover what is right and what is wrong, one must observe what other people are pleased or pained by. To correct for the problem, Hume considered the passions of everyone involved. In many cases, this does not even require surveying everyone who is affected. To determine whether it is a good idea for Sylar or Peter to explode in Kirby Plaza, one need only look at the reactions of everyone who is gathered in the plaza that night. Only Sylar seems to think it is a good idea, and Linderman's thinking about the explosion is not shared by anyone else present.

Hume's general point of view will be unsuccessful, however, in situations where some important people who are affected are not present or the people who are involved lack certain emotional responses. A plaza full of Lindermans and Sylars would not reflect the opinions of the average person affected by the blast. Hume failed to consider situations where people seem to have radically different emotional responses to a situation. Fortunately, Hume's contemporary and friend Adam Smith (1723–1790) proposed another solution.

To address the lack of consistency in people's emotional responses, Smith proposed that we all consider our actions in the way a totally impartial spectator would. We should "place ourselves in the situation of another man, and view it, as it

were, with his eyes and from his station. We endeavor to examine our own conduct as we imagine any other fair and impartial
spectator would examine it."[21] If we possess the same passion
that the impartial spectator would have in our situation, then
we have the appropriate passion. And with the appropriate passion, we will be led to the appropriate action. The impartial
spectator is an imagined person and so is not susceptible to the
limitations of the actual general point of view.

Hiro's constant thinking in terms of what Takezo Kensei
would do is a good illustration of how the impartial spectator can correct our passions. By thinking about "Kensei and
the Dragon," Hiro is inspired to take action against Sylar
("Landslide"). Kensei continues to inspire Hiro, even after
Hiro discovers that he is a fraud, because it is the imagined
ideal of Kensei that motivates Hiro to try his best.

The impartial spectator does not merely inspire us to be
moral; he also helps us to restrain our passions when they
might lead us down the wrong path. It seems that any moral
person needs a filter on his or her emotions, if the individual
is going to act well. In the past, Nathan has served as Peter's
filter. From the beginning, Peter sees Nathan as the one who
will help him sort things out. He tells Nathan, "Something
is happening to me, and I have this feeling that you're the
only person that's gonna understand this" ("Genesis"). And
when he is about to confront Sylar in Volume 1, Peter seeks
out Nathan. Despite Claire's skepticism about her biological
father, Peter tells her that they need to see Nathan, "Because
I'm scared. And I need my brother to help us" ("How to
Stop an Exploding Man"). When Peter feels his emotions
overwhelming him and doesn't know what to do, he turns to
Nathan.

Although Nathan is far from an impartial spectator, his natural ambition and self-centeredness can be a good counterbalance
to Peter's excessive involvement in others. Certainly, it is Nathan
who sees a better solution to Peter's out-of-control powers.

Flying Peter away from the plaza is a better solution than asking Claire to kill someone, and it actually ends up saving everyone's life. There is, however, a lot of risk involved in relying on someone else to filter one's emotion. Peter needs to figure out some way to filter his emotions that does not depend on Nathan (be it taking the general point of view, the impartial spectator, or something else entirely). This begins to become apparent at the beginning of Volume 4, when Nathan starts a government program to track down and capture those with powers. But the need for Peter to find a non-Nathan emotion filter is most obvious at the end of Volume 4 when, unbeknownst to Peter, Nathan dies—and I don't think we want Peter using "Sylar/Nathan" as an emotional filter.

Although Peter's ability to copy the powers of others through empathic mimicry is quite impressive, his real strength lies in his empathy with other people's emotions. Without it, he would be no different from Sylar. When Peter loses his empathic mimicry in Volume 3, he also seems to lose some of his ability to empathize and as a result is more willing to do "morally gray" things (in Volume 4). Does regaining one ability renew the other? In any event, Peter shouldn't rely on either ability alone—he needs to keep things in perspective.

NOTES

1. *Wizard Magazine*, interview with Tim Kring, www.heroestheseries.com/tim-kring-previews-heroes-in-2007/.

2. Of course, by Volume 4, Peter appears to have lost his empathic mimicry and merely copies the powers of others by touch and is able to hold only one power at a time. We will ignore this fact for the purposes of this chapter—the power of empathy is much more interesting.

3. There is some variety in how people use the term *empathy*. For example, many people would insist that empathy is a form of understanding or caring. But as we'll see later in the essay, empathy does not seem to require us to really understand or care about the people we empathize with.

4. David Hume, *Treatise of Human Nature*, edited by L. A. Selby-Bigge (Oxford: Oxford University Press, 1978), p. 576.

5. Max Scheler, *The Nature of Sympathy*, translated by Peter Heath (London: Routledge, Kegan and Paul, 1954), pp. 18–19.

6. If "the hunger" is a psychological disorder—and not a part of Sylar's power per se—then Peter's behavior in "I Am Become Death" and "Angels and Monsters" really shows that Peter absorbs more than powers.

7. Edith Stein, *On the Problem of Empathy*, edited by Waltraut Stein (The Hague: Martinus Nijhoff, 1964), p. 11.

8. Hume, *Treatise of Human Nature*, p. 317. Spellings have been modernized in this quotation. Admittedly, Hume was talking about "sympathy," but, as mentioned earlier in the essay, the word *empathy* was not a part of the English language in Hume's time. Yet what Hume described seems to fit the contemporary psychological definitions of *empathy*.

9. Ibid., p. 427.

10. G. Rizzolatti and L. Craighero, "The Mirror Neuron System," *Annual Review of Neuroscience* 27 (2004): 169–192. It should be noted that the existence of mirror neurons in human beings has not yet been proved, but based on the studies of monkeys and other data, many neuroscientists are confident that we possess mirror neurons.

11. For more on the philosophical issues surrounding mind reading, see chapter 14, "Understanding Other Minds: Philosophical Foundations of *Heroes*' Mind-Reading Powers," by Fabio Paglieri.

12. See V. S. Ramachandran, and Sandra Blakeslee, *Phantoms in the Brain* (New York: Quill, William Morrow, 1998), chap. 3.

13. Copying specific brain structures is probably how Matt Parkman reads the thoughts of others, but I have no idea how that would work, either. For more on Matt's mind-reading skills, see chapter 14, "Understanding Other Minds: Philosophical Foundations of *Heroes*' Mind-Reading Powers," by Fabio Paglieri.

14. You might think that Isaac's drawing skills are a part of his power, yet recall that Sylar also acquires Isaac's powers, but his drawings are much more crude than Isaac's and Peter's ("How to Stop an Exploding Man").

15. Admittedly, this is a dream sequence at the beginning of the episode, but Peter's dreams of Charles always seem to have a special quality and, at least, could be based in memory. Also, it is not clear whether Charles thinks he has made a bad pick or is simply making fun of him for thinking like a businessman.

16. Or maybe it's just that empathy isn't easy to maintain on a regular basis, and that's what makes Peter so special. Thankfully, Peter's empathy is not something that Arthur Petrelli can take away.

17. Interestingly, Sylar's power of "intuitive aptitude" (and the hunger that goes with it) seems to challenge this explanation, because Peter can't seem to copy the power. He has to fix the watch to get access to it (and the hunger). The writers of *Heroes* have said, however, "Peter probably had already absorbed Sylar's power—but he had no idea how to access the ability," and said that they were asked to cut that explanation out of the script (Joe Pokaski and Aron Coleite, "Behind the Eclipse: Week 4," www .comicbookresources.com/?page=article&id=18544). I would even speculate that Peter subconsciously avoids using Sylar's power precisely because it is the power of a serial killer, and Peter doesn't want the emotions attached to this stirred up. But fixing the watch gets him into Sylar's head and therefore into Sylar's power.

18. Stein, *On the Problem of Empathy*, p. 82.

19. In effect, both problems stem from an inability to limit our empathy toward particular people. In the case of overidentification, we allow their perspectives to carry too much weight because we become too invested in it (and therefore are unable to enter other perspectives). And in the case of treating all perspectives the same, we do not limit our particular empathy toward people who have shown themselves to have a skewed or biased perspective on the situation.

20. And we might also worry about being too overwhelmed by emotion in general. People have criticized Peter's poor decision making (such as walking straight into his dad's arms and losing his powers) and the fact that he seems to forget what an array of powers he has at his disposal, but this is a result of his getting too emotional. It may frustrate us to see Peter make these mistakes, but we should remember that this is the danger of relying on emotion so much that we get caught up in how we feel right now, and this interferes with our ability to think things through.

21. Adam Smith, *The Theory of Moral Sentiments* (Indianapolis, IN: Liberty Fund, 1984), vol. III, pp. i, 2.

PART FIVE

VILLAINS, FAMILY, AND LYING

SIXTEEN

ARE THE HEROES REALLY GOOD?

Peter S. Fosl

Superhero stories usually make no secret of who the good guys and the bad guys are. Superman good, Lex Luthor bad. Batman good, Joker bad. *Heroes* began this way, too: Peter good, Sylar bad. Heroes good, Company bad. But as we discovered in Volume 3 ("Villains") things are not always so clear; heroes can become villains and villains can become heroes. By the end of Volume 4 ("Fugitives"), our heroes have become the Company and Sylar has even become Nathan. Even the series' signature icon—the eclipse—signals that the *Heroes* moral universe is more complex and, in fact, darker. Plato (c. 424–c. 328 BC) had used the sun, in his magisterial dialogue *Republic*, as a symbol of goodness, and the light of the sun for him symbolized the intelligibility of goodness.[1] *Heroes*'s iconic eclipse might, accordingly, be interpreted as suggesting that the characters of the show (and maybe all of us) have lost sight of goodness and that goodness no longer remains intelligible to us—or, anyway, that it's become harder to discern. If this is so, it might be a good idea to try to follow whatever leads *Heroes* does manage to offer us for distinguishing goodness from evil. Personally, I'm attracted to the dark side of things. So, let's focus our investigation on what emerges as evil among the *Heroes*.

Evil as Ignorance

Socrates (469–399 BC) believed that no one does wrong knowingly.[2] People do bad things only because they do not know or understand what goodness really is; they mistake evil for goodness. An evildoer might not appreciate the suffering that his or her actions cause, might not understand the duties that goodness requires, or might not know how superior is the happiness that results from a life of virtue. Perhaps most important, according to Socrates, evildoers do not understand that their conduct actually harms themselves. So, if Socrates is right, in *Heroes* we should be able to identify the villains by their ignorance and the heroes by their knowledge. Can we?

Mohinder Suresh and his father, Chandra, are both professors, men of knowledge. And their initial extraordinary goodness, even in a show full of heroes, is perhaps a sign that with great knowledge comes great virtue. It certainly was Mohinder's knowledge that helped save the world from the Shanti virus. Chandra even tries through his book *Activating Evolution* and Mohinder through his lectures to spread goodness by spreading knowledge, explaining to the world (the ordinary, the superpowered, and the Company alike) how the superpowered have appeared naturally through evolution and how they hold great promise for the world.

On the flip side of the coin, ignorance seems to underwrite evil. Suresh's naiveté (a form of ignorance) has led him to collaborate with the Company, assisting it in its malign plans for control and repression (Volume 2, episodes 5–11).[3] Maya Herrera's ignorance of Gabriel Gray's true character leads her to help Sylar return and succeed with his evil aspirations ("The Line"). Claire Bennet's ignorance of her adoptive father's clandestine work and his determined efforts to protect her nearly lead her to run off with West Rosen and abandon her family ("Cautionary Tales"). Moreover, ignorance doesn't merely appear in *Heroes* as a means to evil; it appears as an evil itself in the form of the amnesia that the Haitian inflicts on people.

One might still argue, however, that *Heroes* proves Socrates wrong. In *Heroes*, knowledge is not sufficient for goodness. Those who run the Company seem in many ways evil, even though they possess a great deal of knowledge. Would Takezo Kensei have become the evil Adam Monroe if he didn't know about Hiro kissing Yaeko ("The Line")? And maybe ignorance isn't even necessary for evil. Sylar is generally conceived as evil, but Sylar's evil seems deeply tied to his ability to acquire knowledge about how things work. Even the gruesome way he murders his victims (slicing off their scalps and ransacking their brains) seems to symbolize that in the universe of *Heroes*, as it was in Adam and Eve's Garden, acting immorally and possessing knowledge are perfectly consistent.[4] And ignorance doesn't seem to be sufficient for evil, either. Both Molly Walker and Micah, despite the knowledge their powers yield, are largely ignorant, simply because as children there is much they do not know.

But perhaps this isn't the kind of knowledge and ignorance that Socrates had in mind. Socrates suggested that evil is always accompanied not simply by ignorance but by a specific kind of ignorance—moral ignorance, ignorance of what's right and wrong. With that in mind, *Heroes* seems to confirm Socrates' suggestion; those who do wrong in *Heroes* believe they are doing what is right. This is particularly clear when they try to justify their conduct. Angela Petrelli, for example, does not argue that she knows that blowing up New York City is morally wrong and that she is going to help bring it about, anyway. She argues that destroying New York City will result in something good, a "better future" ("The Hard Part"). Likewise, Bob Bishop argues so convincingly that the Company is morally good that he confounds even Mohinder. Nathan Petrelli, at the beginning of Volume 4, seems to think that rounding up his fellow heroes is a good thing ("A Clear and Present Danger"). Even Sylar seems to suggest that his actions are not wrong, that becoming something greater than an ordinary human being justifies breaking ordinary moral rules ("Six Months Ago").

Evil as Privation and Rebellion

Still, it doesn't seem enough to say that Sylar simply doesn't know any better. After all, Sylar seems to willfully acknowledge that his actions are wrong but does them anyway. Think of when he finally kills Elle Bishop in "The Eclipse: Part II." After making a change for the better and acknowledging that he is (as Hiro would say) a bad man, he goes back to being the way that he was, suggesting that "nobody ever really changes" and that he is "damaged goods." Thankfully, there are, however, other streams in philosophy that better explain Sylar's conduct. Instead of a kind of ignorance, perhaps evil is better understood as a form of rebellion. Along these lines, Augustine (354–430) observed that not only do people sometimes know what is morally wrong but do it anyway, they often do it *because* it is morally wrong.

There is reason, though, to interpret Sylar's conduct not exactly as rebellion but instead as weakness. Aristotle (384–322 BC) argued that even if one acquires moral knowledge and through it understands what is right and wrong, immoral conduct is still possible because of what he called *akrasia*.[5] In one of its forms, akratic conduct happens through "impetuous" acts. As when Hiro kissed Yaeko ("Out of Time"), people can be suddenly overwhelmed by impulse before they have had a chance to think. But even when people do have time to think, they can also suffer from what might be called simple akratic "moral weakness," unable to resist acting on their desires simply because those desires are

PETER S. FOSL

so powerful. Paris running off with Helen in the *Iliad* seems a fair example of this. So does Mohinder's injecting himself with Maya's adrenaline to give himself superpower, even knowing it may well be a bad idea ("The Butterfly Effect").

Sylar's suffering from *akrasia* is evident when his evil persona emerges. Recall what Mohinder and Eden discover scrawled across the walls of Sylar's Queens apartment ("One Giant Leap"). Hidden behind a tarpaulin, the two find messages like "Forgive me," "I have sinned," and "Damned" painted in blood. This suggests that on some level Sylar knew that what he was doing was morally wrong, even from the beginning. The haphazard arrangement of the messages suggests great inner torment—perhaps his moral knowledge tearing against his overwhelming drives. Covering the remarks indicates perhaps that he wishes to hide his moral knowledge not only from the rest of the world, but from himself. Covering rather than eliminating the words reveals a countervailing need to preserve the messages, as if to remind himself that as long as they exist, the moral dimensions of his persona have not disappeared.

This understanding of weakness is part of a larger tradition that considers evil a privation—a lack—of character. Traditionally, philosophers have conceived of virtue as a set of personal qualities or dispositions: habits of feeling and thinking. The proper tuning of these dispositions is characteristic of good and bad. Vice, by contrast, is characterized by an excess or deficiency of these dispositions: a privation of their proper tuning, harmony, and proportion.

Being "properly tuned" has often been described as being temperate, moderate, and self-possessed. Heroes like Sam Spade, John Wayne, and Sherlock Holmes are good examples. Sylar, by contrast, epitomizes someone out of tune. He lacks temperance and suffers from excessive, wild, and uncontrolled desires; he even admits to being controlled by his hunger for power.[6] Consider Sylar's uncontrolled rage against his adoptive mother, Virginia Gray, a twisted desire to punish her by becoming something greater in a grotesque and destructive way; consider, too, his pitiful self-hatred (he is always trying to become something he is not). Sylar flees from the ordinary, viciously and violently—such as when Noah Bennet, who sees clearly what he is, calls him Gabriel and reminds him that he is just an ordinary watch repairman ("Fallout").[7]

But, ironically, Sylar flees the ordinary because he has been denied the ordinary. He is not allowed to be, despite his wish to be, satisfied as one of us. Sylar's evil is not rooted in his desire to raise himself above others. Instead, Sylar's evil stems from his inability to be like others. Think again about the end of "The Eclipse; Part II." Sylar reveals to Bennet that he wants to be like him, a family man. When Bennet convinces Sylar that he never could be—he is not the Petrellis' son and he killed his potential wife's father, after all—Sylar turns back to being the way he was. Because he is not permitted to become a part of ordinary humanity, Sylar seeks furious revenge against it. Maybe he should be compared to Frankenstein's monster: a creature with superhuman powers who turned against people (and rebelled against his "parent") only after having been repeatedly rejected by them. Sylar continues this pattern in Volume 4, when he meets his real father in "Shades of Gray" and essentially leaves him for dead.

The Superhuman

Trying to understand Sylar through the lens of Frankenstein's monster, however, doesn't quite work. Action labeled "immoral" by virtues ethics usually results in a privation of humanness. To become virtuous, for Aristotle, is to become fully, perfectly human. In fact, the ancient Greek word for "virtue" was *aretē*, "excellence." Virtuous humans are extraordinary because they are extraordinarily and excellently human. But curiously, Sylar's evil seems to emerge when he evolves—or realizes he has evolved—into something more than human, something super-human. Sylar's powers (like those of the other heroes) are not the result of a technological accident (such as Spider-Man's). They are the next stage in natural human evolution, as the Sureshes would put it. Sylar struggles with his condition, there-fore, not as the result of social pathology or science run amok, but because he is trying to come to terms with his own develop-ing nature.

One might say, then, that identifying Sylar as an evil char-acter repudiates Friedrich Nietzsche's (1844–1900) moral vision of a coming superhuman, the Übermensch.[8] Nietzsche rejected the ideals of equality, self-sacrifice, nonviolence, and compassion, which he said had infected Western cul-ture since the dawning of Christianity and Platonic philoso-phy. In their place, Nietzsche wished to recover the sense of "good" and "bad" as they were used before. "Good," accord-ing to Nietzsche, was a word originally used to designate the strong and the capacities of the strong. To be good was to be stronger, better, superior. And goodness in this sense licensed a measure of cruelty over those who were weaker or who stood in the way of the expansion of strong people's power. The Greek hero Achilles, for example, by Christian-Platonic standards is an intemperate, selfish, vengeful, brutal man. But in pre-Christian-Platonic times, he was heroic because of his power. It gave him license to define good in his own terms. Beowulf, too, becomes heroic not through extraordinary knowledge or personality traits but instead through success-fully kicking butt. This is not to say that among those with a non-Christian-Platonic idea of goodness, victory is required to be a hero. In Norse mythology, the godlike warriors (Einherjar) of Valhalla become heroes despite being destined to defeat at the forces of evil at the battle of Ragnarok. And the three hundred Spartan soldiers who held off the Persian army at the pass of Thermopylae were seen as heroic as well, despite their ultimate defeat.

Today, a Nietzschean Übermensch would be someone who had overcome Christian-Platonic morality. He or she would be rejected by contemporary society and would live a relatively solitary existence. The Übermensch would not only possess moral freedom; this person's conduct would enhance his or her power (including biological power) and would prepare the next stage in cultural evolution. Similarly, Sylar, who preys on those weaker than him, assimilates their powers. This, at least in his own mind, has placed him beyond the claims of ordinary morality. His new moral philosophy makes it possible for him to expand his power, to become stronger and more powerfully alive. And, anyway, aren't ordinary people sort of like cattle or apes with regard to a being like Sylar? Why should we not regard Sylar as a heroic figure like Achilles who triumphs over all challengers and achieves greatness, despite what in ordinary people would be character flaws? Is it really right to judge this extraordinary being by the standards of ordinary morality? It might be harder than it looks to object to this line of reasoning. Today, we humans commonly justify our exploitation and consumption of other animals by our so-called superior powers and the fact that devouring these lesser beings nourishes us and expands our own power. Why shouldn't a superior being like Sylar do the same?

As if to preemptively rule out facing these very questions, our culture commonly requires both that heroes be like us (Clark Kent, Peter Parker) and not be like us (Superman, Spider-Man). Perhaps to reassure us that they won't establish dominion over us, we require them to remain somehow on equal terms with us. Perhaps this is part of the legacy of the most popular hero with a dual identity, Jesus of Nazareth. Although superheroes often possess sufficient power to take control of the world's governments, we prefer that they, like Hellboy, choose to work for humanity and remain on the side of the Abrahamic deity. Like Moses, they turn against the forces of evil in order to protect us; and like Hercules and Xena, they vanquish those who would do us harm with superior firepower or at least canny cleverness. But unlike Moses, today's heroes must, it seems, after their victories, be prepared to retire to their lairs, to tuck themselves away somewhere in an unthreatening place.

It may be an unsettling dimension of Hiro's character, then, that he finds it difficult to return to ordinary life after saving the world, twice. In "The Second Coming," we find him bored with the ordinary (even if for most people extraordinary) wealth and power that come with owning a large corporation. He selfishly tells us that he really cares only for finding his own personal destiny. (Why not use his powers to help the poor and suffering of the world or perhaps help others find their own destinies?) From where he now sits, to be ordinary is to be nobody. He is happy only being extraordinary.[9]

This is all a sort of psychological explanation for why we can't endorse the Sylar of Volume 2 as a hero and why Hiro has come to seem suspicious. But there's a philosophical reason, too. One of the privations that philosophers have regarded as evil is the loss of happiness. Although Sylar's conduct increases his own power, it does so at the cost of producing pain and depriving others of happiness. This is true of most *Heroes* villains. The evil of the conspirators planning to blow up New York City, for example, is evident in their willingness to inflict suffering on others in order to achieve their objectives.[10] Noah Bennet is figured as evil when he inflicts suffering on others or when he, like the Company, deprives people of the capacity for happiness. This sort of evil is most evident in his interaction with Ivan in the Ukraine ("The Line"). Erasing part of Ivan's memory clearly caused Ivan great unhappiness, and Bennet killing him also deprived him of the pleasure of seeing his granddaughter grow up. And "Level 5" villains presumably are evil because of the extraordinary suffering they have inflicted upon others.

Evil as Not Caring

The best explanation of evil on *Heroes* is the kind of immorality implied by what philosophers call an "ethics of care." In her 1982 book *In a Different Voice*, psychologist Carol Gilligan identified a distinctive type of moral deliberation that is characteristic of girls. Boys, she observed, tend to appeal to rules and principles in making moral judgments. She called their way of thinking the "ethics of justice."[11] Girls, she argued, tend instead to appeal in their deliberations to particular characteristics of the personal relationships in which they are involved. Girls' ways of thinking Gilligan dubbed the "ethics of care." Many have argued that men, too, should adopt ethics of care. So, from the point of view of an ethics of justice, it might be wrong for someone like Jean Valjean, the protagonist of *Les Misérables* (1862), to steal in order to feed his hungry family (because doing so breaks the rule that prohibits stealing). But from the point of view of an ethics of care, his theft might be perfectly proper.

Care, rather than justice, seems to be the driving force behind many of the moral decisions in *Heroes*. It is not a refusal to violate moral principle, various rights, promises, or duties that defines the heroes as heroes. Hiro's vigilante quest to kill Sylar and his deception in pretending to be Takezo Kensei are both examples of heroic (in the series' terms) violations of the ethics of justice. Bennet's illegal abduction and imprisonment of Sylar and other super-miscreants ("Fallout," "Blindsided"), as well as Matt Parkman's similar handling of his father, the Nightmare Man ("Out of Time"), are also portrayed as good, even though the heroes' conduct is contrary to many ethics of principle and duty.[12] Heroism in this sense seems clearly to operate outside the rule of law. One might say that love conquers all in Hollywood movies, but care signifies goodness in the universe of *Heroes*.

Correspondingly, the lack of care signifies evil. Peter's goodness is signaled by his chosen career as a hospice nurse. Angela's evil is evident in her willingness to incinerate millions of New

Yorkers, her ice-cold instructions to Matt to kill her son Peter if necessary ("Powerless"), as well as her chilling, emotionless acknowledgment that killing her other son, Nathan, is acceptable. Bob Bishop seems sinister not simply for the way he and his Company relentlessly hunt down, abduct, torture, coerce, manipulate, experiment on, vivisect, and control people.[13] His evil is also characterized by his cold and careless (ab)use of his daughter as an instrument of the Company's designs, despite the danger in which it places her or the effect it has on her character.[14] Sylar, the scythe of death, of course, fails to care for his adoptive mother, just as she apparently failed to care for him, and he seems utterly without the capacity to care about those he slays. Nightmare Man Maury Parkman seems particularly detestable for the lack of genuine care he exhibits for his son. By contrast, the goodness of Maury's son, Matt, is made evident in the care that Matt exhibits for young Molly in Volume 2 and Daphne Millbrook in Volume 3, and for the way that he took one look at his baby son (Toddler Touch and Go) in Volume 4 and fell in love.

Bennet presents perhaps the most fascinating case of a character torn across the complexities of care. He is nothing if not loyal, as Bishop remarks ("Cautionary Tales"). At first in the series Bennet is a cold-blooded and loyal tool of the Company—the only one, by the way, who is determined and resourceful enough to capture Sylar (despite not possessing any superpowers of his own). But once Bennet comes to care for Claire, his loyalties change, and, for the sake of protecting her, he finds it proper to break many rules of justice, including the rule that prohibits killing. Even his name signals his role as a good protector: the Bible's Noah protected the world's animals, and his last name, Bennet, echoes *bene*, the Latin word for "good" or "well." Noah's willingness to give up his livelihood and his position, his willingness to risk his life taking on the Company—one of the most powerful and dangerous institutions in the world—and perhaps most remarkably his willingness to sacrifice his memories and his life with Claire for the sake of protecting her are some of the most remarkable acts of heroic self-sacrifice in the series.

But in the language of virtues ethics, Bennet's concern for Claire and his family seems excessive. Moreover, in the language of feminist care ethics, Bennet's conduct, though in many ways admirable, also seems patriarchal and too narrowly circumscribed. He seems to go too far, killing Ivan, shooting Nathan, attempting to kill Bishop, threatening Mohinder (after Mohinder joins the Company)—the list could go on. His care for Claire and his family may be profound, but it manifests itself in authoritarian directives ("Claire, thou shalt have no boyfriend") and by his exercising nearly unlimited authority over his wife and children (dictating where they will live, as well as what memories they will have). Bennet not only— perhaps too eagerly—resorts to violence to accomplish his objectives, he also largely goes it alone, not working together with his wife, refusing to let Claire accompany him on his quest to find the Level 5 villains, and taking on Sylar as a partner only after being forced to do so (however, one can understand his reservations). Though perhaps in pursuit of Level 5 villains Bennet does seem to have expanded his circle of concern, his care for the most part seems restricted almost exclusively to his family and magnified to the point where in his view almost anything seems justifiable to protect them. Even in his project of capturing the Level 5 bunch, Bennet tells Claire that he's doing it so that she doesn't have to ("Butterfly Effect").

Bennet, then, may be a remarkable and caring hero, but he is also a decidedly flawed one. Of course, the challenges that comic-book heroes and villains confront represent the real-life problems that the world faces, and moral decisions that comic-book heroes confront regarding their superpowers symbolize our own struggles to make the right moral decisions in a frightening world. Almost certainly, the characters' difficulties in *Heroes* express the struggles with powerful corporations, diseases, and weapons of mass destruction that today's aging generations have left their offspring to inherit. The way the rising generation deals with the problems it inherits, then, will determine whether it earns heroic standing.

We can congratulate the rising generation of *Heroes*, for their trend of not choosing to use their powers for self-aggrandizement and dominion—as clearly many of the older generation of heroes have. The young heroes have undertaken to chart a course for a better world, not by recovering or restoring the values of tradition, the command of religious authorities, or the principles of justice and duty. They have instead looked to nothing beyond their capacity to care for one another to light their way as they confront the evils stalking the world and lurking within themselves.[15] At least, that is, until they re-formed the Company at the end of Volume 4. Have they ultimately fallen prey to the bad habits of the last generation? I'll let you decide.

NOTES

1. The character Glaucon in Plato's *Republic* tells the story of a young man named Gyges (gījēz) who acquires a superpower, the power to become invisible and to move about undetected. Now, unlike the characters in *Heroes*, Gyges' power has nothing to do with his biological constitution. He is no *X-Men*–type mutant. Like *Lord of the Rings*'s Frodo, Gyges acquires the power of invisibility from a ring—a ring he removes from the hand of a giant he discovers buried underground. *Heroes* repeats this moment in the Gyges-like scene of the episode "One Giant Leap," where Niki, as she discovers her own superpower, unearths the corpse of a large violent man and, yes, removes a ring from his hand. The title of the episode, too, slyly alludes to things gigantic. For more on Gyges, see chapter 7 of this book, "Plato on Gyges' Ring of Invisibility: The Power of Heroes and the Value of Virtue," by Don Adams.

2. Compare Plato, *Meno* 77–89b, *Crito* 49a–50a. This claim has come to be known among philosophers as the "Socratic Paradox." Xenophon also attributes it to Socrates, *Memorabilia* III.9.5; as does Aristotle, *Nicomachean Ethics* 1145b:26–27.

3. Though, of course, it is also possible that clever Mohinder may have enlisted the unwitting Company to help serve the ends of goodness. Perhaps Mohinder's heroism is—like that of Odysseus, the hero of the Homeric epic poem *The Odyssey*—grounded in his cleverness.

4. Although in the third volume it begins to appear as if Sylar does not actually cannibalize the brains of his victims, can we be so sure? In any case, the Genesis-oriented nomenclature raises the question of whether Adam Monroe is named Adam because he

is the first of the new superhumans. Does Hiro's kissing Adam's Eve, Yaeko, in a gardenlike orchard full of fruit trees signal the imminent fall of the first (super)man from goodness into sin? Is it significant that the first volume is called "Genesis," the book of the Bible containing the story of Adam and Eve, and not "Beginnings"? And is it significant that the strange heroes icon looks kind of like a serpent?

5. Aristotle, *Nicomachean Ethics*, VII, 1–10.

6. For more on why Plato would say this makes Sylar immoral, see chapter 7 of this book, "Plato on Gyges' Ring of Invisibility: The Power of Heroes and the Value of Virtue," by Don Adams.

7. Sylar's retort to Bennet is that he is "special" even among those with superpowers because he can acquire many powers—which, of course, pairs him against Peter.

8. The concept of the Übermensch is advanced in Nietzsche's famous anti-Scripture *Thus Spoke Zarathustra* (1883).

9. Mohinder, along similar lines in "The Second Coming," is delighted, despite Maya Herrera's protestations, at the prospect of transcending the ordinary through his discovery of how to give people superpowers. Nathan, too, is rapturous at the thought of being an angel and not merely a superman.

10. Indeed, that the series selects a young Japanese man to play a central role in preventing the detonation of a nuclearlike explosion in an American city can be interpreted as a repudiation of the U.S. justifications for incinerating Japanese cities in order to achieve a better world after World War II.

11. Compare Virginia Held, *Justice and Care: Essential Readings in Feminist Ethics* (Boulder, CO: Westview Press, 1995).

12. Matt Parkman tellingly distinguishes himself from his father, Maury, at the moment he imprisons the old fiend by declaring that he, Matt, is a better father than Maury will ever be. What counts here is not living up to principles (both he and his father act outside the law and imprison people in nightmares) but acting in a caring way. Indeed, Matt's and Mohinder's capacity for care is emphasized by their refusal to inject Maury with the virus ("Out of Time"). Matt's imprisoning, rather than infecting, his father, oddly then, is portrayed by the show as the caring option.

13. Bennet's conversation with Claude Rains in "Company Man," as they drive to the bridge where Bennet will attempt to kill Rains, suggests that the Company is involved even in acts as gruesome as vivisection.

14. Elle, as a result, seems to become a cold and even sadistic young woman, taking pleasure in the pain she inflicts on others. She also seems burdened by a frustrated longing for love and care from a father who will not deliver it. In "Powerless," Bennet tells Elle about the way Bishop treated her as a child: "They wanted to see how much wattage you could discharge; enough to power a flashlight, a street lamp, an entire city block? During testing, you would pass out from the strain. We all wanted to call it a day, but Daddy said, 'No, my girl's tougher than that.' You were seven."

15. I am grateful to my student Dustin Smyth for first bringing the connection between Plato and *Heroes* to my attention and to the rest of my senior seminar class of 2008 (Jon Hoffman, Zach Horn, Noel McKay, Eric Sidwell, and Thomas Wynne) for the many contributions they have made to this essay. I am also grateful to those who build, maintain, and contribute to HeroesWiki (http://heroeswiki.com) for the exceedingly helpful reference the site provided to me.

SEVENTEEN

HEROES AND FAMILY OBLIGATIONS

Ruth Tallman and Jason Southworth

Most people would say that *Heroes* is about powers or how to be a hero. But the series is also about a more fundamental issue: families and our moral obligations to our families. Most of the main characters in the series do not act in isolation but rather under the influence of, in reaction to, and out of consideration for their families. There are several moral theories that seek to explain the nature of family obligations—the ethics of universal justice, care ethics, and Confucian ethics are three of them. The sometimes seemingly incomprehensible actions of our heroes can be understood in terms of these moral viewpoints.

Universal Justice

According to the ethics of universal justice, we should not treat members of our family any differently from how we would anyone else; to give our family members special treatment would be unjust. To illustrate this, consider a conversation Socrates once had with a man named Euthyphro, who brought legal charges against his father for the murder of one of his family's servants. Socrates expressed astonishment that Euthyphro could do such a thing in good conscience. But Euthyphro was confident in his action, saying, "It is ridiculous . . . to think that it makes any difference whether the victim is a stranger or a relative. One should only watch whether the killer acted justly or not; if he acted justly, let him go, but if not, one should prosecute."[1] Socrates pressed Euthyphro, wondering how he could be sure he was doing the right thing by betraying his father in this way. Euthyphro continued to maintain that it is always right to prosecute lawbreakers, regardless of their relationship to you.

The Ethics of Care

Clearly, Euthyphro accepted the ethics of universal justice, but should he have? Shouldn't we favor and protect our family members, even when they have done something wrong? Shouldn't we shelter our family from the law, if we can? Don't we have higher duties to family than to the greater good of our nation or humanity? Advocates of care ethics would answer these questions differently from how Euthyphro did. Care ethics, which was developed by feminists in response to the ethics of universal justice, holds that our duties and obligations are strongest for those we care about most. So, it is morally right to be partial to your loved ones over strangers.

How partial should we be? Some care ethicists think we should be like Jessica (Niki Sanders's evil alter ego), who makes the well-being of her son, Micah, the person she cares most about, her *only* concern. But because this would justify things like Jessica's haphazard murder ("Genesis") and blackmail ("Collision"), most care ethicists think that the well-being of strangers should also be considered in our ethical decisions, although to a lesser degree. They think we should be like Niki, who will protect Micah at high cost, but not at any cost. Because she is likely to kill (many) again, she has herself locked up, even though it means she can't protect Micah.

Confucianism

For China's leading philosopher, Confucius (551–479 BC), morality is dictated by the roles people play. There are five primary relationship types, and each has certain duties and obligations. Most important for our family interest in *Heroes* are three of these relationships: parent-child, husband-wife, and older sibling-younger sibling.[2] Each relationship is reciprocal but not identical. A parent has duties and obligations to her child, and the child has duties and obligations to his parent, but they differ depending on the role. The child, for instance, owes the parent obedience, which the parent does not owe back, but the parent owes the child education and moral guidance, which the child does not owe back. Confucius captured the spirit of this relationship in Book Four of the *Analects*: "In serving your parents you may gently remonstrate with them. However, once it becomes apparent that they have not taken your criticism to heart you should be respectful and not oppose them, and follow their lead diligently without resentment."[3]

Likewise, in Confucianism, the obligations of spouses are asymmetrical. Husbands owe their wives protection and are responsible for making decisions for the family. Wives owe their husbands obedience and day-to-day creature care, such as the provision and maintenance of a comfortable home. Although Mrs. Suresh and Sandra Bennet probably have not read much Chinese philosophy, they both fit a Confucian model, understanding their moral duties in terms of their roles as wives. Mrs. Suresh supported and even encouraged Chandra in his decision to leave her and Mohinder behind to pursue his research in America. Sandra allows herself to remain blind to Noah's many deceptions, accepting his edicts, no matter how unreasonable they seem. She obeys, without question, simply because the orders are issued by her husband, the head of her household. Sandra also expects and depends on Noah's protection. She remains unworried in the face of danger, resting calmly in the notion that her husband will fulfill his role and keep her and their children safe from harm. Sandra's peace of mind shows us why the subservient role can actually be attractive for some people. Sandra must obey her husband, it is true, but in exchange for obedience, she is relieved of many responsibilities that Noah willingly shoulders. (Of course, it couldn't have been that great. She eventually left him.)

Confucius had very specific duties in mind when he wrote about human relationships. One need not adopt these specific duties to be considered to have a Confucian view of the family. To be Confucian in this way is simply to believe that one's duties and obligations depend on the roles one holds. Confucian duties and obligations are not determined by an impartial concern for humanity, nor (in contrast with care ethics) are they determined by feelings or affections one happens to have. (Although one might also have these feelings, for the Confucian, it is the role, not the affection, that is the motivation for action.) Furthermore, one need not be a Confucian in other aspects of life (religious practices, for example) in order to adopt a Confucian stance regarding family obligations.

Now that we are acquainted with some theories of family obligation, we can take a look at the families that populate the world of *Heroes*. We can determine which moral code the various characters seem to be adopting, and this in turn will help us understand their behavior and the conflicts that sometimes arise between family members (due to conflicting moral codes).

The Bennets

Noah Bennet has spent much of his life working for what he sees as the greater good: hunting down people with powers, studying them, and helping to determine whether they pose threats to society. He acknowledges that he has ordered and done terrible things, but he rests easy in the belief that all of these actions have been performed in the name of the greater good. Noah clearly lines up with an ethics of universal justice, priding himself on his ability to do tough things that need to be done—things from which weaker men would shrink.

Noah's resolve and priorities take an unexpected turn, however, when it comes to Claire. Noah recognizes one clear set of rules for powered people in general but uses a separate set of rules for his adopted daughter. Noah's actions in a time of crisis show that his commitments, though divided, are ultimately Confucian. These actions put Noah at great risk (one plan of his to save Claire actually involves his being shot and injured) and also jeopardize others who are involved. Noah goes rogue against a company to which he has devoted most of his life, in order to give Claire the best chance at safety. In Volume 4, he agrees to help the government track down the gifted only to ensure that Claire gets a "free pass" ("Cold Wars"). He sees his role as Claire's father and protector to be more important than his role as protector of humanity. Keep in mind his constant response to Claire—"I'm your father, Claire Bear." Though he clearly loves and cares for her, his sense of duty arises primarily from his understanding of the role of a father.

Claire is a teenager when the series begins and does not yet seem to have a fully formed ethical code. As Claire's character develops, we see her struggling with a sense of conflicting obligations. She clearly feels ties of both love and duty to her adoptive family, but she also has a deep desire to meet her biological parents. She feels an instant connection with her biological uncle,

Peter Petrelli. And, despite Nathan Petrelli's apparent indifference and discomfort, Claire struggles to develop some sort of relationship with her biological father.

Claire's sense of obligation toward her adoptive family, the Bennets, is best understood in terms of care ethics, because the basis of her actions toward them stems from affection, rather than from preordained roles. But her drive to connect with and help members of the Petrelli family is more Confucian. She wants to learn more about her biological family simply because they are her family.

Despite these conflicting pulls toward two families, Claire also begins to develop a sense of universal justice. Influenced by her uncle Peter, Claire disobeys the (conflicting) wishes of both her adoptive father, Noah, and her biological grandmother, Angela, to join the band of heroes seeking to save and better the world. And we see Claire do the same type of thing—disobeying instructions intended to keep her safe to go off and help save the world—throughout the series. Seeing Claire as having competing intuitions about the way we ought to treat our families makes sense of her claims of helplessness and her confusion about how she ought to act.

The Petrellis

Nathan Petrelli talks as if he is a Confucian. Consider the many occasions when he gives his brother, Peter, advice. During these interactions, Nathan tells Peter that he needs to "think about the family" ("Don't Look Back"). Nathan implies that Peter is putting himself before the rest of the family. But if we analyze Nathan's actions, we see that he is not practicing what he preaches. Nathan appears to be acting based on an egoistic ethical system, in which his own goals are primary. He wants Peter to conceal his powers and appear normal for the sake of Nathan's political campaign. Nathan does not see his brother as a family member to be helped and supported, but rather as an embarrassment to be covered up. So, He doesn't fall under any of our views of family obligation. He is usually an egoist—he thinks the family and everything else should work to his own personal ends.[4]

Peter, on the other hand, acts according to the ethics of universal justice. Although he understands that his brother's political campaign is important to Nathan personally, Peter sees saving the world as obviously more important than Nathan's winning an election. This is why, contrary to his brother's advice, Peter continues to try to learn more about his power, and why he ultimately decides to go to Texas to "save the cheerleader." This is also why Peter is bound and determined to kill his own father: "The world isn't safe with my father in it" ("Our Father"). In Volume 4, Peter gladly refrains from supporting his brother's efforts to round up the gifted, believing that Nathan is wrong. The source of the Petrelli brothers' conflict, then, stems from their differing ethical starting points.

The tension in the relationship between Claire and Nathan also hinges on their different understandings of the value (and definition) of family. The Confucian in Claire feels that she must look to her biological father for guidance and that he owes her his concern and protection. It also makes her feel let down when Nathan refuses to acknowledge any sort of duty to her as his daughter. Although there cannot be much, if any, true affection between a father and a daughter who don't even know each other, Claire places importance on the role that Nathan simply does not see. This is further evidence that Nathan is not a Confucian, despite his outward rhetoric. Nathan views Claire as he viewed Peter, as an embarrassment to be hidden, rather than a daughter to be protected.

The Petrelli parents are another matter. The flashbacks to Angela's childhood show us that Angela, although she cares deeply for her family, has given universal justice top priority. She left her sister behind at the prison camp when she and the others escaped. Angela could have gone back to look for her sister, but she chose not to, because she did not want to risk compromising her larger project. Angela has continually compromised her sons and pitted them against each other in an effort to achieve her primary goal. She even told Matt Parkman to kill Peter if necessary at the end of Volume 3. It is clear that Angela loves Peter, so her willingness to sanction his death shows that she gives priority to the good of the world even if it means personal pain. Still, Angela protects and nurtures her family whenever she can. She seems to hold the position that you ought to care for your family whenever you can do so without compromising universal justice.

Arthur's motives, on the other hand, seem to be far less noble. He too is willing to sacrifice much to achieve his goals, but rather than saving the world Arthur wants to rule it, and he will sacrifice those who stand in his way. He deceives his family into believing he is dead, indicating that he perceives his own interests as separate from theirs, in choosing to work apart from them to get what he wants, rather than including them in his plan—despite what he says and thinks in the graphic novel chapter "Truths." His disregard for human life (he kills Adam Monroe and countless others, needlessly), and even the life of his family (he comes very close to killing Peter, and seems quite willing to do so), indicates that Arthur is an extreme egoist who will manipulate and feign caring to get what he desires.

The Nakamuras

Hiro Nakamura has been raised to believe that his proper role is to work for his father, Kaito, and eventually take his father's place as the head of his company. On discovering his powers, however, Hiro leaves his family, his father's company, and his country, to serve the greater good. Although his father urges him to return home and take up his place within the family, Hiro resists. The family may have needs, he acknowledges, but the needs of the world and his ability to do more good as a hero than he could do working for the family business lead him to refuse his father's request to return home. Hiro acts in accord with the ethics of universal justice, defying his father's Confucianism.

Kaito Nakamura acts like a Confucian who values traditional roles. He looks past his oldest child, Kimiko, due to her gender, and expects his son to take over the business. Motivated by care ethics, Kimiko acts out of love and is hurt that Kaito seems not to notice her competence and devotion to him and to the company. Unmoved by Confucian considerations, Hiro sees no problem with a daughter serving in a role traditionally reserved for a son and encourages Kaito to make Kimiko the head of the Company. Overjoyed at being put in charge of the company, Kimiko hugs Hiro—a sign of caring, rather than any particular principle or duty; she acts from emotion and affection. Hiro's smile and shrugging response are characteristic, of both his personality and his ethics of universal justice. He does not respond to Kimiko with any particular affection (not any more than we have seen him show complete strangers). He seems to have helped Kimiko—not out of love or because of his role, but rather out of his sense that it is the right thing to do; it is for the greater good.

Hiro learned of the legendary Takezo Kensei from childhood stories told by his Confucian father, who understood himself to be in the role of moral teacher to his son. Years later, Kaito acts as a guide to his son, teaching him how to use his sword and thus equipping him with the tools he needs to embark on his heroic journey. Kaito does this because his son needs the instruction, and there is nobody else to fill the role of teacher. Even though he disagrees with the goals Hiro has set for himself, Kaito still gives him the instruction to protect him, because that is the duty of a good father ("Landslide").

Rounding out the family is Hiro's mother, Ishi. We don't know a lot about her, but she does seem to adopt an ethics of care. In "Our Father," despite Kaito's objection to Hiro's qualifications for carrying the catalyst (aka "the light")—based on Hiro's obsession with video games and comic books—Ishi wants to give it to Hiro. Thus, she seems to favor her family over the common good. (After all, despite Hiro's assurance that he can protect the catalyst, it takes Hiro about five minutes to let Arthur steal it.) And, again, it is the different ethical starting points—in this case, Confucianism versus an ethics of care—that causes the conflict between Kaito and Ishi.

Hawkins and Sanders

The members of the Hawkins-Sanders family come into conflict because Niki is motivated by an ethics of care, but Micah and D.L. are Confucian. For Niki, consideration for the person she loves most, Micah, takes primacy over concerns for the preservation of the family and family roles. When she sees her husband as a threat to Micah's well-being, she has no problem cutting him off. D.L., on the other hand, acts like a Confucian, emphasizing the importance of keeping the family together and believing that it is his duty to provide for the family, and his failure to do this thus causes him extreme distress ("Better Halves"). Even when D.L. is in jail, Micah considers him a source of protection for himself and Niki. Micah understands his father to be a person who will be there for him, even when this seems unlikely. Even after it is clear to Micah and D.L. that Niki (or rather, Jessica) has committed terrible acts of violence, Micah wants to be with her and wants to help her, simply because she is his mother. Keeping the family together in its traditional form is very important to Micah; that's why, while on the run, he disobeys D.L.'s explicit instructions and calls his mother ("Nothing to Hide").

When D.L. visits Niki in jail (after she has herself arrested so that her alter ego, Jessica, will also be incarcerated), we get a clear picture of the difference between Confucian and care obligations. The Confucian D.L. pleads with Niki to allow him to help her escape, out of concern for Micah. Although the child is in his custody, D.L. insists that Micah needs his mother.

He tells her that he can't take care of Micah on his own because he cannot fulfill the role of Micah's mother. Niki, on the other hand, argues that the important thing is not that Micah be with his mother and father, but that he be with someone who cares about him and can protect him. Because she cannot control Jessica, Niki feels that it is better for Micah to be without his mother ("The Fix").

In Niki's death, we see how far she will take her ethics of care. Unlike Micah and his cousin Monica, who feel a deep pull toward the greater good, Niki's concerns are very localized. She gives her life not to save the many, but to save one, whom she cares for deeply. It could appear that Niki made a mistake in giving her life, because that sacrifice meant Micah was left parentless. However, Niki had already made arrangements for Micah in settling him in with his paternal family, so Niki's death did not mean he would be alone in the world.

The Sureshes

Chandra Suresh acts in accord with an ethics of universal justice when he leaves his family behind in India in order to pursue his research in New York City. Chandra sacrifices a day-to-day relationship with his wife and son (a small group, which he might be inclined to prefer) in the name of scientific research, which will benefit a much larger group: the world's population. Unlike his father, who sacrificed duty to family in order to promote the greater good, Mohinder Suresh demonstrates a solid Confucian commitment to his role as son. Although he might argue that powered people in general have duties to use their abilities for the greater good, Mohinder seems to see his duty as a nonpowered person to be directly related to his role as Chandra's son. After his father's death, Mohinder recognizes a strong moral duty to continue the work that his father has started. He also seems driven by a duty to his dead sister—to work to help others live. This displaced feeling of duty probably contributes to Mohinder's decision to take part in raising Molly Walker with Matt Parkman. Although Shanti was actually his older sister, she remains in Mohinder's eyes the five-year-old child she was at her death. Mohinder's attachment to Molly represents his second chance to successfully fulfill the sibling role that he missed with Shanti.

The Parkmans

Janice Parkman is another follower of the ethics of care view. Although she does seem to value family and her considerations are very localized, Janice does not appear to place particular value on her role as wife but rather sees her duties as based on the particular relationship she has with Matt. Thus, when that relationship becomes unstable, and she feels that Matt does not care for her, she sees adultery as justified ("Nothing to Hide"). The reason for this is that obligations arise and dissolve based on the level of care, rather than on roles.

Matt appears to experience moral growth and development throughout the series. When we are first introduced to the character, Matt simply acts and reacts, without reflection. He uses his powers to help, but he also uses them to get himself out of trouble and to make himself look good. He seems to think in terms not of right and wrong, but of getting in and out of trouble. As Volume 1 progresses, however, Matt begins to develop morally. He does not adopt a Confucian ethic or an ethics of care; if he did, he would have taken care of his pregnant wife, instead of gallivanting around the country trying to save the world at the end of Volume 1. (Despite Janice's affair, Matt is still her husband and still cares for her and his child.) Rather, he understands his powers in terms of an ethics of universal justice; the world's safety is more important than his family.

By Volume 2, however, Matt's moral code seems to have evolved into an ethics of care. He is part of a strange modern family, composed not of members holding traditional Confucian roles, but, rather, of people who simply care for one another. He and Mohinder, though not lovers, have joined together to act as parent figures for Molly, whose family was killed by Sylar. Matt now sees keeping Molly safe as his highest priority, trumping his earlier feelings of obligation to humanity in general. His previous sense of duty to Janice has faded along with his love for her, to be replaced by new care-based commitments. This trend even continues in Volume 3 when he meets Daphne Millbrook in "Dying of the Light." After receiving a vision of the future that depicts him and Daphne as married with children, his devotion to her is unwavering, while he tries to convince her not to be a villain and even comforts her when she loses her powers ("The Eclipse: Part I"). Matt's devotion to Daphne continues until she dies, but it is immediately replaced by a devotion to his newly found son (Toddler Touch and Go) and making his relationship with his ex-wife, Janice, work.

"Collision"

Ultimately, the three views of family obligations are not independent theories. Many people mix them. The Haitian is a great example. He is willing to kill his own brother, Baron, because Baron is a villain. When Baron pleads with him, "Don't do this. You still love me. I'm still your brother," the Haitian replies, "That has no power over me" ("The Eclipse: Part II"). Here, the Haitian explicitly ignores an ethics of care and endorses an ethics of universal justice. And yet he views it as his role to stop Baron *because* he is his brother; the Haitian won't let anyone else do it—it is his role. So, he seems to also endorse some kind of Confucian ethics.

How do you treat the members of your own family? Is your behavior consistent? Do conflicts arise because the members of your family subscribe to different ethical codes? Or perhaps problems arise because you and your family members aren't consistent—accepting one code in one situation and switching codes in the next. (How dare they!) What code do you accept? Do you have good reason to? Are you consistent? (You should be!) These are all questions worth considering. Just as they helped us understand the families of *Heroes*, answering these questions will help you understand yourself and your family better—it might even help prevent or resolve conflicts.

NOTES

1. Plato, *Euthyphro*, translated by G. M. A. Grube, in *Plato: Complete Works*, edited by John M. Cooper (Indianapolis, IN: Hackett, 1997), p. 4.

2. Confucius lived in a patriarchal society and was primarily concerned with male-male relationships (except for husband-wife). In this chapter, we discuss the relationships in a gender-neutral way, because today we no longer accept a male-biased way of thinking about relationships.

3. Confucius, *Analects*, translated by Edward Slingerland (Indianapolis, IN: Hackett, 2003), p. 35.

4. Nathan does have a bit of a change of heart, at the end of Volume 3, when he sides with his father, Arthur, and Pinehearst, but he does so not because Arthur is his father but because he believes it will accomplish the greater good ("The Eclipse: Part II"). However, in Volume 4, as Nathan uses the government to track down the gifted, he does often show favoritism toward his brother.

5. She tells Matt (via his mind-reading power) to kill Peter, if necessary, in "Powerless."

EIGHTEEN

CONCEALMENT AND LYING: IS THAT ANY WAY FOR A HERO TO ACT?

Michael R. Berry

Truth, justice, and the American way. That is what Superman fought for. I won't comment on the "justice and the American way" part, but he was pretty lousy at fighting for truth. He lied all the time! He lied to Lana Lang about his abilities during high school, he lies to trick criminals (consider the end of *Superman II*), and (as Clark Kent) he lies to everyone about being Superman. Ironically, lying is an important part of a hero's life, and the heroes of *Heroes* are no different. In Volume 1, Peter Petrelli lies about being able to fly so that he won't ruin his brother's chances at getting elected. Claire Bennet lies about her abilities because she is afraid she will get carted off if anyone finds out. Parkman lies about being able to read minds, to get confessions out of people and get promoted. Noah Bennet, for a time, lies to his entire family about (basically) his entire life—they think he works at a paper factory, for crying out loud. Angela Petrelli lies to Sylar about being his mother in order to manipulate him and get him to do her dirty work. But isn't lying wrong? How can our heroes lie repeatedly and still be heroes?

What Is Lying?

To answer our question, we need to know exactly what a lie is. Although the answer may seem simple, things never are. You might think a good definition for *lie* would simply be "an untrue statement," but this doesn't work. For one thing, if what you say isn't true, but you *think* it is, we can hardly say that you are lying—you are merely mistaken. In "Four Months Later . . . ," Angela tells Nathan that Peter is dead, when in fact he isn't. Even though she is wrong, because she thinks Peter is dead, we can't say that she was lying. Second, if you think that what you say is false and you say it to make someone believe it, but it turns out to be in fact true, well, you're still a liar (just a stupid one).

You might think that lying should be defined as "deception." To deceive someone is to make that person believe something that you don't think is true. But you can do this without lying. The Haitian deceives the Bennets by wiping their memories (repeatedly) so that they think that Noah is a normal family man, when he is anything but. Clearly, the Haitian deceives them, but we can't say that he *lies* to them—he doesn't even talk to them. This teaches us a couple of things. For one, a lie is something that is communicated. If you can't communicate, you can't lie. Second, you can deceive without lying. If you are not the Haitian, you can deceive without lying by simply being silent (when doing so conveys a false message). Nathan does this, for example, when Peter first mentions flying. Nathan neglects to mention that he can fly, leading Peter to believe that he can't. Another good example is when Hiro pretends to kill Ando to impress Knox (Benjamin "Knox" Washington) and Daphne Millbrook, proving himself a badass ("Angels and Monsters").

Hiro goes back in time to give Ando a fake blood pack and himself a retractable sword to make it look as if he killed Ando, when he didn't ("Dying of the Light"). Clearly, Hiro is deceptive, but because he never says, "I killed Ando," although he hasn't, he doesn't lie. So lying is a *kind* of deception but not the only kind.

Contemporary philosopher Sissela Bok said that a lie is "any intentionally deceptive message which is stated."[1] But this might not be right, either. In 2008, when Sarah Palin accepted the Republican nomination for vice president, she said, "I told Congress, 'Thanks but no thanks,' on that bridge to nowhere [bill]," but she failed to mention that she had supported the bill before she opposed it, and she still took the money proposed by the bill and spent it on other projects.[2] This was clearly an intentionally deceptive message—she wanted you to think that she had opposed the bill from the start and had saved money by doing so—but it wasn't technically a lie. Just as you used to do with your mother when you came home too late on Saturday night, Sarah Palin simply left a few things out.

So, perhaps we should say that one lies when one says something that one believes is false with the intention of deceiving others. A perfect example of lying occurs in "Truth and Consequences" when Bob Bishop tells the Bennets that Noah is dead and that Bishop had him cremated, even though Bishop knows full well that Noah is alive and in captivity.

You'll often hear people use this as an excuse: "I didn't lie; I just didn't tell the whole truth." Although often technically true, this doesn't get you off the moral hook. If lying is morally wrong, it is because deception is morally wrong. Pointing out that you engaged in another kind of deception (leaving out information) is just as bad. But the question remains: are deception, in general, and lying, in particular, morally wrong?

Kant and Lying

The philosopher Immanuel Kant (1724–1804) thought that lying was always wrong, regardless of circumstances and consequences. Kant said that for any given action (including a lie), one can determine its moral worth with the *categorical imperative* "Act only according to that maxim whereby you can at the same time will that it should become a universal law."[3] What would it mean to be able to "will that something should become a universal law"? Think of it this way. If everyone doing something led to a contradiction—if everyone doing it meant that no one could do it—then you can't will that it should become a universal law. Take killing, for example. If everyone did it, then everyone would be dead, and then no one could kill anymore. You cannot will that it be a universal law.

Kant thought that lying is immoral because one cannot will it to become a universal law. Lying is a form of communication, but communication requires trust between the participants. If I think that what is coming out of your mouth is untrue, you do not communicate anything to me. And if everyone lied all the time, no one would trust what anyone said and thus no one could communicate; and if no one could communicate, no one could lie. You can't will lying to be a universal law. This, Kant said, is why lying is immoral.

But objections to Kant are plentiful. Suppose that Sylar comes to you asking where your friend is, so that Sylar can kill him and take his power. Sylar forces you to answer, threatening the death of another person if you don't. You know your friend is down the hall, defenseless, but you could lie to Sylar and tell him that your friend is downstairs—where (you happen to know) Noah and a host of others are waiting and ready to capture him. What should you do? Kant considered a similar situation and suggested that you should *not* lie—you are morally bound to tell the truth, regardless of the consequences. By not lying, you will not be guilty of your friend's death, Kant argued; it's not your fault that the *truth* will lead to your friend's death—you simply have the obligation to tell the truth, regardless of the consequences.[4] But this is just ridiculous. If you can save your friend's life and get Sylar captured by doing something as simple as lying to Sylar, you should. Your friend's life and preventing Sylar from killing others are more important than not telling a lie. Kant was clearly misguided. Lying is not always wrong.

What's Wrong with a Little White Lie?

It seems that the reason it is okay to lie to save your friend's life but not (for example) to get a promotion is because the consequences of the first lie are good and the consequences of the second lie are bad—someone else may have earned that promotion. "Little white lies" are usually deemed morally permissible because their consequences are small and inconsequential. In "Hiros," when Hiro tells Nathan he is pleased to meet him, and Nathan says—obviously annoyed at Hiro's enthusiasm—"Thank you," I doubt that Nathan is truly thankful. But his lie is hardly immoral.

The bigger that lies get—the greater their consequences are—the morally worse they seem. Think of Jackie (Claire's fellow cheerleader from Volume 1) taking credit for Claire's heroic action of rescuing the fireman from the burning train ("Don't Look Back"). Usually, we think the greater the harm done by the lie, the morally worse the lie is. In fact, if you don't think little white lies are okay, it is usually because you think that they force one to tell bigger and bigger lies to cover them up, and the consequences become much larger. (This has been the plot of one too many sit-coms.)

What harm can a lie do? The harmful outcomes of lying are most noticeable in the person who is the target of the lie; the extent of the damage depends on whether the lie is discovered. If it is, the target may lose the ability to trust others, negatively affecting his or her ability to function in society—we have to trust someone. In addition, the target's integrity may be compromised. We value our freedom, but our freedom is compromised if we don't know the truth—we can't make informed decisions. Also, the one lied to may feel manipulated and used. Even the liar is affected; this person becomes corrupt, thinking that he or she can get away with lying again and again.

Utilitarianism is the philosophical theory that the morality of an action is determined by its consequences, specifically by how much happiness or pain it produces. If an action produces, overall, more happiness than pain, then it is good; if it produces more pain than happiness, then it is bad. When applied to lying, this would seem to square with our intuition that the more harm a lie does, the worse it is.

At first, utility might seem to get us what we want: an answer to why and when lying is wrong. If a lie does no harm, then the lie is not immoral. In fact, if a lie does good, it is actually morally praiseworthy. And this seems right, given what we said about Kant. It's okay to lie to save your friend's life, but not okay to lie to get a promotion. So when Victoria Pratt, the woman who invented the Shanti virus, lies to Peter and Adam about the location of the last remaining vial of the virus, she is morally right to do so. The lie is justified because the truthful disclosure of the lab's location will result in Adam's releasing a plague that will cause 93.7 percent of Earth's human population to die ("Truth and Consequences"). The lie, though perhaps a little evil, results in a greater evil being eliminated. The end (saving the world) justifies the means (the lie).

But there is a problem with this, as intuitive as it might seem. Using utility to define morality is difficult. To know whether a lie is good or bad, we would have to know all of the consequences associated with it, but that seems impossible.

In addition, it seems that utility can be used to justify outrageous lies. Plato (429–347 BC) proposed such a lie; he called it the "noble lie."[5] The society that Plato described in the *Republic* has three classes: the rulers, the warriors, and the workers. It functions correctly only when each class does its job, but Plato was afraid that some people would be dissatisfied with their position in society and the means by which they acquired that status (through government-run testing, training, and education), and they might rebel. To prevent this, he proposed telling the citizens that their testing, training, and education were a dream—a dream they had while they were being fashioned in the earth before being spat out, ready to go. This would cause them not only to be satisfied with their testing, training, and education, but to defend their land as their mother and consider all of their fellow citizens their "earthborn brothers." In addition, to prevent discontent regarding social class, citizens would be told that while being fashioned in the earth, the god who made them instilled metals within them to determine their social classes: gold in the rulers, silver in the warriors, and iron and brass in the workers. The noble lie, although a lie, keeps society running smoothly—Plato thought that the ends justified the means. But it's not clear that it does.

This is not unlike the Company's reasoning, and Linderman's in particular when he suggests that it is acceptable to sacrifice .07 percent of the world's population (by allowing New York City to be blown up). The sacrifice would benefit the world population as a whole, by unifying it under fear of people with superpowers (".07 %"). Even if the explosion would do less harm than good, it clearly isn't justified. The same is true of Nathan's plan to round up everyone with powers for the greater good. The ends do not always justify the means. So, although it may be clear that some lies, if they do good, are morally acceptable, this is not always the case. Ultimately, utility is an inadequate way to determine why lying is wrong.

Machiavelli

In *The Prince*, Nicolò Machiavelli (1469–1527) argued that a prince or a ruler is allowed to use any means that is necessary to ensure the continued smooth operation of his reign. Lying, therefore, is among the tools in the prince's arsenal to maintain power.[6] The prince does not weigh all of the consequences of lying, as the utilitarian does. He examines only the potential benefits and costs *for his rule (for him)*; the costs to the public at large are ignored.

It is easy to think this means that Machiavelli thought that a ruler can simply lie when, how, whenever, and about whatever he wants, but this is not the case. To make sure that his lying works to his favor, the prince must be very judicious when doing so. The credibility of the prince is important. If the image of the prince is that of a liar, then no one will believe his lies, and the lies will do him no good. But if the ruler can lie and get away with it and do himself good—Machiavelli said that this is morally justified.

Machiavelli's philosophy is played out by "President Sylar" in "Five Years Gone." Recall that Sylar takes on Nathan Petrelli's image. (Nathan was president, but Sylar killed him and took his place.) The only way to achieve the power that he craves is through lying. The effectiveness of this lying is further enhanced by the layering of the lie with his duplication of Nathan's appearance and mannerisms. Sylar takes Nathan's good character and uses it to achieve great power—just as Machiavelli suggested.

Critics have indicted the theory as being next to useless. First, most of us aren't rulers, so this theory isn't helpful for figuring out if and when we should lie. Second, when a ruler lies like this, trust is destroyed, relationships are damaged, and the targeted population's freedom of choice is severely compromised. This seems to make it wrong. Another complication is that most lies are eventually discovered, and this can have long-lasting consequences. For example, Angela Petrelli maintains power for her husband, Arthur, with the lie that his attempts at suicide were heart attacks ("Don't Look Back"). When she has to confess her lies to her son Peter because of her concern that Peter may also be suicidal, Peter immediately distrusts her. In the same way, President Richard Nixon believed that he was protecting the public by lying, but eventually the work of Bob Woodward and Carl Bernstein led to his ouster from office. And who can forget Angela's (and Arthur's) Volume 3 lie to Sylar about his parentage? Sylar's discovering the truth not only led to Arthur's death, but made Sylar worse than ever.

The Presumption against Lying

Bok argued that there is a general presumption against lying and that truthful statements are to be preferred in the absence of special considerations.[7] Telling the truth does not need a defense, but lying will always require an explanation. Bok suggested the following process to determine the moral acceptance of a lie.

First, the lie should be told only in circumstances in which truthful alternatives are inadequate. If a lie and a truthful statement can achieve the same end, then a person is obligated to tell the truth. Second, the significance of the context of the lie must be understood. If the context is Sylar asking where your friend is so that Sylar can kill him, you can lie. Third, one must weigh the potential good and evil that the lie will generate. Again, this will allow good ends to justify the means. Fourth, one has to construct arguments for and against the particular act. Engaging in a two-sided argument leads to a more deliberative process that may cause the person to reconsider his or her action. Fifth, special consideration must be given to how the lie will affect the general principle of veracity. A liar must consider whether the lie will become a tipping point against the general presumption against lying. Finally, after having provided satisfactory answers to these reservations, the liar must test the answers in the court of public opinion. Bok asserted that the liar must consult an audience of both peers and persons who have a different outlook to determine whether the lie is justified.

The Bok approach seems reasonable because this process would allow some of our lies to be justified but would exclude most of them. Many of us probably go through a similar process when we consider whether to lie—especially if we believe the lie to have important ramifications. We generally consider the context of our potential lie, the good and bad impacts the lie might have, and the resulting view that others might have of us. What separates Bok's test from what most of us normally do is the presumption against lying embedded in the first consideration and the prior consultation of peers in seeking the approval to lie. This systematic cognitive processing of the act of lying should prevent most of us from lying in the vast majority of cases.

In principle, Bok's approach is reasonable, but a closer examination reveals some significant problems. First, unless you are Hiro and can freeze time, you will not have the opportunity to go through all of these steps and provide the kind of detailed, thoughtful answers that Bok seems to require. Second, human beings will engage in self-deception to achieve their ends. A person who is considering lying will inevitably tilt the information to fit into his or her worldview. If Jackie, the cheerleader, had considered the good and evil that might result from her lie, she would likely conclude that the good outweighed the bad. No one would get hurt (no evil), and she would look like an altruistic person, which would not only benefit herself but would also reflect well on the cheerleading squad as a whole. If she sought the approval of her peers, as Bok suggested, it is highly unlikely, given the lemminglike nature of her squad, that they would disapprove.

If she sought the approval of people who have a different mind-set, they might not tell her the truth about her untruth. Claire certainly has a different mind-set when it comes to taking credit for heroic acts and would likely be glad that someone other than herself was taking the credit.

Although Bok's approach is difficult, attempts to go through such a process seem worthwhile. We may never be able to fully complete each step, but attempting them will yield better results. This more reasoned but incomplete process is seen when Bishop and Mohinder are discussing whether to inject Monica with a variant of the Shanti virus ("The Line"). They go through most of the steps outlined by Bok. They (as people who disagree with each other) discuss how the vaccine will help remove Monica's power (the good) and how the vaccine might create an incurable strain that crosses over to the general population (the evil), and they weigh the two possible outcomes. Special consideration is given to the experimental medical nature of the process that the lie will facilitate. After Mohinder decides not to lie to Monica about the treatment, he and Bishop discuss how they are keeping ethical checks on each other. The process works in this instance.

Should We or Shouldn't We?

The heroes of *Heroes* are different from ordinary people. They have extraordinary power to create and destroy, to mimic and to change, to create illusion and to remain invisible. But what their powers don't allow them to do is escape the moral complexities of life. They are constantly thrown into situations that test whether they should lie. Various characters answer in different ways, just as philosophers over time have answered the question concerning lying differently. Some choose to lie and reap rewards, while others choose to lie and suffer greatly. Some characters will tell the truth and suffer as a result, while others will tell the truth and gain great power.

The essential nature of ethics is a complex field that generates very few black-and-white answers. Life would be much simpler if human beings had clear guidelines to steer their choices. Life, however, is not easy, and therefore we must struggle with our own consciences. We struggle with the choices we make and determine whether we are acting ethically. Genetic mutations allow the inhabitants of *Heroes* to perform incredible deeds, but these abilities offer no guidance as to the question of when it is ethically correct to lie. Only by thinking through their own morality can Claire, Noah, Angela, Peter, Sylar, and the other characters of *Heroes* determine the circumstances where lying would be acceptable. The same principle applies to ordinary human beings. Whatever the justification, the label of "hero" or "villain" will be attached. The question is, "Are you a hero?"

NOTES

1. Sissela Bok, *Lying: Moral Choice in Public and Private Life*, 3rd Edition (New York: Vintage Books, 1999).

2. Nathan Thornburgh, "How Sarah Palin Mastered Politics," *Time* (U.S. edition, vol. 172, no. 11, September 04, 2008.

3. Immanuel Kant, *Grounding for the Metaphysics of Morals*, 3rd Edition, translated by James W. Ellington (Indianapolis, IN: Hackett, 1993), p. 30.

4. For Kant's whole argument, see "On the Supposed Right to Lie from Altruistic Motives," by Immanuel Kant, in *Modern Philosophy*, 5th Edition, edited by Forrest E. Baird and Walter Kaufmann (Upper Saddle River, NJ: Pearson/Prentice Hall, 2008), pp. 653–656.

5. Plato, *The Republic*, translated by G. M. A. Grube, revised by C. D. C. Reeve, in *Complete Works*, edited by John M. Cooper (Indianapolis, IN: Hackett, 1997), pp. 414d–415b.

6. Nicolò Machiavelli, *The Prince*, translated by N. H. Thompson (Buffalo, NY: Prometheus Books, 1986), p. 56.

7. Bok, *Lying*, pp. 30–31.

CONTRIBUTORS

Our Heroes

Don Adams received his B.A. from Reed College in 1983 and his PhD in philosophy from Cornell University in 1988. He has taught philosophy at several colleges and universities across the United States, including California State University at San Bernardino; Middlebury College in Vermont; Hobart and William Smith Colleges in Geneva, New York; and Bentley College in the Boston Area. Since 1998 he has been at Central Connecticut State University. His primary area of expertise and publication is ancient Greek philosophy, especially the ethics of Socrates and Plato. He has also published work on the medieval philosophy of St. Thomas Aquinas and more recently has been analyzing elements of ancient philosophy in modern American popular culture, including the music of James Brown, 50 Cent, and Nas, as well as the television series *Buffy the Vampire Slayer*. Recently, at pizza restaurants, Don has discovered that he has the uncanny ability to know which pizza is his even before they call his name.

Erik Daniel Baldwin is a graduate student (ABD) at Purdue University in West Lafayette, Indiana. His primary areas of philosophical specialization and research include philosophy of religion and epistemology. He also has strong research interests in Asian philosophy and Eastern philosophy of religion, ethics, and Islamic philosophy. He has published articles on religious epistemology, Asian and comparative philosophy, and Islamic philosophy. He has written a chapter for *Battlestar Galactica and Philosophy: Knowledge Here Begins Out There*. He has the power to do whatever he feels like he wants to do.

Michael R. Berry is currently the director of debate and an assistant professor of speech communication at King's College. Among his research interests are presidential debates, baseball, and deception. He is proud to be a hero to both of his sons, Seth and Noah. His biggest hero is his wonderful wife, Cindy. He recently discovered that he possesses the ability to automatically identify any fallacious argument at twenty paces—but if it's any closer or farther away, he has to think about it.

David Faraci is a graduate student in applied philosophy at Bowling Green State University. David's philosophical interests include a broad range of metadisciplinary topics, although his primary focus is metaethics. Currently, he is working on his dissertation on normative error theory; however, David is capable of producing suspiciously reasonable-sounding excuses for not working on said dissertation, seemingly from thin air. This is both a blessing and a curse, as the powers so often are for our heroes.

Peter S. Fosl is a professor of philosophy at Transylvania University in Lexington, Kentucky. He is the coauthor of *The Philosopher's Toolkit* (Blackwell, 2003) and *The Ethics Toolkit* (Blackwell, 2007) and the coeditor of *Classic Readings in Philosophy* (Wiley-Blackwell, 2009). A specialist in skepticism and a frequent contributor to *The Philosophers' Magazine*, Fosl also explores philosophical topics in the philosophy of religion, political philosophy, and the history of philosophy. He has contributed to *Metallica and Philosophy*, *Lost and Philosophy*, and *Terminator and Philosophy*. An actual Kentucky colonel (HOKC), Fosl possesses the uncanny power of never getting a hangover from bourbon, no matter how much those around him drink.

David Kyle Johnson is currently an assistant professor of philosophy at King's College in Wilkes-Barre, Pennsylvania. His philosophical specializations include philosophy of religion, logic, and metaphysics. He has also written chapters on *South Park*, *Family Guy*, *The Office*, *Battlestar Galactica*, *Batman*, and *The Colbert Report* in this series. He has taught many classes that focus on the relevance of philosophy to pop culture, including a course devoted to *South Park*. Kyle has recently discovered that he possesses a genuinely uninteresting ability: when opening doors, he never pushes when he should pull and never pulls when he should push.

Andrew Zimmerman Jones writes and edits the About.com physics site at http://physics.about.com/ and maintains www .azjones.info/ as his home on the Web. He has a degree in physics from Wabash College, with minors in mathematics and philosophy, and an MS degree in mathematics education from Purdue University. His work has appeared in various sources, most notably as the author of the upcoming *String Theory for Dummies*. While writing his book, Andrew discovered that when deadlines near, he gains the ability to subsist on only four hours of sleep and a can of Diet Mountain Dew, although this causes him to be weakened by sunlight the following day.

Peter Kirwan is currently a philosophy graduate student at the University of California, Irvine. He specializes in moral philosophy, broadly understood, and has the ability to survive in Southern California without a car.

Morgan Luck is a senior lecturer in philosophy at Charles Sturt University and a fellow of the Centre for Applied Philosophy and Public Ethics (CAPPE). Morgan completed his MA and PhD in philosophy at the University of Nottingham and a PGCE in religious education at the University of Cambridge. His areas of research include philosophy of religion, metaphysics, and epistemology. Morgan discovered that by intentionally driving a DeLorean into a police box, you are able to travel five years into the future—three with good behavior.

J. K. Miles, like Charlie Andrews, developed an eidetic memory. He is quick to point out that he is a *mutate*, not a mutant. He claims his powers are the result of being bitten by a gamma-irradiated mosquito growing up in the deep South. To his disappointment, his enhanced memory has not helped him in his current position as a PhD candidate at Bowling Green State University because, so far, his powers are confined to *Star Wars* trivia. His philosophical specializations include political philosophy and applied ethics. This is his first essay in pop culture and philosophy.

Fabio Paglieri is currently a researcher at the National Institute for Cognitive Sciences and Technologies (ISTC-CNR) in Rome, Italy. His specializations include philosophy of mind, cognitive science, and artificial intelligence. He has published and lectured on social cognition, rational choice theory, belief change, argumentation, intentional action, and goal-directed behavior. Over the last year, Fabio realized that he has developed an uncanny gift: in a crowded public place, he can subtly alter his appearance so as to repel any attempt at polite conversation or idle chatting from strangers. So, if you remember spotting a person you really wouldn't want to talk to, that was probably Fabio using his powers on you.

Christopher Robichaud is an instructor in public policy at Harvard's Kennedy School of Government. His philosophical interests rest primarily in the areas of metaphysics, epistemology, and ethics. He is pursuing an ongoing project of examining various ethical issues that arise out of superhero narratives and has written articles about Batman, Iron Man, and the X-Men, among others. Happily, Christopher possesses the ability to generate devastating counterexamples to philosophical theories. Sadly, he's learned that he can direct this power only at his own theorizing.

Robert Sharp is an assistant professor of philosophy at Muskingum College in New Concord, Ohio. His specialty is ethics, especially moral dilemmas and conflicts of value. He teaches on a wide range of topics, however, from ancient philosophy to advanced moral theory. He has contributed chapters to the *Family Guy* and *Battlestar Galactica* books in this series. Robert has at least two confirmed superpowers: He can completely remove memories from his own mind, especially when he most needs them. He also emits an electromagnetic pulse that allows him to attract all animal hairs in his house before leaving for work. So far, neither power has saved the world, but it's only a matter of time.

Tyler Shores received his BA in English and rhetoric from the University of California, Berkeley, where he created and for six semesters taught a course on "The Simpsons and Philosophy" (inspired by William Irwin's book of the same name). He has worked at Google, as part of the Authors@ Google lecture series. While writing for this book, he was working as project manager at the Center for Civic Education, a nonprofit organization dedicated to promoting greater civic and political awareness in students across the nation. He is currently pursuing a master's and eventual doctorate at Oxford University. Tyler also has the superpower to see one second into the future, if he stops to think about it long enough.

Jason Southworth is an ABD graduate student at the University of Oklahoma in Norman, Oklahoma, and an adjunct instructor of philosophy at Fort Hays State University, Hays,

Kansas. He has contributed articles to several pop culture and philosophy volumes, including *Batman and Philosophy*, *Stephen Colbert and Philosophy*, *X-Men and Philosophy*, and *Final Fantasy and Philosophy*. Like Wendy and Marvin the Wonder Twins, Jason's superpower works only in the presence of his animal companion, Ruth Tallman. Together, they can put a stop to anyone's attempts at meaningless small talk with their super-Socratic-method power and a complete disregard for whether this upsets their interlocutor.

Ruth Tallman is an ABD graduate student at the University of Oklahoma in Norman, Oklahoma, and an adjunct instructor of philosophy at Fort Hays State University, Hays, Kansas. Like Wendy and Marvin the Wonder Twins, Ruth's superpower works only in the presence of her animal companion, Jason Southworth. Together, they can put a stop to anyone's attempts at meaningless small talk with their super-Socratic-method power and a complete disregard for whether this upsets their interlocutor.

Andrew Terjesen is currently a visiting assistant professor of philosophy at Rhodes College in Memphis, Tennessee. He taught previously at Washington and Lee University, Austin College, and Duke University. His main philosophical interest is in the relationship between empathy and moral judgment, especially attempts to work out that relationship in the eighteenth century. He has a long-standing interest in discovering the philosophy lurking in pop culture topics (especially anything related to his only passion outside philosophy, comic books) and has written essays on the philosophical aspects of *Family Guy*, *The Office*, *Battlestar Galactica*, *Watchmen*, and *X-Men*. He has even taught four classes on philosophy and comic books. After reading a radioactive comic book, Andrew exhibited the ability to determine what comic book stories are in continuity for any character (although some people refuse to accept his superhuman judgment on these matters).

CHANDRA SURESH'S LIST

A Catalogue of Powers, Both
Natural and Synthetic

Tables are organized by powers' first appearances.

Major Characters

Character	Power (the Ability To)	First Manifestation
Claire Bennet	Rapid cell regeneration: Heal from any wound without scarring	Genesis
Hiro Nakamura	Space-time mastery: Manipulate time and space (time travel, time freezing, and teleportation)	Genesis
Matt Parkman	Mental access: Project thoughts, suggestions, and dreams into others' minds, as well as read their thoughts	Genesis
Nathan Petrelli	Flight: Fly	Genesis
Peter Petrelli	*Natural Power:* Empathic mimicry: Copy the powers of others by empathizing	Genesis
	Mimicked Powers: Precognitive dreaming: Dream future events that will (likely) occur	Six Months Ago (from Angela Petrelli)

(Continued)

Major Characters (Continued)

Character	Power (the Ability To)	First Manifestation
Peter Petrelli (continued)	Flight: Fly	Genesis/Dual (from Nathan Petrelli)
	Precognitive painting: Paint future events that will (likely) occur	Hiros (from Isaac Mendez)
	Space-time Mastery: Manipulate time and space (time travel, time freezing, and teleportation)	Collision (from Hiro Nakamura)
	Rapid cell regeneration: Heal from any wound without scarring	Homecoming (from Claire Bennet)
	Mental access: Project thoughts, suggestions, and dreams into others' minds, as well as read their thoughts	Fallout (from Matt Parkman)
	Invisibility: Become transparent	Godsend (from Claude Rains)
	Telekinesis: Move objects by will alone	Unexpected (from Sylar)
	Radioactivity: Generate radioactivity	The Hard Part (from Ted Sprague)
	Enhanced strength: Have above-normal muscular strength	How to Stop an Exploding Man (from Niki Sanders)
	Intangibility: Pass through solid objects and have them pass through you at will	Four Months Ago (from D.L. Hawkins)
	Electric manipulation: Create and direct electricity	Four Months Later (from Elle Bishop)
	Pyrokinesis: Create and control fire at will	I Am Become Death (from Flint Gordon Jr.)
	Intuitive aptitude: Intuitively understand how complex things work (with a hunger to acquire powers)	I Am Become Death (from Sylar)

Character	Power (the Ability To)	First Manifestation
	Super speed: Move at high rates of speed	I Am Become Death (from Daphne Millbrook)
	Powers Mimicked in the Explosion Future:[a] Electric manipulation: Create and direct electricity	Five Years Gone (from an unnamed guard in GN: Walls, Part 2)[b]
	Super speed: Move at high rates of speed	Five Years Gone (from an unnamed guard in GN: Walls, Part 2)
	Pyrokinesis: Create and control fire at will	Five Years Gone (from Meredith Gordon)
	Powers Mimicked in the Exposed Future:[c] Persona insertion: "Place" one person in another's body	Powerless
	Illusion: Control what others sense with their five senses	Powerless
	Powers Possessed via Touch: Freezing: Freeze objects by touch	A Clear and Present Danger (from Tracy Strauss)
	Shape-shifting: The ability to take the form of anyone you touch	An Invisible Thread (from Sylar)
Sylar (Gabriel Gray)	*Natural Power:* Intuitive aptitude: Intuitively understand how complex things work (with a hunger to acquire powers)	Genesis
	Stolen Powers: Freezing: Freeze objects by touch	Don't Look Back (from James Walker)
	Enhanced memory: learn and retain large amounts of information	Seven Minutes to Midnight (from Charlie Andrews)
	Telekinesis: Move objects by will alone	Six Months Ago (from Brian Davis)
	Melting: Melt any object	Runl (from Zane Taylor)

(Continued)

Major Characters (Continued)

Character	Power (the Ability To)	First Manifestation
Sylar *(continued)*	Enhanced hearing: Hear sounds beyond normal human ability	Unexpected (from Dale Smither)
	Precognitive painting: Paint future events that will (likely) occur	.07% (from Isaac Mendez)
	Radioactivity: Generate radioactivity	Landslide (from Ted Sprague)
	Rapid cell regeneration: Heal from any wound without scarring	The Second Coming (from Claire Bennet)
	Clairsentience: Perceive the history of an object by touching it	One of Us, One of Them (from Bridget Bailey)
	Voice amplification: Produce very loud sounds with one's voice	One of Us, One of Them (from Jesse Murphy)
	Remote shattering: Shatter objects from a distance	Villains (from Trevor Zeitlan)
	Electric manipulation: Create and direct electricity	It's Coming (from Elle Bishop)
	Lie detection: Tell when others are lying	Our Father (from Sue Landers)
	Imprinting: Make forged signatures appear by mental will alone	GN: Out of Town . . . on Business (from Joe Macon)
	Shape-shifting: Take the form of anyone you touch	Into Asylum (from James Martin)
	Disintegration: Break down any object into small pieces at will	I Am Sylar (from Tom Miller)
	Flight: Fly	An Invisible Thread
	Powers Possessed in the Explosion Future:	
	Flight: Fly	Five Years Gone
	Illusion: Control what others sense with their five senses	Five Years Gone

Character	Power (the Ability To)	First Manifestation
	Intangibility: Pass through solid objects and have them pass through you at will	Five Years Gone
	Powers Possessed in the Exposed Future	
	Radioactivity: Generate radioactivity	I Am Become Death
	Precognitive painting: Paint future events that will (likely) occur	I Am Become Death
Angela Petrelli	Precognitive dreaming: Dream future events that will (likely) occur	The Second Coming
Ando Masahashi	Ability supercharge: Enhance the powers of others and discharge harmful red electricity from one's hands	Dual
Mohinder Suresh	Enhanced strength: Have above-normal muscular strength	Dual[d]

[a] "Explosion Future" denotes the future being prevented in Volume 1 that bears the effects of New York City after an explosion.
[b] GN refers to the graphic novel.
[c] "Exposed Future" denotes the future being prevented in Volume 3 that bears the effects of public access to the formula that gives powers.
[d] Mohinder's original powers included the ability to climb walls and spin webs, but he lost those particular abilities in the episode "Dual."

Minor (On-Screen) Characters

Character	Power (the Ability To)	First Manifestation
Niki/Jessica Sanders	Enhanced strength: Have above-normal muscular strength	Genesis
Isaac Mendez	Precognitive painting: Paint future events that will (likely) occur	Genesis
James Walker	Freezing: Freeze objects by touch	Don't Look Back

(Continued)

Minor (On-Screen) Characters (Continued)

Character	Power (the Ability To)	First Manifestation
Eden McCain	Persuasion: Force others to obey one's commands	Don't Look Back
The Haitian	Negation (power/memory): Erase others' memories and cause others to not be able to use their powers	One Giant Leap
D.L. Hawkins	Intangibility: Pass through solid objects and have them pass through you at will	GN: Snapshots
Ted Sprague	Radioactivity: Generate radioactivity	Nothing to Hide
Sanjog Iyer	Dream manipulation: Manipulate others' dreams	Seven Minutes to Midnight
Charlie Andrews	Enhanced memory: Learn and retain large amounts of information	Seven Minutes to Midnight
Micah Sanders	Technopathy: Control and manipulate electronic machines	Six Months Ago
Brian Davis	Telekinesis: Move objects by will alone	Six Months Ago
Claude Rains	Invisibility: Not be seen	Godsend
Meredith Gordon	Pyrokinesis: Create and control fire at will	The Fix
Zane Taylor	Melting: Melt any object	Run!
Dale Smither	Enhanced hearing: Hear sounds beyond normal human ability	Unexpected
Candice Wilmer/ Betty	Illusion: Control what others sense with their five senses	Company Man
Daniel Linderman	Healing: Heal other life forms by touch	.07%
Molly Walker	Clairvoyance: Locate people and things, regardless of distance	Landslide

Character	Power (the Ability To)	First Manifestation
Maya Herrera	Poison/disease emission: Give others nearby a sickness that blackens their eyes (and one's own) and kills them quickly	Four Months Later
Alejandro Herrera	Symptom absorption: Counteract the ability of his twin sister, Maya	Four Months Later
Bob Bishop	Alchemy: Turn any object into gold	Four Months Later
West Rosen	Flight: Fly	Lizards
Adam Monroe	Rapid cell regeneration: Heal from any wound without scarring	Lizards
Monica Dawson	Adoptive muscle memory: Mimic any action once seen	The Kindness of Strangers
Maury Parkman	Mental access: Project thoughts, suggestions, and dreams into others' minds, as well as read their thoughts	Fallout
Elle Bishop	Electric manipulation: Create and direct electricity	Fight or Flight
Kaito Nakamura	Accelerated probability: Predict the probability of events	Season 2, Deleted Scenes
"Chameleon Girl"	Dynamic camouflage: Blend into any environment, remaining hidden	Season 2, Deleted Scene
Robert Keep	Impenetrable skin: Not be penetrated by anything (e.g., fire and bullets)	Season 2, Deleted Scene
Benjamin "Knox" Washington	Fear manipulation: Smell the fear of others and use it to enhance strength	The Second Coming
Flint Gordon Jr.	Pyrokinesis: create and control fire at will	The Second Coming
The German	Magnetism: Manipulate metal objects	GN: Berlin, Part I

(Continued)

Minor (On-Screen) Characters (Continued)

Character	Power (the Ability To)	First Manifestation
Daphne Millbrook	Super speed: Move at high rates of speed	GN: Our Lady of the Blessed Acceleration, Part 1
Tracy Strauss	Freezing: Freeze objects by touch	The Butterfly Effect
Stephen Canfield	Vortex creation: Create mini black holes	The Butterfly Effect
Usutu	Precognitive painting: Paint future events that will (likely) occur	The Butterfly Effect
Eric Doyle	Remote body control (puppetry): Control the bodily actions of others	The Butterfly Effect
Jesse Murphy	Voice amplification: Produce very loud sounds with one's voice	One of Us, One of Them
Bridget Bailey	Clairsentience: Perceive the history of an object by touching it	GN: Into the Wild, Part 3
Arthur Petrelli	*Natural Power:* Power absorption: Steal the powers of others without killing them	Dying of the Light
	Absorbed Powers: Rapid cell regeneration: Heal from any wound without scarring	Dying of the Light (from Adam Monroe)
	Electric manipulation: Create and direct electricity	Dying of the Light (from Peter Petrelli)
	Telekinesis: Move objects by will alone	Eris Quod Sum (from Peter Petrelli)
	Poison/disease emission: Give others nearby a sickness that blackens their eyes (and one's own) and kills them quickly	Eris Quod Sum (from Maya Herrera)
	Telepathy: Read minds	Villains (from unknown)

Character	Power (the Ability To)	First Manifestation
	Mental manipulation: Project thoughts, suggestions, and dreams into others' minds	Villains (from unknown)
	Memory wiping: Erase others' memories	Villains (from unknown)
	Precognitive painting: Paint future events that will (likely) happen	It's Coming (from Peter Petrelli)
	Space-time mastery: Manipulate time and space (time travel, time freezing, and teleportation)	Our Father (from Peter Petrelli)
Danny Pine	Metal mimicry: Change parts of one's body into metal	Villains
Trevor Zeitlan	Remote shattering: Shatter objects from a distance	Villains
Baron Samedi	Impenetrable skin: Not be penetrated by anything (e.g., fire and bullets.)	The Eclipse, Part II
Ishi Nakamura	Healing: Heal other life forms by touch	Our Father
Scott (the Marine)	Enhanced strength: Have above-normal muscular strength	Our Father
Sue Landers	Lie detection: Tell when others are lying	Our Father
Luke Campbell	Microwave emission: Emit microwaves	Truth and Blood
Alex Woolsly	Underwater breathing: Breathe underwater	GN: The Swimmer
Samson Gray	*Natural Power:* Intuitive aptitude: Intuitively understand how complex things work (with a hunger to acquire powers)	Shades of Gray
	Stolen Powers: Telekenisis: Move objects by will alone	Shades of Gray
	Sedation: Sedate people at will	Shades of Gray

(*Continued*)

Minor (On-Screen) Characters (Continued)

Character	Power (the Ability To)	First Manifestation
Matt Parkman Jr.	Touch and go: Activate objects and powers	Cold Snap
James Martin	Shape-shifting: Take the form of anyone you touch	Into Asylum
Alice Shaw	Weather control: Cause weather disturbances	1961
Mr. Shaw	Seismic burst: Push away objects and people with a burst of sound from one's hand	1961
Tom Miller	Disintegration: Break down any object into smaller pieces at will	I Am Sylar

Characters from the Graphic Novels

Character	Power (the Ability To)	First Manifestation
Hana Gitelman	Transmission manipulation: Generate and alter transmissions	Wireless, Part 1
Au Co	Plant growth: Accelerate plant growth	War Buddies, Part 4
Unnamed agent	Electric manipulation: Create and direct electricity	Walls, Part 1
Unnamed agent	Super speed: Move at high rates of speed	Walls, Part 1
Guillame	Bliss and horror: impart feelings of happiness or terror in others	It Takes a Village, Part 1
Rollo Fusor's accomplice	Dehydration: Remove water from any object or person	Golden Handshake, Part 1
Unnamed teenager	Electrical absorption: Absorb and release electricity	Blackout, Part 1
Maarten	Pyrokinesis: Create and control fire at will	Team Building Exercise
Liquid Man	Water mimicry: Mimic (turn into) water	Team Building Exercise

Character	Power (the Ability To)	First Manifestation
Unnamed traveler	Omnilingualism: Understand all languages	The Last Shangri-La
Evan	Self-cloning: Create duplicates of oneself	Revolutionary War, Part 1
Marcus	Crumpling: Crumple any object	Normal Lives
Richard Drucker	Transmission manipulation: generate and alter transmissions	The Golden Goose
Matt Neuenberg	Enhanced memory: Learn and retain large amounts of information	The Man with Too Much Brains
Abu Aswan	Levitation: Levitate heavy objects	History of a Secret
Khufu	Levitation: Levitate heavy objects	History of a Secret
Linda Tavara	*Natural Power:* Aura absorption: See auras and steal them	War Buddies, Part 7
	Absorbed Power: Mediumship: See dead people	Moonlight Serenade (from Ida May Walker)
Howard Grigsby	Luminescence: Emit light from one's body	Blindsided
Ben Franklin	Electrical absorption: Absorb and release electricity	A Lesson in Electricity
Piper	Elasticity: Stretch one's body beyond normal	Different and the Same
Ida May Walker	Mediumship: See dead people	Moonlight Serenade
Donna Dunlap	Telescopic vision: See in the dark and magnify one's own vision	Donna's Big Date, Part 1
Felicia Brooks	Disintegration touch: Undefined (the effects of the power are unclear)	Donna's Big Date, Part 2
Leonard Cushing	Acid secretion: Secrete acid	Trust Issues, Part 1
Connie Logan	Appearance alteration: Alter the appearance of others	Faces, Part 1
Unnamed NYC resident	Nerve gas emission: Sweat nerve gas	Faces, Part 1

(*Continued*)

Characters from the Graphic Novels (Continued)

Character	Power (the Ability To)	First Manifestation
Manuel Garcia	Teleportation: Disappear in one place and instantly appear in another	Faces, Part 1
The Croatian	Weather control: Cause weather disturbances	Faces, Part 1
Bianca Karina	Lung adaptability: Adapt one's lungs to process oxygen in any environment	Root and Branch, Part I
Julien Dumont	Self-cloning: Create duplicates of oneself	Root and Branch, Part 2
Paulette Hawkins	Ability supercharge: Enhance the powers of others	The Kill Squad, Part 1
Brendan Lewis	Plant manipulation: Create and mimic plants	The Kill Squad, Part 1
Unnamed agent	Sound absorption: Absorb sound waves	Going Postal, Part 1
Samir Mellouk	Intangibility: Pass through solid objects and have them pass through you at will	Our Lady of Blessed Acceleration, Part I
Unnamed terrorist	Magnetism: Manipulate metal objects	Resistance
Michael	Laser emitting: Generate a laser from one's finger	Doyle
Abigail	Force-field projection: Create and manipulate force fields	Sum Quod Sum, Part 1
Tina Ramierez	Chlorine breath: Exhale chlorine	Viewpoints
Michael Fitzgerald	Enhanced strength: Have above-normal muscular strength	Viewpoints
Anna Korolenko	Neurohindrance: Hinder the upper-brain function of others nearby	Red Eye, Part 1
Ricardo Silva	Primal rage: Induce rage in others	Red Eye, Part I
Perrin Crocker	Spike protrusion: Make spikes protrude from one's body	Under the Bridge, Part 1
Donald Essex	Water mimicry: Turn into water	Under the Bridge, Part 2

Character	Power (the Ability To)	First Manifestation
Joe Macon	Imprinting: To make forged signatures appear by mental will alone	Out of Town . . . on Business
Harmon	Wall climbing: Scale walls effortlessly	Liberated
Angie	Flight: Fly	Liberated
Misha	Telekinesis: Move objects by will alone	Liberated
The Russian	Age shifting: Change one's age	Comrades, Part I
Howie Kaplan	Oil secretion: Secrete oil from one's hands	Hanging by a Thread
Gordon Hovey	Sand transmutation: The ability to change objects and persons into sand	Exodus
Mary Krause	Acidic blood: Have blood with acidic properties	Exodus

Characters from the Webisodes

Character	Power (the Ability To)	First Manifestation
The Constrictor	Constriction: Mimic the abilities of a boa constrictor	Going Postal, Part 1
Echo DeMille	Sound manipulation: Create any sound, anywhere, from any distance	Going Postal, Part 1
Santiago	Accelerated probability: Predict the possible outcomes of events	Destiny, Part 1
Iris	Pyrokinesis: Create and control fire at will	Destiny, Part 1
Elisa	Water mimicry: Mimic (turn into) water	Destiny, Part 1
Edward	Accelerated probability: Predict the probability of events	Destiny, Part 4
Rachel Mills	Teleportation: Disappear in one place and instantly appear in another	The Recruit, Part 1
Leona Mills	Life force transfer: Transfer the life force (age) between objects and persons, including herself	The Recruit, Part 5

All Others Powers Revealed in Other Ways

Character	Power (the Ability To)	First Manifestation
Albert Rossling	Weather control: Cause weather disturbances	Assignment tracker map[a]
Lukas Bahn	Evolved human detection: Detect gifted individuals	Assignment tracker map
Robert Ferguson	Size alteration: Alter one's own physical size	Assignment tracker map
Paul Harding	Hair manipulation: Manipulate all hair on his body	Assignment tracker map
Sebastian Shell	Object displacement: Displace objects by touch	Assignment tracker map
Felipe Acerra	Intangibility: Pass through solid objects and have them pass through you at will	The Map[b]
Byron Bevington	Precognition: See the future	The Map
Tracy Chobham	Teleportation: Disappear in one place and instantly appear in another	The Map
Amid Halebi	Radioactivity: Generate radioactivity	The Map/Unaired Pilot
Abe	Light absorption: Absorb light	The Agent iStory, Chapter 407
Crazy Tom	Outfit Morphing: Change one's clothes at will	The Agent iStory, Chapter 409
Syn Anders	Empathic manipulation: Alter others' emotions and feelings after physically touching them	Habbo[c]

[a] "Assignment tracker map" refers to an interactive map that can be found at primatechpaper.com.
[b] "The Map" refers to an interactive map that can be fount at NBC.com.
[c] Habbo is a social networking Web site that hosts *Heroes Evolutions* content.

These tables were compiled using information found at heroeswiki.com.

INDEX

The Power of Omniscience

Page references in *italics* refer to illustrations.